Democracy and Human Rights in Africa:

The Politics of Collective Participation and Governance in Cameroon

Peter Ateh-Afac Fossungu

Langaa Research & Publishing CIG
Mankon, Bamenda

Publisher:
Langaa RPCIG
Langaa Research & Publishing Common Initiative Group
P.O. Box 902 Mankon
Bamenda
North West Region
Cameroon
Langaagrp@gmail.com
www.langaa-rpcig.net

Distributed in and outside N. America by African Books Collective
orders@africanbookscollective.com
www.africanbookcollective.com

ISBN: 9956-790-15-X

Table of Contents

Introduction

One important fundamental preoccupation of constitutionalism is the avoidance of governmental tyranny through the abuse of power by rulers pursuing their own interests at the expense of the life, liberty, and property of the governed. A major challenge faced by constitutional engineers has been to design a system of governance that maximizes the protection of individual members of society while minimizing the opportunities for governments to harm them [Fombad, 2005: 301].

Since the mid-80s, there has been much federalism talk in Cameroon where federation (said to have been created in Foumban in 1961) had supposedly been 'overwhelmingly' rejected in 1972 by Cameroonians. It is cleanly hard to see how all of this could be conveniently explained except by the words, 'confusion' and 'manipulation', enormously greased with corruption and selfishness – confusioncracy, for short; a system of rule that has since equated federalism with secession. Is federalism in fact a vehicle for self-determination or one for secession? This main question, and many more democracy issues that are incidental to it, can be best answered through adequately understanding the politics of secession in Cameroon. This politics finds its roots in the concept of federalism through which the country's English-speaking minority thinks it can feel protected in the larger state. Thus, Konings (1999: 290) has posited that "the political agenda in Cameroon has become increasingly dominated by what is known as the 'Anglophone problem'"; with Eko (2003: 80) regarding it as "an important issue that must be dealt with." This problem, to Eko (2003: 81), is an assemblage of political, cultural, economic and social grievances expressed by the English-speaking minority in the predominantly French-speaking Republic of Cameroon (formerly called the United Republic of Cameroon); an issue which Anyefru (2010: 85) thinks "has attracted significant [international] attention since the mid-1980s."

Cameroon and Human Rights

Much as this book centres on it, it is not only about the Anglophone Problem. It is principally about human rights and their excessive violations resulting directly from what Konings (1999: 289) decries as "this approach

[that] fostered political monolithism and the entrenchment of presidentialism, at the expense of constitutionalism." The Anglophone problem then cannot but be central to the book because it "touches on the distribution of political and economic power, the institutional structures of the society, the educational system, and the relationship between the government and the governed" (Eko, 2003: 81). This book largely condemns the Cameroon government for incessantly singing democracy and rule of law at the same time as it is massively torturing and wantonly killing citizens that dare to question the confusion. I think only the ignorant would now think that the international community is not unaware of the Anglophone Problem. As Anyefru (2010: 85) clearly makes known, "The aim of the [numerous Anglophone] petitions against the new state [of Cameroon] has been to draw the attention of the UN and the international community to the injustices inflicted upon minority English-speaking Cameroonians by the ruling government. The Anglophone elites believe that by making their plight known to the international community, the latter might intervene to restore the statehood of Southern Cameroon."

The international community is thus quite aware of the Anglophone problem but it seems that it is unaware of the degree of the unsettling human rights atrocities in this country most probably because of the confusioncracy that has been deeply and widely embedded in and around human rights issues in Cameroon. For example, Cameroon is signatory to all the international conventions on human rights; but what the international audience may not quite know, as far as Cameroon is concerned, is that signing and ratifying those conventions and treaties is one thing and actually abiding by them is another; an issue further complicated when its inhuman and degrading treatment of citizens would be wrapped with the cloak of national unity. Furthermore, the United Nations (that most Africans continue to look up to) usually is incapacitated by the 'interests-politics' of the gear-lever states of the UN; interests that would often hide behind the 'sovereignty of states' (non-interference) principle; only to quickly invoke "humanitarian intervention" when that is solely in the invokers' own interests, as many incidents in Africa can clearly show; leading many critics to wonder when Africans would then ever grow up and stop waiting to be spoon-fed by the others – especially when they count so much on the UN that Cassese (1986: 396) says "now increasingly indulges in the highly questionable practice of begetting ever greater number of resolutions, as if to conjure up problems and provide for their solution on paper served to settle them in real life."

I strongly share the position that a state like Cameroon must be seen to ensure that its laws and other practices accord with its international commitments in order not to lengthen the documented list of its human rights violations to an extent "unlike anything the world has ever known, with manifestations of genocide, torture, 'disappearances' and slavery for which historians must search long and hard to find equivalents."[1] The Cameroon regime is plainly guilty of gross violations against humanity, contrary to its commitments under international human rights law and practice as this book largely demonstrates. In a way, it calls on the international community to see to it that this state's crooked regime, party to all the known treaties and conventions on human rights, be made to respect its international commitments and stop the massive brutalization and killing of its citizens. Said international community cannot be knowledgeable of the real situation until one has conveniently capped or excluded the great amount of confusioncracy in the federalism and other collective participation (democracy) theses or arguments from both sides – the English-speaking minority and the Cameroon administration. A lot of West Cameroonians have been quick to pin the human rights problems in Cameroon solely on the Francophone-dominated government. This book however strives to apportion the blame accordingly, showing how the English-speaking minority is, in large measure, enormously contributing to its own oppression and propping up the Ahidjo-Biya dictatorship that is oppressing Cameroonians generally, not just the linguistic minority.

Gorji-Dinka (1996) narrates that many young English-speaking Cameroonians do not understand and wish to know "How do we come to be ruled directly from Yaounde?" The youths' query is seeking to comprehend why there is no separation of powers in Cameroon when the country is incessantly singing democracy and rule of law. The youths' probing must have to be squarely addressed; the more so as Cameroon's President Biya

---

[1] William A. Schabas, *International Human Rights Law and the Canadian Charter: A Manual for the Practitioner* (Toronto: Carswell, 1991) at v. See also Daniel D. Nsereko Ntanda, "Victims of Abuse of Power, with Special Reference to Africa" 28:1 *University of British Columbia Law Review* (1994), 171 at 188-191; H.M. Kindred *et al*, *International Law chiefly as Interpreted and Applied in Canada* (Toronto: Edmond Montgomery Publications Ltd., 1987) at 663; and Susan Marks, "Civil Liberties at the Margin: The U.K. Derogation and the European Court of Human Rights" 15 *Oxford Journal of Legal Studies* (1995), 65 at 81-82.

(1986: 9) thinks that more than "Twenty-five years after our political independence, and at this stage in our economic, social and cultural development, I feel the time has come to elucidate [in a straightforward manner] on the doctrines that [have been used to mis]guide the Cameroon [and African] People." This misguidance, paradoxically, is being carried out by those who should rather be showing the way forward by shedding light on what Konings (1999: 289) sees as "The current debate on democracy in Africa [which] has once again raised the issue of what form of constitution is appropriate to accommodate the enormous ethno-regional diversities within the framework of a broader national unity."

Criticism, Provocation, and Construction

This book is written with the trilogy of criticism, provocation, and construction in mind; employing the first two towards reconstructing a new society in the Hinge of Africa or Cameroon that ensures respect for fundamental human rights and certain basic shared values that were dolefully mistreated by the Foumban arrangement and Federal Constitution (Fossungu, 2013:2). My belief and hope are that this unassuming contribution would, among other goals, help Cameroonians particularly and Africans generally to understand certain basics of federalism; a device which I find to be the best or authentic modern vehicle for multiculturalism or the political management of ethnic/cultural diversity. In particular, Africans should be able to comprehend that, when it is what it is or ought to be, federalism cannot be detached from effective multiparty politics or constitutional democracy; that it must guarantee judicial independence, fundamental human rights, and local values and minority concerns. If this understanding is enhanced by the book, as I earnestly hope it will, then proper allowance and place would have been made for a governmental and constitutional arrangement in diverse Africa (specifically represented here by Cameroon) that should permit and foster governance with due regard for human rights generally and minority and other disadvantaged groups' concerns in particular. My firm belief is that Cameroon should be uniting Africa rather than further splitting the continent into incapable mini-states vis-à-vis the changing world stage.

I argue that this noble task cannot be realized until the confusing theses have been adequately capped or excluded from the scene altogether. That explains why this book is a general but pin-pointed critique of both the academia and the political elites in Africa with respect to the myriad of dishonest and confusing postulations that they have been and continue propagating to date. I must reiterate here with both Rovere (1979: v) and Newman (1968: xi-xiii) that criticism has been practised not only in arts and letters and philosophy but as well in politics and government – with Tremblay (1993: 65) seeing government as 'including all the organs that exercise state powers'.

The book thus unabashedly casts a cold eye on what has been discovered in Africa, reporting it with a heavy emphasis on the critical, an accentuation of the negative because I agree with Archer and Reay (1966: 107) that criticism of abuse is necessary to make governments uncomfortable and keep the public conscience alive. Any protest that will keep this conscience awake must therefore be encouraged and promoted because during a lure the public conscience may fall asleep, and history can sufficiently furnish many communities where its slumber was seen only too late to be the sleep of death. According to Rovere (1979: iv) also, the highlighting of bad news is the helpful kind since it can be turned into cease-and-desist and never-again orders – thus improving the ratio of good news to bad news. Good news is the kind that is rarely concealed while bad news is frequently concealed. The easiness or difficulty of this concealment of bad news is thus shown in the book to largely depend on the type of academy, media, and legal profession in place.

The provision of straightforward non-manipulative responses to the queries posed by the younger generation (some of which have been raised in this book), is particularly important for a host of reasons but the main ones are simple. First, Cameroon's Federal Constitution[2] (which I see as the firm base of the country's one-culture multiculturalism, one-man democracy, and one-state federation, and several other One-Manish concepts) has been so unnecessarily praised by most of the intellectuals for its solid human rights guarantees that, today that Cameroonians are fervently seeking and yearning for democracy and the respect for human rights, there are persistent calls

[2] See *Loi N° 61-24 du 1er septembre 1961 portant révision constitutionnelle et tendant à adapter la constitution actuelle aux nécessités du Cameroun réunifié* [Federal Constitution]. This constitution (in English) is appended to Rubin (1971: 215–227) while the authentic French version (by virtue of its article 59) is appended to Benjamin (1972: 216-237).

"for a return to the 1961 Federal arrangement and Constitution."[3] Demands like this one forcefully portray to me that a lot of Cameroonians have not yet learnt anything from the past fifty-three or so years, most probably because of the confusioncracy. That they are still to come to grips with the fact that the personification of public debates in this country and the associated alarming human rights questions are intimately rooted in the events that took place before and during the Foumban Conference,[4] their embodiment being that same '1961 Federal arrangement or constitution'.

The failure to grasp this important issue is evidenced by the theories on separation of powers and arguments in the various secession/coup d'état theses in Cameroon, all of which do essentially hypothesize that changing the name from the Federal Republic of Cameroon (FRC) to the Republic of Cameroon (*en passant par la République Unie du Cameroun*) is tantamount to secession on the part of French-speaking Cameroun from the Foumban union. Or that changing, through the *2 June 1972 Constitution of the United Republic of Cameroon* from the FRC to United Republic of Cameroon (URC) is 'a coup d'état staged upon Cameroon by President Ahidjo'. The secession-from-federalism theses in this country have no firm bases except those of calculatingly blinding Cameroonians of the need to look to countries like Canada, Belgium, Germany, and Switzerland for ground rules to the type of society they are now seeking. These 'secession-from-federalism' and 'coup d'état' theses mostly from West Cameroonians, and the government's counter theses of federalism-is-secession and democracy/federalism-is-foreign-to Africa, etc, have now come to dominate political discourse regarding national unity in Cameroon and are elaborately critiqued and capped in the Chapters below.

On Tradition, Style, and Additional Usefulness of Book

Squarely focusing on and comprehending federalism and democracy questions in Cameroon would be greatly assisted by some important issues

---

[3] See, for example, SCFAQ (Question 5); Gorji-Dinka (1991); and Ngwana (2009). Ngwana, the chairman of the Cardinal Democratic Party (CDP), an opposition party in Cameroon, theorizes that "For the Anglophone Problem to stop, Cameroon must revert to the 1961 Federal Constitution......"

[4] See *Record of the Conference on the Constitutional Future of the Southern Cameroons, Held at Foumban 17th to 21st July 1961* (Buea, 1961)

that I have to immediately straighten out. This levelling out could be vital to understanding and appreciating this study. Having studied and lived in a tradition-loving environment for quite long, I am not unaware of the fact that the somewhat 'out of the ordinary' style I have used in this study may also raise questions from most tradition-loving readers and/or book editors. I hope and believe though that these readers/editors would equally comprehend that exceptional phenomena (like 'advanced democracy' – confusioncracy, to be accurate) would call for innovative and tradition-breaking styles or approaches. Innovation would, of course, hardly be one if it is not unlike the traditional. Moreover, I have discovered that others (before me) that have 'foolhardily' approached the subject otherwise have ended up woefully failing to grasp the amoeba-like confusion.

Moreover, I also think that it is about time traditional (Western) scholars and publishers open up to other 'unfamiliar' approaches and modes. This will help in spicing up the discussions, to begin with. Opening up is a thing they must do if they care as much about cross-pollination as well as a proper understanding of what they have so far 'traditionally' lumped up as the "Third World" – a world whose interests, aspirations and opinions do not seem to matter very much to them, as Okafor has more elaborately dwelled on.[5] As a long-time teacher, I have also realized that concrete or real life illustrations often help reinforce points evoked.

I think an *informed* knowledge of the Cameroon Republic could greatly help Belgians and Canadians (for instance) to better appreciate their own society. From my experience of over ten years as a researcher in the Canadian legal academy, I have come to recognize that a lot of Canadian scholars often quickly take offence when I say certain things about the Canadian governmental system and society that will generally tend towards praising them. I find this attitude particularly amusing because, most often, what is said in those regards is not directed to saying just what said scholars often think I am implying – that the Canadian system is a perfect one, requiring no further enhancement. If in a discussion with them I call Canada 'a veritable federation', I am by no means saying that Canada has no constitutional and other problems of its own. A 'veritable federation' is surely not the synonym for a 'federation without problems'.

---

[5] See Obiora Chinedu Okafor, "Newness, Imperialism, and International Legal Reform in Our Times: A TWAIL Perspective" 43.1 & 2 *Osgoode Hall Law Journal* (2005), 171-191.

Their manner of reacting to my use of 'veritable federation' (for example) can simply be attributed to their failure to learn about what holds elsewhere (outside the USA, Europe and South-East Asia); a necessary learning that can greatly aid them in better understanding and appreciating what, as Canadians, they have.[6] Cameroon is obviously one of those countries that Canada could be very carefully monitoring in this respect. Both Cameroon and Canada do not only have almost similar colonial "pasts" (British & French hegemony) but are also very often (perhaps erroneously) thought of as birds of the feather or "uniquely similar" because of their (multi-ethnic, multicultural,) *bilingual* and *bijural* nature. It would thus be good for Canadians to know about, and juxtapose the Canadian system with, that of Cameroon since comparison has been found by Magstadt (1991: 4) to be an excellent antidote to ethnocentrism or a narrow view of the world based on one's own culture, religion, nationality, and so on. Indeed, as Magstadt has largely admonished, there is no better way to gain perspective on one's own society than to view it from afar, through the eyes of others.

It is my thought then that I would not be doing Canadians in particular (and the academic community at large) any service if I do not provide an accurate or true picture of Cameroon (with which they can do the juxtaposition), with my sole excuse being because I could not use a 'free' or non-traditional writing or discussion style in doing so. What I am saying simply is that I must refuse to allow traditional conformity bar me from sharing vital information on an un-traditional governmental system. Doing it any other way could be doing great disservice to a huge amount of scholarship that would otherwise have been made readily available regarding the world's 'democracies' which, in any case, are not all of the traditional type.

---

[6] Canadian law journals and other publishers also are fond of refusing to extend publication to manuscripts such as this one for reasons such as: "it deals with an issue that may not be well known by our Canadian readership" [so, when will they ever know until they begin somewhere and somehow?]; "The manuscript assumes a detailed knowledge of Cameroonian affairs which our readership would not possess, and its main disciplinary links seem to be more with political science than law"; "the Editorial Board was uncomfortable at times with the tone of the article. The Board thought this is partly due to the author's strong understanding of the subject, which can have the result of alienating a reader who is less familiar with the subject. One solution could be to provide more context for the reader who is unfamiliar with Cameroon politics"; "While it can add colour to the article, the Editorial Board felt that the author should avoid overly using familiar language"; etc.

Georges Védel (*Manuel de Droit constitutionnel*, Paris: Sirey, 1949) has generally seen the emergence of so-called "popular" democracies as raising stiff classification problems not hitherto known to the classical sense of the term. To that problematic classification must have to be added the 'advanced' which is peculiar to Cameroon. The Cameroonian additional (or subtractional?) description of democracy must certainly disturb the equanimity of political and constitutional pundits because they would spend all their lives digging into treatises and books on democracy and never come across anything like advanced democracy (*la démocratie avancée*) – except, of course, they happen to read what Jua has described to Ndi Chia (1995b) as "Communal Liberalism that is the bible of political theology in this country."

This is a unique type of democracy that this unique African country is so loudly boasting of being ready and capable of exporting to the rest of the world, according to Tegha who could not help questioning with amazement: "Is it not this same *Kontchoumeter* who had the audacity to tell USA, Britain and the rest of the world that Cameroon was so advanced in democracy (*démocratie avancée*) they could not teach Cameroon any democracy? He even had the effrontery to shamelessly declare that Cameroon was capable and ready to export her own system of democracy. The learned *Kontchoumeter* is undoubtedly indomitable."[7] Is it not only trite then that the rest of the world should know exactly what they would be importing from Cameroon? This book therefore addresses some of the questions prospective buyers and other perplexed constitutional and political experts could want properly addressed before they go ahead and place their importation orders.

The Issues and Questions

I do not purport however to be providing the rest of the world with a 'perfect comprehension' of the democracy and separation of powers confusion in Africa. Purporting to be doing so will itself be just as confusing as Cameroon's 'advanced democracy' that is intended to appear like a better type of the government that North Americans, for example, are used to. A perfect understanding of confusion is near the impossible (a thing that is paradoxically not something Cameroon knows). In brief, it is hard not to be

---

[7] Epo Joseph Tegha, "Kontchoumeter Spawns Lies Again" *The Herald* N° 470 (11-12 June 1997), 4.

lost in "a disorderly jumble", as Pearsall (1998: 387) has defined confusion. Put differently, therefore, it is hard to understand political and constitutional confusion in Cameroon without being confused: confused here being derived from the act of "caus[ing] surprise or confusion in (someone), especially by not according with their expectations" (Pearsall, 1998: 386). The intention in this book therefore is not to further but to curb this confusion through largely understanding and/or exposing it.

To comprehend the confusion in Cameroon called advanced democracy (and its corollaries of federalism, separation of powers, etc) I would, in keeping with Pearsall (1998: 2016),[8] simply attempt to do one, two, three, and/or four things out of four on it. I would try, first, to perceive the intended meaning of the democracy's pieces of confusion; striving to perceive the significance, explanation, or cause of the confusion. I will also strive to be sympathetically or knowledgeably aware of the character or nature of the confusion; and interpret or view this confusion in a particular way – a way that not many, if any at all, have so far interpreted or seen this advanced democracy. This democracy is all pervasive but the understanding of it is here anchored on its unique federalism (and its relationship to secession and self-determination), bicephalism, and bicameralism, as forms of both separation of powers and the preservation of ethnic, cultural, and/or historical, diversity.

The necessity for separating state powers has been stressed in all systems that hinge on people's rule. This does not seem to be the case in Cameroon, especially with its 1996 Constitution[9] which wants to present the country as a bridge between parliamentarianism and congressionalism. Congressional is preferred in this book for references to, or description of, the American (presidential) system in order not to have it confused with other world

---

[8] To put in the other official language of Cameroon, *comprendre quelque chose c'est:*

- *de le contenir, de le renfermer en soi, de l'englober,*
- *de le faire entrer dans un ensemble, dans une catégorie,*
- *de saisir par l'esprit sa raison d'être ou sa signification,*
- *de l'interpréter,*
- *de représenter avec plus ou moins d'indulgence ses mobiles, de l'approuver, et*
- *de le représenter, de connaître sa nature.*

Grand Larousse encyclopédique Vol. 3, at 342.

[9] See *Loi N° 96-06 du 18 janvier 1996 portant révision de la Constitution du 02 juin 1972.*

regimes (including Cameroon's) that do have so many "presidents",[10] although being very far indeed from the system in the United States, where, moreover, parliament has a distinct role and existence. For parliament in any democracy (congressional or parliamentary) to be both representative and the almost exclusive legislation-making organ, there must be a proper constitution (written and/or unwritten). A constitution is proper in the sense, first, that it is the supreme law of the land and, second, that it is balanced and does not give any room for any organ (or person) to be able to confiscate or arrogate all or most state powers (see generally Wade, 1980; Fombad, 2005; and Fossungu, 2010). These imperative features of a proper constitution are wanting in Cameroon's system which is better to be known as confusioncracy.

The relationship between the status of a country's government and its constitutional scholarship is not a very difficult one to establish. Any academic worth the name cannot but be very critical of the manner in which most of the scholars in Cameroon twist plain facts. The facts-twisting is especially accentuated in regard of the Foumban Federation or Constitution about which there are numerous confusing theses on separation of powers, human rights guarantees, full citizen participation, etc. It is even doubtful if one should continue referring to the facts-twisters as intellectuals since, by definition, they are supposed to be shedding light on the issues, not emasculating them; issues that are so numerous and include the following. Magstadt (1991: 91-92) would like to know where to situate the Cameroonian governmental system. Is it with the British unitary and centralized model that vividly contrasts with the federal system found in Canada, Germany and the United States? Is it one of collective ministerial responsibility, a two-party (multiparty) system? Is it the national fusion of powers of Britain, or the USA congressional separation of powers that bars members of Congress from holding a cabinet office concurrently?

Magstadt is quite justified in his queries since the combined potential

---

10 What would, for instance, be chief justice, speaker, chairman, etc. in other jurisdictions would all be 'president' in Cameroon. I would therefore have to shorten president of the republic to POR in order not have this personality (if shortened to 'president') confused with the myriad of other "presidents" that this country is infested with; even though only of them is made to think and breathe for 19 million people. It is even known that in Cameroon it is very easy to find someone who is president of just himself or herself. See Peter Ateh-Afac Fossungu, "Cameroonian Love of the President Title" *The Herald* N° 607 (13-14 May 1998), 4.

and/or effect of Cameroon's numerous constitutions or laws and decrees and their employment of certain concepts (such as *premier ministre*, vote of confidence, *motion de censure*) will be to lead people into thinking that the country is a parliamentary democracy like Britain, Canada or Germany, where parliament is almost exclusively the focal point of state powers. But that is not all because the impression is also given that Cameroon is like the United States of America, when its constitutions talk of the two houses (one of which is even not yet 'created') meeting in *congress* as well as specifying a host of incompatibilities of posts and functions. On the other hand, the fact that said constitutions/laws/decrees also talk of a *President of the Republic*[11] – rather than King or Emperor – will impress on people that Cameroon is (unlike the United Kingdom but) like France which has been shown to bridge the gap between the parliamentary and congressional systems.

Questions emanating from Cameroon's democracy confusion do not always end. Some critics like Fossungu (1998a) would want to also know if the Third World (a conspicuous part of which Cameroon is) should only practise Western-style democracy or must they refurbish their own brand? Asif Hasan Qureshi (cited in Fossungu, 1998: 44 n.182) appears to have been addressing this particular issue when he pondered aloud to some international lawyers in The Hague, The Netherlands, about democracy being a Western mechanism for the imposition of its own value system.

Is democracy a Western mechanism for the imposition of its own value system? This question is relevant because if one is concerned about tensions between countries which have democratic systems and those that do not, one must address the question of whether that is, in part, a cause. If one is to make the institution of democracy attractive, one must deal with the possible suspicion that the avocation of democracy is in fact a disguised call for the imposition of Western value systems. If the institution of democracy is to be sold then it must come across as though it is not an imposition of a value system. I do not think that it is too far-fetched to be suspicious of these calls for democracy given that Western… governments are not too eager to talk about democracy when it comes to the [Third World dictatorships that foster their interests to the total disregard of those of the indigenous people].

Qureshi's suspicion would seem to be graphically brought out,

---

[11] See 1996 Constitution, Part II, Chapter I (articles 5-10); and Federal Constitution, Title III (articles 8-15).

> For example, [by] the stereotyped images of Africa that served to justify European exploitation of the continent during the colonial era [and which] belonged to a European universe of discourse that facilitated countless individual projects designed to enrich Europeans and enhance their power over others [Bjornson, 1991: xii].

Now, it can be and has actually been specifically asked by Fossungu (1998a), if the Third World countries are entitled to stick to their own value systems by having their proper democracy like Cameroon claims to have done, how can their homemade democracy co-exist with associated (Western) concepts such as federalism, bicameralism, judicial independence and constitutionalism? Should they also refurbish their own versions of these latter concepts? How is the age-old question of who guards the guardian (*qui custodiet ipsos custodies*) to be addressed in their democracy? In other words, as Fossungu (1998a) concludes his questioning, can the Camerounization of democracy rather than the democratization of Cameroon be justified, if at all? How? By what means can the justification be made?

In attempting responses to some of the numerous issues raised, and for a better comprehension of the Southern Cameroonsian case at the portals of international human rights law, the internal confusing theses have to be first capped or excluded from the discussion table. Chapter 1 will first circumscribe federalism in the context of the FRC, including the role of intellectuals; and then focus on the coup d'état and/or annexation theses, including whether the Federal National Assembly was the sole legislative organ. Chapter 2 handles the invisible hand of federalism in the context of the lessons in patriotism, sincerity and brotherhood; all within the meaning of the relationship between federalism, political geography, and independence. Chapter 3 examines federalism and the politics of self-determination and of secession; squarely tackling the issue of federalism being foreign to Africa, as claimed by most of the continent's leaders; examining as well their equation of federalism to secession; the understanding of both theses being essential to a correct grasping of the self-determination and/or secession debates under international human rights law and practice. An indication of what I see as the best pathway for Southern Cameroonsians (assuming they really want to have an independent state of their own) is proffered. Chapter 4 looks at bicephalism and bicameralism as forms of separation of powers; debunking the new creations (of the prime ministry, senate, and regions) as mere instruments of further concentration of powers in the midst of "paper" multipatism. The book generally recommends the combination of federalism and the parliamentary system of government as a better way of protecting rights of both citizens and state institutions in Africa.

Chapter 1

Laughing at the Academia: The Federal Republic Of Cameroon (FRC) And The Definition Of Federalism

One of the areas of study I intend to pursue is intellectual and individual responsibility and human rights in Africa. This is based on the belief that the elite has a great many responsibilities towards the population. These responsibilities, I intend to argue, have not been properly discharged. Instead, the elite has engaged in both justifying and participating in most of the political activities responsible for the current malaise in Africa [El Obaid (1996: 311-312 n.203)].

On The Importance Of Federalism And The Issues

Federalism is such an important human rights protecting instrument in governance that it was a principal topic of discussion at one of the triennial congresses of the International Political Science Association, held in 1964 in Geneva. Majeed (2008: 5) sees federalism as an important method of good governance in which political accommodation and understanding become sound practices in the midst of conflicting ideologies, disparate groups, and seemingly irreconcilable positions. Given that a decline of the legitimate political order results in a decline of the moral authority of the nation-state, he concludes, the link between the need for good governance and federal power-sharing is obvious. Federalism has thus been prescribed and applied as a remedy to a great variety of political, economic, social, cultural, and other ailments at all levels of state organization. Federalism is not a fixed point on the map but a tendency that is neither unitary nor separatist. In Aristotelian terms, federalism is the median between those two polar positions, and thus the true opposite of the two (Trager, 1968: ix & x). Federalism has been prescribed and applied around the world with varying degree of success. Why has it not succeeded (or will not succeed) in Cameroon? It is simply because of confusion and manipulation from the intellectuals and other political elites; thus calling for the role of the intellectual in politics as well as the meaning of "intellectuals in politics".

The Role Of The Intelligentsia

Federalism and the New Nations of Africa contains contributions that are based on a symposium sponsored by the University of Chicago's Law School Centre for Legal Research (New Nations) February 12-17, 1962. Three years after the formation of the FRC, David P. Currie could not have phrased it any better, when introducing said book:

> There has never been a greater challenge to the wisdom and ingenuity of the statesmen, lawyers and scholars whose task it is to establish forms and institutions of government. For although constitutions alone cannot ensure the freedom, the vitality, or the economic health demanded by the new nations, the creation of a sound institutional structure cannot fail to have a deep and salutary influence on the course of history.[1]

The curiously intriguing case of Cameroon concretely proves the professor's thesis here; especially again because the status of its Federal Constitution is not even clear. Purportedly the very first political and constitutional document of re-united Cameroon (Le Vine and Nye, 1964: 31 would disagree here), it is only normal that the Federal Constitution has enormously dictated the pulse and rhythm of events since its inception. I demonstrate in this book – contrary to what has so far been presented – that, had Cameroon's statesmen, lawyers and scholars been endowed with any wisdom and ingenuity at all, the country could not be mired in its present unfortunate and precarious politico-constitutional atmosphere; a situation significantly tied to the issues of democracy and federalism or self-determination. These are human rights concepts about which the "intellectuals in politics" say Cameroon's versions are so advanced that even Americans can struggle all their lives and will never catch up with Cameroon's.

This has obviously prompted questions that specifically seek to know what the intellectual has to be doing in politics that is infested with political chameleons. "What is the role of an intellectual? Should the intellectual be an active participant or a seer in politics? How can he [or she] avoid brushes with political chameleons?"[2] In response to the queries, de Smith (1964: 280)

---

[1] David P. Currie, "Introductory Note" in David P. Currie, ed., *Federalism and the New Nations of Africa* (Chicago: University of Chicago Press, 1964).

[2] Canute C.N. Tangwa, "Siga Asanga's Death and the SDF" *The Post* N° 0067 (8 May 1998), 4.

has held that the scholar must become involved in the events themselves, as an adviser, a commentator, or a partisan; and if he or she ends by being none the wiser he or she will at least be better informed. Again, I ask, is that what they are, or have been, doing in Cameroon and Africa generally? There is no better way to respond than by demonstrating the veracity or otherwise of their various theses through the meaning of federalism and associated concepts.

Has Cameroon ever been a federation? That is, as Wheare (1963: 33) would want to know, did the "system of government [in question] embody predominantly a division of powers between general and regional authorities, each of which, in its own sphere, is co-ordinate with the others and independent of them?" Upon the answer to this central question (and those following) lies the heart of the entire confusion in Cameroon regarding multiculturalism and human rights. The other associated questions are: Does a federation exist by the mere fact that "federal" is affixed to the name of a centralized unitary country? What are some of the most conspicuous features of the Foumban Constitution that are inimical to the federal spirit and form? The city of Foumban is regarded in Cameroon as Philadelphia is in the USA (or as Charlottetown is in Canada): Is this analogy sensible or simply a subtle part of the confusion?

Did the President of the Federal Republic (shortened to PFR to also differentiate from the unitary POR) stage a coup d'état upon Cameroon in 1972? In other words, did the Foumban Constitution (1961-1972) guarantee fundamental human and institutional rights and especially minority concerns, as most West Cameroonian intellectuals do claim? If the answer is yes, then why did the FRC very *peacefully* terminate in 1972 without the existence of two or more countries (such as was the case with Ethiopia and Eritrea)? If the answer to the issue of rights being guaranteed is no, why did the FRC not protect those rights? Did federation (if there was any) in Cameroon *end* in 1972?

I think giving genuine answers to these questions is an important step toward comprehending the groundless theses on human rights guarantees by, and surrounding, the FRC; and therefore also civilizing the current federalism and multiculturalism (and, therefore, human rights) debates in Africa generally and Cameroon in particular. Aimed at securing a deeper understanding of the law as a social phenomenon in Cameroon, therefore, this book, though looking at the issues of confusion in governance and human rights there through the eyes of a lawyer, goes a step or two further by viewing the whole Cameroonian system intact. It does not scrutinize just the legal or concerned constitutional enactment in isolation. I think it is through research *on* (and not just *in*) Cameroon law[3] (risky and over-ambitious as it obviously is[4]) that the Cameroonian confusion can be largely understood, if not entirely grasped.

---

[3] For the distinction of research *in* and *on* law, see Arthurs Report (1983: 66). Experts like Dunlop (1991) of the University of Alberta do prefer to employ research *about* law in opposition to *in* law. Talking about the two predominant influences, Dunlop (1991: 67, note omitted) has declared that research *in* law

> is necessarily narrower, though a more coherent, activity than research *about* law. Research *in* law often (perhaps always) consists of doctrinal analysis of legal texts such as cases and statutes. It often (perhaps always) makes assumptions about some aspects of the legal order, for example, the primacy of the reason and the nature of legal reasoning, as well as political assumptions about the value of a legal system and of the rule of law as a necessary part of the good society. Another characteristic of research *in* law is that it tends not to involve empirical study of the actual working of the legal order or of its economic or social consequences. It becomes the study of a limited set of texts rather than an examination of the actual workings of legal institutions. Finally, legal research *in* law usually does not cross disciplinary boundaries, at least when the operational and political assumptions noted above remain unquestioned.

See also Tamanaha (1993: 197 – distinguishing legal sociology from lawyers' internal perspective of law).

[4] Dunlop (1991: 68 & 67) has understandably warned that research *about* law is a much larger and riskier enterprise, with all the inherent dangers involved in an over-ambitious interdisciplinary research. All this is because law in this instance can be discussed as an historical phenomenon, as a cultural, philosophical, or political idea, or as an institution having social, political, or economic consequences that can be examined empirically. Here, Dunlop pursues, law can be read as a story without necessarily making assumptions about rationality or value that the research *in* law tends to involve; seeming always to involve disciplines other than law. One is driven, the Alberta professor concludes, to examine history, the social sciences, cultural studies, philosophy, and literature to carry out the project. The global view adopted by this study appears to somehow combine and overshadow Arthurs Report's (1983: 65-66) research classification into conventional, legal theory, law reform, or fundamental: which it respectively defines as (1) one designed to collect and organize data, to expound legal rules, and to explicate or offer exegesis upon authoritative legal sources; (2) one designed to yield a unifying theory or perspective by which rules may be understood, and their application in particular cases evaluated and controlled – usually including scholarly commentary on civil law known as *doctrine*; (3) one that aims at accomplishing change in the law, whether to eliminate anomalies, to enhance effectiveness, or to secure a change in direction; and (4) the type designed to secure a deeper understanding of the law as a social phenomenon, including research on the historical, philosophical, linguistic, economic, social or political implications of law.

This global approach has an unrivalled advantage. Above all else, it enormously aids anyone capable of managing it to grasp and master a lot of the confusion within/about Cameroon's constitutional and political set-up. As I would continue to say throughout, most of these issues continue to largely baffle the majority of black-letter lawyers and academics who cling to a single constitutional provision, without considering the entire document as a package. Equally significant to any sane discussion of Cameroon's nation-building, therefore, must be the relative importance of the non constitutional factors such as religion, culture, language, distribution of resources, political geography, and, above all, personal and psychological factors like charisma, commitment, friendships, rivalries, and personal ambitions. One can clearly not go beyond the mere words of the constitution (as advised by Benjamin, 1972: 13) without these enumerated elements, most of which also go into making Cameroon political and constitutional history.

Looking at all the historical factors (constitutional and non-constitutional alike) in the case of Cameroon, one cannot help but be very critical of the academia in this country for the shaky or outright confusing stance they take on important human rights issues; whereas their role is to shed light and improve the common good of humanity. The problems of society are no doubt very complex; with this complication being accentuated in multiethnic and/or multicultural polities. And, of course, no one would deny that "Cameroon is a multicultural, multiethnic, multi-lingual and multi-religious State" (Ngwana, 2009). In such societies, as has been pointed out, the role of the intelligentsia in the creation of a sound institutional structure and the influence of the latter on the course of history cannot be doubted. The vital role of lawyers and other scholars in any society would hardly require overemphasis.

Legal education, according to Professor Allott, refers to the experiences and training that help different kinds of people to understand and use the law in society.[5] This means that one does not necessarily need to be a *lawyer* or *law* student to interest oneself with the law and especially with the Constitution and its issues.[6] Intellectuals (lawyers and jurists or not) simply cannot escape from the issues, if they must retain those descriptions given

---

[5] Cited in J.B. Ojwang and D.R. Salter, "Legal Education in Kenya" 33-1 *Journal of African Law* (1988-89): 78-90 at 78.

[6] Marc Gold, "Constitutional Scholarship in Canada" 23 *Osgoode Hall Law Journal* (1985), 495-518 at 496-98.

them since, by definition, "the task of any intellectual inquiry is to raise people (the oppressed) to a level of 'true consciousness' because only when they truly appreciate how oppressed they are, can they act to transform the world."[7] The contrary is what largely holds true for Cameroon with the rampant confusioncracy, thus making it almost impossible for the oppressed to 'act to transform the world' since they cannot 'truly appreciate how oppressed they are'. Most of the intellectuals in Africa have been described with the Janus-like phrase 'intellectuals in politics' and this may be the right moment to discuss this confusing phraseology.

'Intellectual In Politics': What Does It Mean?

The confusion and manipulation in Cameroon are yet to find an area where they are excluded. A better comprehension of the issues will be greatly assisted after I have neatly distinguished the various forms of intellectualism that may be involved in African politics. The description 'Intellectual in Politics' would itself further aggravate the confusion that is characteristically Cameroonian. It has been used specifically to describe Dr. Fonlon who was the interpreter/translator in Foumban and therefore the key-holder to the creation of the FRC. The phrase keeps occurring in this book and other discussions of Cameroon's 'fascinating federalism subject which demands a very careful and thorough investigation.' The accentuated study (in Chapter 2) of the translator/interpreter's impeccable but largely emasculated anti-federalism role in the Foumban Enterprise should be understandable. A professor at the School of Medicines (CUSS) of the University of Yaoundé, Lantum (1991: 21), on Thursday 6 June 1991 in his very lengthy piece in the Special Political Issue of *Le Messager* talked of the Foumban bilingual translator's

> Pursuit with grand style political engagement… the central theme of this fascinating [federalism] subject which demands a very careful and thorough investigation. It is thus the principal concern of this paper. How did he achieve this? What were the consequences? What was his special preparation for this important role? What does it prove? These

---

[7] Egon C. Guba, "The Alternative Paradigm Dialog" in E.C. Guba, ed., *The Paradigm Dialog* (Sage Publications, 1990), 17 at 24. See also Editor-in-Chief Richard L. Abel of the University of California at Los Angeles (UCLA) Law School, "From the Editor" *African Law Studies* N° 14 (1977), 1.

are some of the questions which we will be answering in the next few paragraphs.

These said 'next few paragraphs' that do span six newspaper pages (and which Lantum, 1991: 20, addressed to "political scientists, sociologists, historians, political sociologists, philosophers, and jurists") have declared in the third paragraph (*ibid*) that "Since I consider this paper as the forum-setter for a long and elaborate debate on the phenomenon of F[ederal]ism, I have no apologies to tender. It is my wish and hope that erudite scholars will continue and develop this subject to its full ramifications in order to do justice to Dr FONLON [-] himself an illustratrious [sic: illustrious? Illustrative?] son of Cameroon and the country he served as politician." There are a few preliminary points to straighten out here.

First, it is my belief that we do not need to make any apology especially when we are discussing public matters since "The right of freedom of expression and of criticism, upon matters of public policy and public administration, and the right to discuss and debate such matters, whether they be social, economic or political, are essential to the working of a parliamentary democracy."[8] These public matters certainly include what Lantum (1991: 20) describes as "the paper [which] is purported [sic] to examine the political significance of Dr Bernard FONLON's life, with Dr FONLON being focused upon as an intellectual – not just any Cameroonian citizen." It is also my conviction that ordinary Cameroonian citizens in particular are now seeking to know how confusing and manipulative (or otherwise) the Foumban Federalism Enterprise is/was. These ordinary citizens want to understand, in addition, whether or not the architects of the FRC were completely ignorant of the federalism theories of some of the experts listed below and therefore relied solely on the translator. Their question is apt because what came out of Foumban seems to be completely beyond reasonable imagination, in view of the West Cameroon proposals for union, as discussed in Chapter 2.

The phrase *intellectual in politics* must therefore have to be given a particular attention because of its tendency to conceal a people's true history from them; or, if it does not completely hide this history, it confuses it. The

---

[8] Justice Abbott in *Switzman v. Elbling* [1957] S.C.R. 285 at 326, cited in Keith Dubick, "Freedom to Hate: Do the Criminal Code Proscriptions against Hate Propaganda Infringe the Charter?" 54 *Saskatchewan Law Review* (1990) 149, at 157 n.39.

vague and ambiguous description, some critics like Fossungu (1998b) have charged, has been well chosen solely to confuse and emasculate the issues and/or some forms of intellectualism. Fossungu could hardly be wrong because Lantum (1991: 20 – quoting James Wilford Gamer, Professor of Political Science at the University of Illinois – without specific reference) thinks *intellectual in politics* "is open to the objection that it possesses several meanings and, when used without qualification or discrimination[,] leads to confusion if not misunderstanding." What then are the possible meanings to be qualified in order to eschew misconstruction and confusion?

According to Fossungu (1998b), *intellectual in politics* can mean more than one thing. In the first place, he indicates, the phraseology can mean that the person being described by it is an intellectual in the *art* of politics. I think political scientists probably come within the ambit of this first meaning, since Lantum (1991: 20, quoting James Wilford Gamer, emphasis as in original) says Jelineck has stated that the "*task of political science is to study in their fundamental relations the public powers, to examine the conditions under which they manifest themselves, their end and their effect, to investigate the state in its inner nature.*" Not only political scientists do all of that though; and this may even be the reason why Lantum has not addressed the "political significance" paper only to them but also to all the other "erudite scholars" named, including jurists like the present writer who (while still 'rooting' himself on his home turf) is nonetheless refusing to be pigeonholed, in order to better comprehend the amoeba-like confusioncracy.

Intellectual in politics, according to Fossungu (1998b), can as well be that the person it describes is an intellectual in something else than politics but is involved *in* politics. I would want to name this second category 'something else politician'. Where then do those in and out of the Cameroon regime fall? Perhaps their postulations on federalism, on history and on independence can help in situating them? It is simply not clear as to which of these possible meanings is intended in Lantum's (1991: 20) famous paper which is devoted to an examination of the political significance of Dr. Bernard Fonlon's life, with Dr. Fonlon being focused upon as an intellectual – not just any Cameroonian citizen; and this because it is hard to gainsay that genuine intellectuals *in* politics (in both senses already proffered) must surely recognize when plain facts are being this much twisted in public affairs. By this type of intellectuals, I am here referring to those who not only recognize, but also actually practise, good governance. To most genuine intellectuals *in* politics, Couloumbis and Wolfe (1986: 3, emphasis as in original) say, "politics could probably be best understood as a person's *concern* with *public affairs*. Public affairs affect collective interests rather than narrow personal interests." Such intellectuals would certainly recognize that the FRC did not approach the definition and practice of federalism and why.

The FRC and the Definition Of Federalism

The book, *Distribution of Powers and Responsibilities in Federal Countries*, presents what Majeed (2008: 3) describes as an objective and balanced description and analysis of the distribution of powers and responsibilities in the federal constitution and actual practice of eleven countries: Australia, Belgium, Brazil, Canada, Germany, India, Mexico, Nigeria, Spain, Switzerland, and the United States. For each federation there is an in-depth examination of such themes as (1) the distribution of governmental, political, monetary, fiscal, administrative, and policy responsibilities; (2) symmetry and asymmetry in the distribution of responsibilities; (3) the reasons and ways in which powers and responsibilities are explicitly and implicitly exclusive, concurrent, or shared in the constitution; (4) the reasons and ways in which responsibilities become divided and shared in actual governmental practice; (5) current controversies over the division and/or sharing of powers and responsibilities; and (6) assessments of the exclusive and concurrent exercise of powers and responsibilities. Is there any home for the 'true federation' logic in Cameroon? This query is another way of saying that it is not clear that Cameroonians have, since 1961, ever known and practised local government, a system of governance that the current 1996 Constitution is also bragging about in its Part X (articles 55-62). As the intellectuals do claim that there were, contrary to what I am saying, a lot of power-sharing in the FRC, marked particularly by judicial review, I will first survey the definition of federalism before outlining those separation of powers theses and then continue to find out how a federation with all those acclaimed features can be so easily 'terminated' without two or more countries resulting from it.

Defining Federalism: Surprising The Experts

Many writers are often bewildered by the actual formation and continuous existence of the FRC or Cameroon. The singularity of the FRC is indeed noted in several respects. For instance, unlike Franck (1968a: 8) whose discussion "touches not upon the failure of what was, but of what might have been," I am here examining what was, although not being in fact what should have been. Yet, the FRC being studied here has, surprisingly, never disintegrated like the West Indian Federation which Flanz (1968: 113) says created at worst hostility and at best apathy, being seldom able to produce the kind of concrete advantages which could have engendered support for the Federation. Neither has the FRC even broken down, in the words of Franck (1968a: 8), into "resembling more those peculiar ex-lovers who, having broken up, still continue to meet and engage in love-hateful domestic bickering that end sometimes in sex but never again in marriage." That is not all that gives the FRC its unusualness.

Writing ten years after its formation, Le Vine (1971: 1) stated that Cameroon's experiment in federalism is not without its unusual aspects. It is thus far the only federal union of French- and English-speaking territories on the continent (not excepting the Ghana-Guinea-Mali union, which never went beyond the rhetorical stage) and the first attempt to blend the political offspring of French, English and United Nations tutelary experiences. The only other African bilingual territorial merger has been that of the Somalis that resulted in a unitary state long before the FRC that is said to have done same in 1972. Did the FRC actually end in 1972?

Awolowo has reviewed most of the political unions around the world;[9] but the FRC could be distinguished from most other broken political marriages such as Britain/Ireland, Northern/Southern Rhodesia, India/Pakistan, all of them, according to Franck (1968a: 8), being profoundly poisoned relations among former partners; as well as from the Scandinavians whose *sang*-Freudian correctness disguises their mutual alienation. To leave most of Cameroon's other distinctive conflict-ridden (but not even clashing[10]) characteristics aside, the *successful* Cameroonian English-French marriage is bound to knock a lot of people off balance: viewing, for example, the experts' (Franck 1968a, 7-8; Southall 1974, 138; Okondo[11]) findings that

---

[9] See Obafemi Awolowo, *Thoughts on Nigerian Constitution* (Ibadan: Oxford University Press, 1966) at 28-48.

[10] See Fossungu (2013:200-203); and Emmanuel Anyefru, "The Refusal to Belong: Limits on the Discourse on Anglophone Nationalism in Cameroon" available at http://www.thefreelibrary.com/The+refusal+to+belong%3A+limits+of+the+discourse+on+Anglophone...-a0279891521 [accessed on 11 February 2013].

[11] Peter J.H. Okondo, "Prospects of Federation in East Africa" in David P. Currie, ed., *Federalism and the New Nations of Africa* (Chicago: University of Chicago Press, 1964), 29-74.

federalism could not even materialize in East Africa (between three English-speaking countries: Kenya, Uganda and Tanzania) despite all the mystique of unity that still remains a reality vividly perceptible to the political sense there. But that surprise must substantially dwindle when some hard facts (that are wrapped in confusioncracy) about Cameroon are grasped.

Other than confusion and manipulation, what could account for the uniqueness of the FRC just noted? Was the FRC actually a federation and why was it formed? The correct answers to these questions are found in the principal and general question(s): What is federalism and what gives impetus to its adoption? As it is usual with almost all institutions, the meaning and purpose of federalism are intertwined. Both its meaning and purpose can be seen in (1) *what* it is adopted to do, and (2) *how/why* it is able (or unable) to do it. While the first point has to do with the sickness to be cured by federalism (see Chapter 3, for example), the second touches on the kinds of principles upon which the federation is based (largely discussed below in this Chapter). Both these factors are principally shaped by (3) the forces pushing for and/or against a federal union; that is, *why* federalism is adopted (see Chapter 2, for instance). All these points are important and are discussed in this study, but the third point (the Invisible Hand of Federalism) is the most important since it is the key to the others and therefore that which directly involves how the institutions and/or history and/or culture of the federating components are/is to be treated in the union.

It has not been an easy task defining federalism to the general satisfaction of all. Using several definitions (all of which he set out), Shapiro (1995: 4) amply demonstrated the striking vagueness of many attempted definitions of federalism, opining that no easy definitions and pigeonholing will prove adequate. This may largely explain why Wheare's (1963) celebrated federal principle has come under fire from Hogg (1996: 99 & 100) for being too rigid in stressing the separate and distinct spheres of both levels of government. Having also catalogued several other contrary (to rigid) contributions, Hogg (1996: 99) has found that those too would have so eroded the concept of federalism that it has become too vague to be useful. It is thus not surprising that another expert had made the same discovery six years before Shapiro when, having extensively examined the various attempted definitions at pages 7-9 of his book, Stevenson (1989: 8) also concluded that possibly no single definition of so elusive and controversial a concept could be satisfactory for all purposes. This could explicate why a number of images, according to Majeed (2008: 4), emerged from the eleven studied countries. There is the image of the "divided federalism" of Canada as a contrast to the "integrated and shared federalism" of Germany, with the "quasi-federalism" of India lying in between. The United States system, Majeed says, underscores a delegation of powers to the national government rather than a distribution of powers between the national and the state governments – but not without an often strongly coercive centralism. Whereas Canadian fiscal federalism is one of the most decentralized forms of federalism, Majeed has concluded, India's is one of the most centralized.

These complex or numerous attempts at circumscribing the concept of federalism cannot however be indicative that definitions should be completely shunned. According to Franck (1968b: 169), what such a definitional problem or diversity simply suggests is not that a single, highly structured definition of federalism is needed. Rather, it is that there be greater understanding of the nearly infinite number of variations that can be played in the federal theme and that the difficulties of engineering a union of nations should only begin when the leaders agree to federate and their subalterns sit down to work out what is too often called "the details". This thesis can again be well seen in *Distribution of Powers and Responsibilities in Federal Countries*. As Majeed (2008: 3) tells us, their study identifies similarities and differences among the eleven federal polities studied with regard to intergovernmental distribution of powers and responsibilities. In all eleven countries the system is part of the constitutional structure; yet there is wide range of variations among these systems. He goes on to exemplify, stating that whereas the United States and Australia present one type of distribution system, Canada and India present another. Even in Europe, he notes, Belgium presents still another; whereas other European federations such as Germany and Switzerland exhibit a division between the allocation of legislative and executive authority in particular areas.

Majeed's (*ibid*) conclusion is also that in view of differences in forms and scope of various distributions of powers and responsibilities, "it can be surmised that there is no pure model of federalism but, rather, several practical variations within the common framework of federal systems." From the foregoing, the definitional problem, according to Franck ((1968b: 169), would also suggest that the content of a federal arrangement need not be governed by any historically fixed pattern; that the concept of federalism is malleable enough to bend with the realities. Indeed, the important conclusion about federation formation which he emphasizes is that it is when the realities are bent to fit into some rigid, historic but unsuitable federal pattern that trouble often begins. This critical and constructive study advances the FRC and the SDF four-state federation project (the latter is discussed elaborately in Chapter 2) as clear candidates in this stark bending of realities.

On "Evaluating Federalism" (Stevenson, 1989: 14-18), it is clear that the FRC is no case from which one can pick certain characteristics to hold out as being the essence of federalism; which is an obvious indication of the fact that there was in reality no federation in Cameroon, notwithstanding Benjamin's (1972: 148) thesis that 'the ideal federal state does not yet exist anywhere' (my translation). Federalism proper, as I see it, cannot exist and function in a society that is wanting in properly enlightened citizens, that is wanting in some basic political and legal institutions, that lacks basic and properly enacted laws, that is marked by the absence of rule of law, and that is defined by the absence of self-control. "At the background of it all," Enonchong (1967: xiii) has explained, "is the age-old idea of the protection of the individual and the right of the national-state to carry out its responsibilities in a democratic and progressive society." This signifies that federalism must further constitutionalism and the protection of human rights, all of which, in liberal-constitutional democracies like Canada, "are inseparable from the doctrine of separation of powers, from parliamentary sovereignty, from rule of law, from constitutional supremacy, and from diversification of power centres" (Tremblay, 1993: 66 – my translation).

Like multiparty politics with which it must marry, federalism is obviously one of the effective modes of separating powers and dividing competence – both institutionally and territorially – so as to save the people and federating entities from autocracy. This is the state form that African states so badly need to be able to effectively tackle their ethnic and other conflict-management problems; as well as to pull together for the betterment of the African peoples' lot on this planet called earth. Lack of vision apart, it is evident that this federal undertaking is something that will not be impossible in Africa: absent confusion and manipulation. The lack of vision is mostly on the part of the officials in power who do regard federalism just as negatively as anything else that preaches the diversification of power centres. But it does not end there because the absence of vision and integrity would seem to cut right across the entire African spectrum (Government and Opposition alike). Truly, as Anyangwe (1987: xiv) has observed, it is only "lack of vision, integrity and commitment on the part of many [that] will continue to clog the wheels of that important [federalism] undertaking [in Cameroon, for example]." A critical and balanced evaluation of the invisible hand of Cameroon's federalism (especially in Chapter 2 below) best illustrates this lack of vision, integrity, commitment, and the accompanying and overriding confusion and manipulation; all of which would not let authentic history play the role that is its own in development or nation-building.

Was the FRC actually motivated by a desire to both protect human rights and avert some imminent problems common to the federating entities? Was the FRC really the result of "history-less" political science or simply that of an "ulterior something"? This issue must be examined because political science without history has been largely condemned for its fruitlessness (see Fossungu, 2013: 141-147). Classical authors on federalism such as Wheare, Dicey, Geoffrey Sawer, Durand, Livingston, Friedrich, Tarleton, Elazar, and Riker certainly formulated their theory without taking "*compte du cas camerounais, trop récent et trop mal connu*" (Benjamin, 1972: 147).That is, without taking 'into consideration the case of Cameroon that is very recent and thus not very appropriately known or studied'. Can it also be said with conviction that the Cameroonian "Fathers of Federation" did not know of the existence of the theories of those experts when they formulated theirs in Foumban?

In addressing this last issue, Enonchong (1967: xii-xiii) has told the questioning youths that ignorance on the architects' part is clearly out of the question "because the framers of the [Cameroon Federal] Constitution frequently adverted to these constitutions [of the United States, Canada, France and Great Britain] at the Foumban Constituent Assembly. This is particularly true of the principles of federalism and judicial review which have been closely modelled, knowingly or unknowingly, on the American idea." The authenticity in most of these issues concerning Cameroon's 'fascinating federalism' will come to light when I examine the theory and practice regarding the formation of, among others, the two federal unions whose constitutions have just been alluded to. Can there really be judicial review without separation of powers? And was there such separation of powers in Foumban?

Power-Sharing in the FRC?

My response, of course, is no. Of course, as Ngwana (2009) rightly points out, "A Federation is the only way by which any multinational and culturally divers[e] communion, has the opportunity for variation in laws, existences, dispensations, that take into account of the motley sensibilities and accordingly concede reasonable autonomy to the constituting units." But I think all these things cannot happen without that 'Federation' being marked by separation of powers both in theory and practice.

> It is here that this study asks how different jurisdictions interact with one another. Their relationships may be characterized by hierarchy, mutual dependence, asymmetrical dependence, or relative independence. To understand these distinctions one has to understand both the formal and informal institutions of the country in question. In addition, any discussion about the distribution of powers and responsibilities must encompass the constitutional mechanisms that have been used for that end. Structural changes have been introduced in many federal countries, and any debate on a distribution of responsibility and of resources remains incomplete if the constitutional provision of the federal structure remains blurred [Majeed, 2008: 5].

Some West Cameroonian intellectuals insist however that there was a great deal of multiplicity of power centres in the FRC; and this involved all levels and branches. To Gorji-Dinka (1991), for instance, the 1961 Foumban Constitution

> shared power: (a) territorially, i.e., between the states and the centre; (b) institutionally, i.e., between the executive, the judiciary and legislature [and] (c) personally-wise, i.e., the Executive power was shared by the President and the State Prime Ministers; while legislative power was shared by State Deputies and Federal Deputies.

This theory is then claiming, first, a clear demarcation of federal-provincial domains; implying that there was "politics of intergovernmental relations"[12] which Eleazu (1977: 267) says "today from the viewpoint of the

[12] For further discussion of this indispensable federal-state cooperation, see, e.g., Shapiro (1995: 26-35 (cooperative federalism in Germany), & 71-73 (cooperative federalism in Belgium)); Hogg (1996: 129-131 (cooperative federalism in Canada)); David C. Nice, *Federalism: The Politics of Intergovernmental Relations* (New York: St. Martin's Press, 1987); Bruce W. Hodgins, John J Eddy, Shelagh D. Grant and John Atchison, "Dynamic Federalism:

states and localities is (1) a right to be heard in the design of programmes and (2) a right to share in the implementation of programmes." In the second place, Gorji-Dinka (1991) claims what Schneider (2008: 130-133) prefers to describe as "Horizontal Division of Powers: The Three Branches of Government", a principle that has been widely adopted because the liberty of the individual lies in the separation of powers – that is, in such an arrangement of the various institutions of government that each should prevent the other from having sufficient power to act tyrannically.[13]

Gorji-Dinka's claim of "The Constitutional Distribution of Powers" (Simon and Papillion, 2008: 97-100) in the FRC has been confirmed by Enonchong (1967: 22) who declares that "The general feature at the national level is, therefore, that the [Foumban] Constitution seeks to separate powers between the executive, legislative and judiciary, with the set purpose that each can be an expert in its own field. The federal legislature is identified with making legislation, the executive with implementing it, and the judiciary with interpreting the rules where necessary." Gorji-Dinka (1991) then concludes that "In this way the guarantee of security for the individual w[as] institutionalised." Enonchong (1967: chapter 7) also discusses the FRC's 'Civil Liberties and Constitutional Guarantees'. The theses on the institutionalization of individual freedoms are highly erroneous or manipulative and would appear to have been inspired by Enonchong (1967: xi-xii) who seems to have led the others to their baseless positions when he posited in 1967 that "Undoubtedly the [Foumban] constitutional instrument had allocated powers to the federal and federated state authorities and among the three governmental bodies, namely, the Executive, the Legislature and the Judiciary."

It must be highlighted over and over that these are confusioncratic (confusing and manipulative) theses, as I elaborately show later; and that they

---

Continuity and Change Since World War I" in Bruce W. Hodgins, John J Eddy, Shelagh D. Grant and James Struthers, eds., *Federalism in Canada and Australia: Historical Perspectives, 1920-1988* (Peterborough, Ontario: Frost Centre for Canadian Heritage and Development Studies, 1989), 19-54; and Malcolm Alexander, "State/Provincial Governments and Federal Power: The Politics of National Development" in Hodgins *et al*, eds., *Federalism in Canada and Australia: Historical Perspectives, 1920-1988* (Peterborough, Ontario: Frost Centre for Canadian Heritage and Development Studies, 1989), 86-103.

[13] H. Finer, *The Theory and Practice of Modern Government* rev. ed. (New York: Holt, 1949) at 84. See also W.B. Gwyn, *The Meaning of Separation of Powers: An Analysis of the Doctrine from its Origin to the Adoption of the United States Constitution* (The Hague: Martinus Nijhoff, 1965); Loewenstein (1967: x-xi); and Dickson (1985: 9 & 22-23).

are coming from intellectuals (mostly lawyers and jurists) who, rather than tell the truth ('and nothing but the truth, so help me God') to the people who are looking up to them, will be busy inventing facts where none exists to further compound and emasculate the people's real situation. I would simply think that all the unfounded claims about the FRC (if not deliberate confusioncracy) could then be purely the result of what Ntenga (1997) vehemently condemns as the "cow dung journalism [and intellectualism]." It is cow dung, as Ntenga (*ibid.*) explains it, because it will not "Take up the spade of the journalist [and intellectual] and go into the field and dig out the root causes of those events and also draw from history" and then "get down to analytical, incisive and objective reporting." Ntenga is absolutely right; and this correctness applies as well to Ntenga's own Solid Edifice Theory that is discussed below. "Once more," another press critic has questioned, "it becomes necessary to question who in Cameroon may be termed a journalist. Is it the young man who can write good sentences in very colourful language or persons trained in activities as well as the ethics of this privileged profession?"[14] Let's find out from their various theses on the country's name-changes.

Secession, Coup D'état and/or Annexation In 1972/84?

It is known from both Njawé and Eyoum'a Ntoh that it is the doing of analytical, incisive and objective reporting (*sans avoir horreur de la vérité*[15]) that

[14] Tadoh Ndikum Munji, "Save the Profession from Hijackers" *The Post* (24 October 1997), 4. See also James Fallows, "The Most Famous Journalist in America" in Charles Peters and Nicholas Lemann, eds., *Inside the System* 4th ed. (New York: Holt, Rinehart and Winston, 1979), 246-266; J. Konana, "Journalists Urged to Avoid Journalism of Excess and Innuendoes" *Cameroon Post* N° 0028 (8-14 October 1996), 4; and Jude Waindim, "Laughing at the Press" *Cameroon Post* N° 0274 (11-18 December 1995), 9 (cataloguing instances of sensational and unhelpful journalism).

[15] See Pius Njawé, "Le vrai débat" *Le Messager* N° 587 (20 février 1997), 1; and Patrick-Thomas Eyoum'a Ntoh, "Qui veut tromper Fru Ndi?" *Le Messager* N° 587 (20 février 1997), 3.

principally, if not exclusively, leads to real debates of/on the issues such as those of federalism, democracy, and multiculturalism in Africa. Pathetically, as I indicated earlier, the reverse instead seems to be the rule in Africa. Local government (or federalism) without an independent judiciary and locally elected officials is not worth the name. In the absence of these institutions there is no reason why anyone would then be using the terms federalism and democracy, except for confusion, a mystification that seems to have become the singular characteristic of the "intellectuals in politics". They claim, for instance, that Biya's 1984 change of name to 'Republic of Cameroon' is secession on the part of East Cameroon from the 1961 union (see Konings, 1999: 305-306; and Fossungu, 2013:23-29). From Pactet's (1991: 85) definition of democracy,[16] it is crystal clear to even any savvy elementary school pupil that secession will not be regarded in the inverted, confusioncratic, and subversive manner (as it is in Cameroon) in a country that is truly democratic. If it is truly a government of the people by the people for the people, secession has already been excluded by self-determination or the absence of repression. Was West Cameroon then repressing East Cameroon in the union for the latter to be seceding from it? It is the reverse that would instead hold. Secession is nothing but the legitimate response to the repression of the universal right to self-determination within the state (see Chapter 3 below for details).

This also means that a democratic society, according to Hogg (1996: 124-25), may even have 'the power to secede' embedded in the constitution. As indicated by Konings (1999: 301), the final version of the Foumban Constitution left no room for legal secession from the federation, although some Southern Cameroons delegates had wanted a provision inserted into the constitution sanctioning the peaceful withdrawal from the federation. Why did they accept what they did not want? And why would there now be such a peaceful withdrawal on the part of East Cameroon? Chapter two might provide an answer; but to provide for secession in the constitution does not however necessarily mean that states or provinces have the right to secede from a federal union *whenever* they just feel like doing so. "If the definition [of federalism] is a valid one," Stevenson (1989: 8-9, emphasis added) has argued, "it follows that in a *true federation* the provinces or states

---

[16] "*La démocratie* peut *être considérée, selon la définition adoptée, comme le pouvoir du plus grand nombre ou le gouvernement du peuple, par le peuple, et pour le peuple ou encore comme le régime qui assure l'identification des gouvernés aux gouvernants.*"

have no right to secede. If such right existed before, they surrendered it when they entered the federal union." This is the elementary lesson; and which is quite normal and logical but does this logic apply to the case of Cameroon? That is, was the FRC a true federation? I answer in the negative; and would therefore think that, as there was no true federation in Foumban, the 'true federation impediment' argument from Southern Cameroonsians cannot stand. That is to say in particular that the Southern Cameroonsian argument that (by the name-change in 1984) *La République du Cameroun* seceded from the Union in 1984 has no firm foundation or any underpinning at all (for more of which, see Fossungu, 2013:67-69).

Let us find out if their treason and coup d'état theses (tied to the 1972 name-change) can also stand. A lot of Southern Cameroonsian writings have scathingly accused late President Ahidjo for having staged a coup d'état upon Cameroon in 1972. Not in any way being Ahidjo's advocate, I am yet to be convinced that such a thing happened *in 1972*. To exclude the charge from the scene and thus make proper allowance for the new political dispensation that Cameroonians now deserve, I will cut to pieces and exclude the coup d'état/annexation theses by scrutinizing (1) the question of how amendments were to be effected in the FRC; including (2) whether the FNA was the sole legislator and thus the only organ responsible for effecting constitutional amendments, and (3) the availability of open-ended emergency powers to the PFR.

Amendments And The Solid Federal Edifice Theory

The secession claim from the English-speaking in this country has already been excluded because there was no true federation. As Scott's (1991: 15) argument goes, "There is no legal basis for any constitutional change – and therefore no right of secession by any province of Canada – except through the means of change provided by the Constitution itself." What then were the means provided by Cameroon's 1961 Federal Constitution that could justify change in Cameroon such as the one(s) in 1972 (and in 1984)? In other words, was the minority state protected in such a way that a nation-wide referendum could not be one of these devices for effecting constitutional change in Cameroon?

In this country, a lot of people just jump into talking wildly about the 'solid federation' without ever having seen the constitutional or political basis of said solid edifice. There are several theories suggesting the affirmative to the query just posed, especially the Solid Federal Edifice Theory. This theory claims that the given constitutional means for change under the FRC protected the minority from any change that they did not favour. In the proper words of Ntenga's (1997) Solid Federal Edifice thesis, the Foumban Federation, "made up of the State of West Cameroon and that of East Cameroon", undoubtedly "was built on a solid foundation known as 'the Federal Constitution.' While laying the foundation stone in Foumban in 1961, the architects and builders of the Edifice agreed that no part of the building shall be modified without the knowledge and express consent of both parties and the sovereign people of Cameroon." Other similar theses[17] such as the SCFAQ's Question 5 (emphasis added) do claim that

> The July 1961 constitutional conference in Foumban defined the structure of the union between La Republique du Cameroun and the Southern Cameroons as a Federation. This agreement led to the Federal Republic of Cameroon that came into being on October 1st 1961. The two parties co-existed happily till 1972 when the President of the Federation Mr. Amadou Ahidjo unilaterally *and in violation of Article 47 of the Federal Constitution (which prohibited any action that would threaten the existence of the federation)* abrogated the Federal arrangement with Proclamation DF 72-270 of February 6th, 1972, abolishing all federal legislative, judicial and administrative institutions and removing *all guarantees that protected the rights of the minority Southern Cameroons* in the Federation.

This contribution or book strongly disagrees with these theories and, to buttress my contrary view, I am going to take a keen look at the constitutional amending formula of only the Solid Federal Edifice, not to go into those of other federal constitutions.[18] According to the amendment

---

[17] According to Ngwana (2009), "Unification was based on Federalism and Equality of status, on Unity in Diversity, on equality of all Cameroonians.... that is why the United Nations gave Southern Cameroons independence on the basis of Federalism. We unified on the understanding that we would operate a Federal System, in which we will live in a mighty, united, economically, strong Cameroon Nation; guaranteeing all citizens of every race and religion, inalienable fundamental and civic rights, equal opportunities and respect for the bicultural character of our people."

[18] For discussion of the amending procedures of several federations, see Wheare (1963: 55-57); and Dumont *et al* (2008: 50-55) (Belgium). For the 'interesting' case of Canada in particular, see Tremblay (1993: 29-35); Anne F. Bayefsky, *Canada's Constitution Act 1982*

formula in article 47 of the Cameroon 'Federal' Constitution (its equivalent being Part XI (articles 63-64) of the 1996 Constitution),

> Any proposal for the revision of the present Constitution which impairs the unity and integrity of the Federation shall be inadmissible. The power to initiate the revision of the Constitution shall belong equally to the President of the Federal Republic, after consultation with the Prime Ministers of the Federated States, and the Deputies of the Federal Assembly. Any proposal for revision submitted by the Deputies must be signed by at least one third of the Members of the Federal Assembly. Proposals for revision shall be adopted by simple majority vote of the members of the Federal Assembly, provided that such majority includes a majority of the representatives in the Federal Assembly of each of the Federated States. The President of the Federal Republic may request, under the same conditions as for a federal law that a second reading be given to a law revising the Constitution.

Every sentence of this amending formula is topic enough for a whole book of its own. I am not going to write those books within this one though. I will just stay on the issues of *coup d'état/annexation in 1972* and of the minority being guaranteed protection under the Federal Constitution, especially against change that they did not want. This will entail finding out (1) whether two simple majorities equal a special majority and (2) whether there was any place for judicial review in the FRC.

1. Two Simple Majorities Equal A Special Majority?

Citing A. W. Mukong (ed.), *The Case for the Southern Cameroons* (Yaoundé, Cameroon Federalist Committee, 1990), p. 18, Konings and Nyamnjoh (1997: 210) have indicated that on 6 May 1972, Ahidjo announced in the National Assembly that he intended to transform the Federal Republic into a unitary state, provided the electorate supported the idea in a referendum to

---

and Amendments Vol. 1 (Toronto: McGraw-Hill Ryerson, 1989); André Tremblay, *La réforme de la Constitution au Canada* (Montreal: Éditions Thémis, 1995) especially at 22-46; Honourable Gérald Beaudoin and Jim Edwards, *The Process for Amending the Constitution of Canada: Report of the Special Joint Committee of the Senate and the House of Commons* (20 June 1991); and Benoît Pelletier, *La modification constitutionnelle au Canada* (Toronto: Thomson Canada Ltd., 1996).

be held on 20 May, thereby abrogating clause 1 of article 47 of the Foumban document which read as outlined above. Even if the constitution were to be amended, they further pointed out that it should not be done by referendum, because clause 3 of article 47 stipulated `that proposals for revision shall be adopted by simple majority vote of the members of the Federal Assembly, provided that such majority includes a majority of the representatives... of each of the Federated States.'

It has thus been largely alleged that Ahidjo staged a coup d'état in 1972 by not respecting article 47's special majority which some scholars like Enonchong (1967: 21, citing Federal article 18) regard as "the entrenchment of special clauses as a necessary safeguard against the imposition of wanton legislation on any unwilling state." Konings (1999: 300), commenting on the praised article, has lengthily observed that,

> Curiously, Ahidjo eventually allowed a Southern Cameroons recommendation to be incorporated into the constitution which created a potential safeguard against the adoption of federal legislation harmful to one of the federated states. Article 18 created a procedure whereby the president might require a bill to be read a second time, either of his own accord or at the request of the prime minister of either federated state. At the second reading, the bill had to receive the approval of a majority of the national assembly members from each federated state. This element of a 'second reading' was one of the few respects in which the constitution envisaged curtailment of the powers of the federal authority through the actions of state representatives. Although this provision could have made a significant contribution to the safeguarding of West Cameroon interests, it was never actually applied.

My view is that it never could have been any safeguard even if applied. It is already stated but I think I should take it over again. Federal article 18 that Enonchong cites in buttressing his "special clauses" thesis, provides that "Before a law is promulgated, the President of the Federal Republic may request a second reading thereof, either of his own motion or at the request of either of the Prime Ministers of the Federated States. On second reading, the law shall be adopted only if the majority specified in the preceding article comprises a majority of the votes of the deputies of each of the Federated States." On its part, the preceding article 17 simply stipulates that "Federal

Laws shall be adopted by simple majority of deputies." The question to pose here is: do two simple majorities equal a special majority? A reading of Cameroon's amendment formula (Federal article 47) and the other articles cited would hardly show any special majority. Lantum (1991: 21) tells us that the "intellectuals in politics" in Foumban in 1961 possessed "An intelligence quotient towering high above the average, to learn and understand the world with unusual perspicacity." This, it must be emphasized, is describing the architects of the FRC, especially the ones from West Cameroon.

I think any ordinary educated person has to appreciate what I am saying without necessarily having to be the 'intellectuals with towering IQs'. But I am sure these ones (if they are really what we are being told they are), would, perforce, even more easily realize that the requirement of a vote by simple majority: provided this includes a *majority* (not *necessarily* a special one, it must be noted) of the representatives – *in the federal assembly* – of each of the two constituent states, does not in any way transform the first simple majority into a 'special majority'. Perhaps the point being made here can become very lucid (if not already obvious) if it is expounded upon mathematically (and there is certainly much more difficult mathematics awaiting these 'intellectual' in Chapter 4). The Federal National Assembly (FNA) had fifty members with one-fifth of them being from West Cameroon.[19] A simple majority of 27/50 in the FNA may then be apportioned as follows: 21/40 (Francophones) and 6/10 (Anglophones). (And do not forget that all members of both camps in the FNA are of the same party – see closing remarks to this Chapter.)

Any genuine 'intellectual in politics' (excepting the Intellectual in Process Manipulation) must then hardly need to be another Lord Denning of England to truly fail to see how a simple majority becomes a special majority simply because there is another simple majority from both sides of the Mungo River right there in the FNA. To further regard the formula for this kind of majority as something which is "even more significant" (Enonchong, 1967: 90), simply beats the imagination; the more so as there would seem to be no independent judge to confirm or disallow it, or even to say whose interpretation (Enonchong's or mine) is the correct. Enonchong (*ibid.*) then proceeds to praise the "special procedure clauses under article 47 of the Federal Constitution for its amendment" before concluding that

19 See *Law N° 64-LF-1 of 24 March 1964*; and Federal Constitution, articles 16 (one deputy to 80,000 inhabitants) & 60 (given population of two federated states: 3,200,000 for East and 800,000 for West).

"Constitutional amendments are the exclusive jurisdiction of the National Federal Assembly." All this is preposterous except the learned doctor is talking about a different enactment than the article 47 that I have laid out above.

The theory positing human rights protection under the Foumban document quickly provokes a series of associated questions that are stiffly posed by the very first sentence of the article-47 amendment formula that everyone seems to be clinging on. Some of these questions have to do with the person or organ that decides on the inadmissibility of the proposal for amendment. Who similarly defines what "impairs" the unity and integrity of the State? In other words, as Enonchong (1967: 227-28) himself wants to know,

> How then must the [various] legislatures and the executives be kept strictly within their constitutional domains? Who will tell each of them that it has overtly or covertly allowed its function to flow out of the pale of its constitutional authority? On the answers to these questions depends the determination of the body in the Cameroon federal system which can and will define the limits of the various powers distributed by the constitutional instrument.

Who decides what "impairs" unity etc when there is no independent judiciary as well as no independent territorial units/institutions? Is the absence of an independent judiciary and of locally elected officials in Cameroon not the main reason (according to their very own secession theses) why East Cameroun was able to so easily "secede" (renege, is the correct term) from the FRC 'by unilateral act' (Hogg, 1996: 127-29), be it in 1972 or in 1984 (and yet still being part and parcel of the FRC)?

2. *Judicial Review of Constitutionality in Cameroon?*

Both democracy and federalism preach and further self-governments of local communities. There can plainly be no self-government of a region (or state or province or canton or *Land*) of a federation in the absence of an independent and influential judiciary as well as multiplicity of power centres (such as effective multipartism). I think that the mere absence of the democratic spirit and form at Foumban must render the FRC not a federation. It also makes the acclaimed power-sharing, marked by judicial review in Cameroon, mind-boggling. According to Alexis Charles Henri Clerel de Tocqueville,

> The end of good government is to ensure the welfare of a people, and not merely to establish order in the midst of its misery. I am therefore led to suppose that the prosperity of the American townships and the apparent confusion of their finances, the distress of the French communes and the perfection of their budget, may be attributable to the same cause. At any rate, I am suspicious of a good that is united with so many evils, and I am not averse to an evil that is compensated by so many benefits.[20]

Judicial review of the constitutionality of laws and administrative acts is largely responsible for the "so many benefits" Tocqueville is talking about here. This power of review is something that is simply unknown in *Democratically Advanced* Cameroon. It should have been a miracle if it were since this power cannot exist in the midst of concentration of powers. That is, in the absence of effective separation (and splitting) of power (centres). This splitting of power, by necessity, must mean having effective multiple political parties and, particularly, keeping the judiciary apart from the other branches. The judiciary (or 'Judicial Power'[21]), as any other non-executive state organ was never and has never been intended to play any independent political or constitutional role of its own in Cameroon's Solid Edifice or "federation" which has never ceased to exist; with its strangely solid "federalness" growing day by day into what Biya (1986: 28) now proudly

---

[20] Alexis de Tocqueville, *Democracy in America* Vol. I (New York: Alfred A. Knopf, 1945) at 91-92 n. 50. As to the important role of the courts that is responsible for these "so many benefits", see Holland (1988); Edmond Orban, "La Cour suprême des Etats-Unies et le processus de nationalisation" in Edmond Orban, ed., *Fédéralisme et cours suprêmes/Federalism and Supreme Courts* (Bruxelles: Établissement Émile Bruylant; Montréal: Presses de l'Université de Montréal, 1991), 59; and Antonin Scalia, "Federal Constitutional Guarantees of Individual Rights in the United States of America" in David. M. Beatty, ed., *Human Rights and Judicial Review – A Comparative Perspective* (Dordrecht/Boston/London: Martinus Nijhoff Publishers, 1994), 57.

[21] See 1996 Constitution, Part V (articles 37-42); and Federal Constitution, Title VI (articles 32-35) ('The Judicial Authority') & Title VII (article 36) ('The High Court of Justice').

defines as the "State [which] is the best politically organized human grouping and the most complete from the standpoint of its system of authority...and a concentration of the most imposing deterrent forces (army, police, prisons) in order to ensure order."

It is not very surprising then that this type of state is filled to the brim with abhorrent laws that even punish a judge for rendering justice (see Anyangwe, 1989: 25; Nyo'Wakai, 1991; and Fossungu[22]); and turning courts into a formidable policing organ.[23] The question of no guarantee of individual rights and freedoms by that 1961 Federal Constitution (as all the others after it) hardly needs overemphasizing, especially in view of the country's Supreme Court which critics[24] – including its own justices (Nyo'Wakai, 1991: 18) – have said is supreme only in name and in the matter of *renvoi.* That is, 'in sending the case back' (*renvoyer*) to the courts of appeal for a new decision. That is the Cameroonian Supreme Court's best function. How can federalism, as generally understood, be feasible in such a setting? Leaving federalism aside, can democracy, under the caption of decentralization, be feasible? A proper answer is provided in Chapter 3 where I discuss 'democratic society and rule of law in Cameroon'.

To cut a long confusion and manipulation Foumban-story short, I will simply posit here that Enonchong's assertions about judicial review in the FRC are not true; otherwise, first, there would not have been the controversial 1972 'Glorious Revolution' that is said to have ushered in the unitary state; and there would also not have been the even more national-unity boat-rocking 1984 name-change that is said to have since sparked off secessionist drives in Cameroon. Above all (and tied particularly to judicial review), both of those name-changing events would not have gone by

---

22 Peter Ateh-Afac Fossungu, "Sentencing Criminals in Cameroon: Tying Judges' Hands and Expecting Them to Do Gymnastics?" 29 *Juridis Périodique* (*Revue de Droit et de Science Politique*) (1997), 84-98.

23 See Peter Ateh-Afac Fossungu, "The Oppressive Policing Role of Courts in Cameroon" *The Herald* N° 710 (15-17 January 1999), 10; and Taku (1995).

24 See Carlson Anyangwe, "Administrative Litigation in Francophone Africa: The Rule of Prior Exhaustion of Internal Remedies" 8 *Revue Africaine de Droit International et Comparé* (1996), 808-826; and Andrew Sone Ewang, "The Cameroon Supreme Court: A Court of Judicial Review or a Cour de Cassation?" 25 *Juridis Périodique (Revue de Droit et de Science Politique*) (1996), 31–33.

without similar Cameroonian decisions like *Reference re Secession of Quebec,*[25] and *Re A.G. Quebec and A.G. Canada*[26] in the last of which Gold says the Canadian Supreme "Court invoked the rhetoric of formalism to obscure its own role in rejecting Quebec's claims."[27]

Writing about this important Canadian federalism case (*Re A.G. Quebec and A.G. Canada*), Banting has stated that before 28 September 1981 (date of the decision of the case), there had never "been such a day in the calendar of the Supreme Court of Canada. Never had a decision been awaited with such intensity, and delivered with cameras rolling and television commentary reminiscent of an election night. Never had a Court judgement had such critical impact on the subsequent course of the political life of the nation."[28] There were basically no cases like the cited Canadian cases in Cameroon in 1972 and/or 1984 principally because there has never been any federalism there, not even an independent judiciary too – all this being intimately tied to the invisible hand of Cameroonian 'federalism' (extensively discussed in Chapter 2) that is completely at variance with that of Canada, for instance.

That is why in Cameroon all the issues are to be decided only by the PFR or POR himself who has been made both referee and player by the same constitutions. By article 32 of the Federal Constitution, it is the president who is the "guardian" of judicial independence. And he obviously has been 'guarding' that independence so well that some experts have observably considered this entire scheme as being "a strong hint of the lack of judicial independence in Cameroon."[29] But that is not all since, in addition, the

---

[25] [1998] 2 S.C.R. 217. For some of the other leading cases, see Peter H. Russell, Rainer Knopff and Ted Morton, *Federalism and the Charter: Leading Constitutional Decisions*, (Ottawa: Carleton University Press, 1990).

[26] [1982] 25 C.R. 793, 140 D.L.R. (3d) 385.

[27] Marc Gold, "The Mask of Objectivity: Politics and Rhetoric in the Supreme Court of Canada" 7 *Supreme Court Review* (1985), 455 at 459-60. See also Peter H. Russell, "The Supreme Court Decision: Bold Statecraft Based on Questionable Jurisprudence" in P.H. Russell, Robert Décary, William Lederman, Noel Lyon, and Dan Soberman (eds.), *The Court and the Constitution* (Kingston, Ontario: Institute of Intergovernmental Relations, 1982), 1.

[28] K.G Banting, "Foreword" in P.H. Russell, Robert Décary, William Lederman, Noel Lyon, and Dan Soberman, eds., *The Court and the Constitution* (Kingston, Ontario: Institute of Intergovernmental Relations, 1982) at vii.

[29] Nelson Enonchong, "Human Violation by the Executive: Complicity of the Judiciary in Cameroon? *The People v. Nya Henry*; *The People v. Dr. Martin Luma*" 47 *Journal of African Law* (2003), 265 at 273. See also Mbeng N. Atem, "The Lack of Justice and the Rule

Federal Constitution in article 8 makes "The President of the Federal Republic of Cameroon, Head of the Federal State and Head of the Federal Government, [who] shall uphold the Federal Constitution and shall ensure the unity of the Federation and the conduct of the affairs of the Federal Republic." Was Ahidjo then not merely 'ensuring *the unity* of the Federation' in his 'conducting of the affairs of the Federal Republic' when *he* thought 'Federal' was not unity enough as 'United' is, in 1972? Cameroon's Unitary Constitutions (being the modified but much more potent equivalent of this Federal article 8) do not only also make '*Le Président de la République*, *Chef de l'État*,' the Courts, judge and umpire over the "*respect de la Constitution*" but also make him the only person who "*définit la politique de la nation.*"[30] Was Biya also not just defining that policy in 1984 when, to him, there was then only 'one Cameroon people', and nothing left to united as implied in the URC? No one will then be wrong to say that any "constitutional tradition" in Cameroon (if there is anything like it at all) "varies with the foot of the POR." That being the case, as Fossungu (2013:134) has asked in regard of multipartism, who can then ever try to engage the POR in debates over these matters without being considered by him (the only and final judge on the matter) as threatening the [head of] State's "unity" that he alone "shall ensure"?

Etinge (1991: 6) has therefore properly pointed out that this type of drafting embedded in Cameroon legislation, done "by the cronies of the executive called *Administrateurs civils*" and "investing powers… [in] one man can only be seen in a dictatorial regime where the legislature is the puppet of the executive." The barrister has therefore submitted that it is not the POR who ought to define the policy of the nation, concluding that it is the Constitution, the supreme document of the land, the sentinel of all freedoms and liberties which is drawn and agreed upon by the people. This expert is obviously right because, by section 14 of the Nigerian Constitution, "sovereignty belongs to the people of Nigeria from whom government through the Constitution derives its powers and authority." As Etinge (1991: 6) has then crowned his brilliant argument, "If the president is invested with

---

of Law in Cameroon" *The Herald* N° 319 13-16 June 1996), 4; and Wa Nfon Bolung, "Cameroon: An Unconstitutional Polity" *The Herald* N° 384 (18-19 November 1996), 4.

30 *Loi N° 91/001 du 23 avril portant modification des articles 5, 7, 8, 9, 26, 27, et 34 de la Constitution* [1991 Constitution], article 5 (*nouveau*). See also 1996 Constitution, articles 5 & 11 which reinforce the same stance.

that power" (as he is in Cameroon), "then fifty Presidents will define fifty policies for a nation." This is axiomatic. Had the Canadian or American Constitutions, for example, been drafted in that manner, then John A Macdonald (for the former) and George Washington (for the latter) would have "defined" their respective country's policies: with their numerous successors having the same opportunities of defining and redefining; which, in effect, simply means amending and re-amending the documents. This would obviously mean (especially in the United States where there is a fixed term of office" – there is none for Canada) that the country would not be what it is today – after no less than forty presidents. For, would some "mad" president not have defined the policy to be the demise of the Union as Mikhail Gorbachev did to the defunct Soviet Union? *Son Excellence* El Hadj Amadou Ahidjo did just that in Cameroon in 1972.

With a one-man system like this one, it is not exactly clear how the people of Cameroon can properly be rejoicing in diversity; especially when their demands for the institution of federalism (which is the proper vehicle for rejoicing in diversity) are being rejected and turned into secession. Federalism has been found to be the suitable medium for effectively managing *diversity* in all of its forms and, at the same time, making diversity a source of strength rather than a weakness. That is how people genuinely rejoice in diversity. Genuinely rejoicing in diversity means the people of a locality must be the ones to decide (through fair and free elections) who their governors should be. It is very probable that Ahidjo would not have easily succeeded in the 1972 'revolution' had the West Cameroon prime minister and other ministers been chosen exclusively by West Cameroonians through elections, rather than being single-handedly appointed and dismissed by Ahidjo. By article 39 of the Federal Constitution (which is now the equivalent of article 58 of the 1996 Constitution – discussed in Chapter 4 below),

> The President of the Federal Republic shall appoint the Prime Minister of each Federated State, who must be confirmed in office by simple majority vote of the Legislative Assembly of the State concerned. The President shall appoint the Secretaries of State [who are] members of the [Federated State] Government on the proposal of the Prime Minister confirmed in office. He [the President] may relieve them of office under

the same condition.

The situation is also likely to have been different if the said prime minister also had nothing to do with the federal government, let alone be its vice president. You can then see why West Cameroonians were ruled directly from Yaoundé from the very start since their head of government was lodged but in Yaoundé, not in Buea. And this, in spite of the incompatibilities of functions, for more of which, see Chapter 4 below. Furthermore, the Foumban Constitution in article 51 made Ahidjo (and his successors from East Cameroon) the automatic president until the end of "his present term of office." Had West Cameroonians therefore magically elected this president even before Foumban? During that "present term of office" which seems never to have ended (see Chapter 4) this same constitution in article 52 gave the vice president position to West Cameroon's Prime Minister Foncha (and his successors).

And this is supposed to be the same constitution that institutionalized the guarantee of individual and organic freedoms? In this unique federation the combination of especially Federal articles 51, 52, and 59 (on the authenticity of only the French text) would provide the roots of the 'second fiddle syndrome' discourse in Cameroon today. "The most tragic fate that can befall a people is their psychological acceptance of defeat or abdication to a subordinate role in society."[31] Why did the West Cameroon leadership (with all their remarkable towering IQs) embrace these untoward constitutional arrangements? This is one of several important questions that normally have to be addressed. But people are hardly telling the young people about all these vexatious issues; they are only being told about the overflowing of power-sharing and lots of human rights guarantees; and that President Ahidjo refused to obey "our" solid constitution and staged a coup d'état upon Cameroon *in* 1972. How and why? Is it because Ahidjo refused to bind himself to his future legal action, when no one else could tell him to do so?

Regarding the first sentence of article 47 that talks of no introduction (or inadmissibility) of amendment that "impairs the unity and integrity of the Federation", Enonchong (1967: 90 & 90-91) has first suggested that the

[31] M.L. Lokanga, "The Second-Fiddle Syndrome" *Le Messager* **Special Political Issue** (Thursday June 6, 1991), 17.

"obvious intention is to deny any part of the federation the right to secede" before positing that "it poses the question as to whether a sovereign can validly bind its future legal action." Can s/he or can't s/he? Unfortunately, one cannot be told anything by Enonchong (1967: xii) regarding these "problems [which] demand[] profound research under academic guidance." He sort of fears speculating about these issues that one would have thought his thesis was out to confront. "The jurisprudential issues emanating from this question", Enonchong (1967: 91) says in answer, "are too speculative and beyond the scope of this thesis" – a thesis which, by the way, is a "surgical analysis of constitutional law" (*ibid*) and "written with the set purpose of explaining specific aspects of Cameroon [constitutional] law."[32] Whatever happened to the scope of Enonchong's thesis? Controversial as the issues may be, the present book refuses to shy away from them, having already handled the issue of 'binding future legal action' above under both the 'true federation' impediment thesis and the stark absence of the independent judiciary and other free institutions, including even the FNA that is said to have had exclusivity in the legislative domain.

Was The Federal National Assembly (FNA) The Exclusive Legislator?

The question here turns on the larger one of the separation of powers between the traditional branches (executive, legislative, judicial) as well as between the national and provincial governments, what Schneider (2008: 129-30) discusses as 'Vertical Division of Powers: The Two Levels of Government'. The incessant praising of power sharing in Foumban as seen above, may somewhat explain why these legal scholars have all construed the amendment formula to the effect that constitutional amendments in the FRC were the exclusive jurisdiction of the FNA. Maintaining this position is to say that the said FNA was the sole legislating organ, which is either to completely ignore the facts or to simply emasculate them so as to further the Foumban Darkness. Like all the others, this particular thesis "is like trying to

32 Enonchong (1967: xi). Did the sponsors of the research limit its scope otherwise than stated? Enonchong, Director of Cabinet etc. in the Ministry of Justice, "was granted study leave under a bilateral arrangement first, between the French Government and the Cameroon Government to study at Grenoble University, and second, between the Cameroon Government and the United States Government, to study at Howard and Georgetown Universities." *Id.*: xii.

teach a pig to sing: it usually succeeds only in annoying the pig."[33] This unnecessary annoyance is plainly evident through a casual look at legislative functions at the federal level as well as the federal-state domains. I will give you just a little of each before finding out if the intellectuals are confused or confusing.

Traditional Federal Level Separation and Federal-State Domains

There is overflowing poverty and manipulation in constitutional scholarship in Cameroon generally but especially in regard of the FRC. Doesn't the second sentence of the amending formula itself even clearly divide this amendment domain *equally* between the PFR and the deputies of the FNA? The critics would further like to find out just how legislative power can be the exclusive domain of the FNA when it is pellucid from article 23 that "[t]he power to initiate legislation" simply belonged "equally to the President of the Federal Republic and the Deputies of the Federal Assembly." Rubin (1971: 141) also thinks that article 24 of the Foumban Constitution entitled only the FNA to legislate on the 'protection of the freedom of the individual' and 'public liberties'. That cannot be correct because said article 24 is not talking of the FNA but "Federal Authorities"; which would include the executive (and more specifically the PFR).

Buttressing the point are the domain-listing Federal articles 5 and 6. Matters that are captured by these two articles as the exclusive domain of the 'federal authorities' would make any talk of the FRC as a federation only good for the study of confusion and manipulation. Articles 23 and 24 also make the point very clear. While article 24 lists matters "within the spheres of Federal Law, within the framework of the powers specified in articles 5 and 6",[34] article 23, in no unclear terms, stipulates that the "[t]he power to

---

[33] Don Macpherson, "Bouchard Not the Life of His Party" *Montreal Gazette* (15 December 1998), B3.

[34] According to article 24 of the Federal Constitution, "The following matters shall be within the sphere of Federal Law, within the framework of the powers specified in Articles 5 and 6

(1) The fundamental guarantees and obligations of the citizen: protection of the freedom of the individual; public liberties; labour and trade-union legislation; the duties and obligations of the citizen in respect of national defence.

initiate legislation" belongs "equally to the President of the Federal Republic and the Deputies of the Federal Assembly." This unadorned fact must even be responsible for Benjamin (1972: 23) having elaborately discussed "*Les pouvoirs <<législatifs>> du président de la République*".

Moreover, nowhere in the entire federal document is there any convincing talk at all of any provincial or state domain(s). Konings (1999: 297) agrees that "No specific list of tasks which were to fall permanently within the jurisdiction of the state governments was provided." What were the states then for, absent confusion? In brief, to be discussing federal-state domains in the FRC makes no sense except in studying manipulation because there were actually no federated states to fight with the 'federal' or national state over any domains; and there was no need for anyone or organ to have to tell them who has exceeded their domain(s). The so-called 'federated states' of Title IX (articles 38-46) simply had no such domain, notwithstanding the fact that article 38 would be trying to prove otherwise when it pretends to be leaving them with residual matters. First, what else could be remaining after the catch-all listings of articles 5, 6, and 24? Second, as Fossungu (2013:92-95) has shown, it is supposed to be the other way round in a true multicultural federation.

Not to just leave the matter hanging confusingly in the air like the 'intellectuals in politics', the Foumban Constitution which is based on lies to the populace put all or most of the matters of grave concern to the English-speaking at the altar of the 'Federal' Authorities. Articles 5 and 6 of the Foumban document (that is being acclaimed for having shared power) simply made all matters relating to justice administration, education and other unique cultural aspects exclusive federal matters. This, to say the least, is like

---

(2) The law of persons and property; nationality and personal status; the law of personal property and real property; the law of civil and commercial obligations.

(3) Political, administrative and judicial organisation with respect to: the electoral system of the Federal Assembly; the general rules relating to the organisation of national defence; the definitions of crimes and offences and the establishment of penalties of any kind, criminal procedure, means of enforcement, amnesty, and the creation of new orders of jurisdiction.

(4) The following questions of finance and property: the currency issue system; the Federal Budget; the institution, assessment and rates of federal taxes and dues of any kind; legislation relating to State lands.

(5) The aims of economic and social action within the framework of the laws, relating to economic and social policy.

(6) The Educational system."

taking all such matters from Quebec's jurisdiction and burying them deep down into Ottawa's graveyard and yet be claiming fuller freedom, self-government and the like for Quebec. For a graphic illustration, the Foumban document in article 5 lengthily enumerated the powers of the "Federal Authorities" to

> embrace the following matters: Nationality; the status of aliens; regulations concerning conflicts of laws; national defence; foreign affairs; the internal and external security of the Federal State, emigration and immigration; development planning, guidance of the economy, statistics, the control and organisation of credit, external economic relations (including trade agreements); the monetary system, the preparation of the Federal Budget and the establishment of taxes and revenue of all kinds to meet federal expenditure; higher education and scientific research; information services and radio; foreign technical and financial assistance; postal services and telecommunications; aviation and meteorology, mining and geological research and the geographical cover of the national territory; regulation governing the Federal Civil Service and the Judiciary; the organisation and functioning of the Federal Court of Justice; the territorial boundaries of the Federated States; [and] organisation of services pertaining to these matters.

Quite a list that must obviously leave anyone with the slightest amount of education (intellectual in political science or not) wondering about much. "Indeed, by claiming for itself nearly all the most important functions of state business, the federal government ensured the redundancy of the governments of the federated states and denied them any *raison d'être,* except a political one" (Konings, 1999: 298). Most of these matters are clearly not to be in the federal domain especially for a multicultural state.[35]

The German Basic Law[36] in its most current form in Chapter VII

[35] For the position in Canada, see André Tremblay, *Les compétences législatives au Canada et les pouvoirs provinciaux en matière de proprieté et de droits civils* (Ottawa: Éditions de l'Université d'Ottawa, 1967); and for Belgium, see Shapiro (1995: 57 & 60); and Dumont *et al* (2008: 38-49).

[36] For the complete English text of this German Constitution (Basic Law), see Gisbert H. Flanz, "Germany" in Albert P. Blaustein and Gisbert H. Flanz, eds., *Constitutions of the Countries of the World* (Release 94-6 Issued August 1994) (New York: Oceania Publications, Inc., & Dobbs Ferry, 1994).

(Federal Legislation – articles 70-82) and Chapter II (The Federation and the Länder – articles 20-37) more clearly divides domains and responsibilities between the two levels before calling on the two to co-operate in certain matters in Chapter VIIIa (Joint Responsibilities – articles 91a & 91b). Schneider (2008: 136-38) has examined "The Logic of the Constitutional Distribution of Powers and Responsibilities" as well as "Cooperation between the Governments (*id* 142-44) of this German system. These are some models for Africans to examine and emulate. But will they want to do so?

As if the Cameroonian article-5 list was not already devastating enough to the Foumban Intellectuals, the next provision (article 6) came in with these further more centralizing and damaging powers:

> The powers of the Federal Authorities shall also embrace the following: Public liberties; the law of persons and of property; the law of obligations and contracts in civil and commercial matters; judicial organization, including the rules of procedure and jurisdiction of all courts (with the exception of Customary Courts of West Cameroon, save as regards appeals from the decisions of such Courts); criminal law; transport of federal importance (roads, railways, rivers, maritime and air transport) and ports; prison administration; legislation relating to State lands; labour legislation; public health; secondary and technical education; administrative organization; weights and measures.

What actually then was not a "federal" matter to those Intellectuals in Politics (that was to be reserved for the Federated States)? In other words, what would be the article-38

> Matters other than those specified in Articles 5 and 6 and other than those which under the present Constitution are to be the subject of a federal law [that] shall lie exclusively within the competence of the Federated States?

Perhaps the intellectuals of the English-speaking Federated State pinned all their hopes on a certain hoodwinking portion of article 6? Said portion (with my emphasis) stipulates that

> So far as concerns the matters enumerated in this article the authorities

> of the Federated States may continue to enact laws and to direct the corresponding administrative services *until such time as the Federal National Assembly or the President of the Federal Republic, as the case may be, shall decide to exercise the powers vested in them respectively.*

This article-6 provision is described as hoodwinking because it does not at all meet the requirements of federalism. Some "insiders" like Enonchong (1967: 169-70) even declared in October 1967 that Cameroon's hoodwinking federal

> Article 38 was intended, in metaphorical terms, to serve as a mirage designed to condition psychologically the minds of the timorous souls that existed at the time of formulating the constitution, while at the same time succeeding in the primary objective of securing a strong reunited Cameroon.

That is exactly what I am vehemently condemning: the all-out search for so-called national unity even through the complete disregard for human rights. Yet, at the same time, the same people acclaim the same Foumban Enterprise for entrenching the guarantee of those same neglected rights.

The question one keeps asking is: where then was the territorial and institutional sharing of powers? It was not even long before the said "federal authorities" began 'federalizing' most of those matters in 1962-1963. By 1964, according to Benjamin (1972: 13), only penitentiary services remained; being solely because of a clash of jurisdiction over it between two federal ministries. As early as 1963, he concludes, there were even open attempts to abolish altogether the so-called federal form. The only problem that even delayed the issue until 1972 was that of what to do with the numerous secretaries (appellation for non-federal ministers) of East Cameroon. Could this be taken as the origin of the inflation of ministerial portfolios that is characteristic of this country? And where are the towering IQs that understand the world with unusual perspicacity? It is not clear how the Cameroon people can be taught the rules of democracy and of federalism (as requested by Biya, 1986: 127) by those whose knowledge of what is to be imparted and learnt cannot be distinguished from that of the students meant to be instructed.

This has truly not failed, of course, to leave the road wide open for the second-classing of some citizens and the like of gross human rights violations in Cameroon without the court being able to say anything. "No one coming from a system in which parliamentary sovereignty has stultified creative legal thinking", Ackerman (1989: 70) has declared, "can fail to be moved intellectually and otherwise by the unfolding history of the American Constitution." The said constitution, no doubt, has been able to be what it has been, is, and will be, doing solely because the judges have made it so. These American judicial officials, I think, could not have done so if they were not independent and influential. They could not have been that independent without public support. Public support can hardly be forthcoming if the citizenry is not politically aware and active. In view of this fact, Frye therefore thinks that teaching the humanities is a militant activity: it has constantly to fight for the freedom that the critical faculty represents against passivity and uncritical acceptance.[37]

Intellectuals in Politics: Confused or Confusing?

As I would keep saying, the Foumban Constitution is so confusing that many experts, even well-groom ones, do easily fall prey to its traps; believing, for instance, that there were functionally three legislatures in the FRC.[38] That is, of course, the impression given but there are some doubts since it is highly disbelieving how East Cameroon could have had twice as many deputies than the entire Federation which had only 50. By article 40 of the Foumban Constitution, "The number of representatives in the Legislative Assembly of East Cameroon shall be one hundred; in the Legislative Assembly of West Cameroon, thirty-seven." By the same constitution's principle of representation, we have 1 deputy to 80,000 inhabitants (article 16); and its population ratio tells us that there were 800,000 West Cameroonians and 3,200,000 East Cameroonians (article 60). The important question to answer now is: How was the Federal article 16 principle respected, to be able to also have 37 deputies for the West Cameroon House? The query is more especially significant because Enonchong (1967:

[37] N. Frye, "Language as the Home of Human Life" in Michael Owen, ed., *Salute to Scholarship: Essays Presented at the Official Opening of Athabasca University* (Athabasca, Alberta: Athabasca University, 1986), 20-33 at 21.

[38] See Barry B. Fohtung, "Parliamentary History in Cameroon 3: The One-Party State" *The Herald* N° 446 (16-17 April 1997), 6.

164 *et seq*) has very elaborately indicated how 'Federal Law [epitomized by the Federal Constitution] Governs Federated State Institutions'. Is this, by the way, the normal arrangement in a true federation?

If so, then why do the experts like Hogg (1996: chapter 5) bother about discussing the essential requirement of "coordination" of both levels? Every expert on the subject, in discussing this important requirement, indicates like Hogg that in federal states (such as Canada) governmental power is distributed between a central government and several regional ones in such a way that *every individual in the province is subject to the laws of two authorities*: the central authority and a provincial authority. For example, anyone in Quebec is subject to the laws of the Parliament of Canada (the central authority) and the Legislature of Quebec (the regional or provincial authority). The central authority and the provincial authorities are "coordinate", which means that neither is subordinate to the other.[39] To shorten the long discussion on the issue, I will continue using Hogg's explanation. To say both level have to be "coordinate" means that neither is subordinate to the other; the powers of the Legislature of Quebec are "not granted" by the Parliament of Canada, and they cannot be taken away, altered or controlled by the Parliament of Canada. And the Legislature of Quebec, even acting with the other nine provincial and two territorial Legislatures, is likewise incompetent to take away, alter or control the powers of the Parliament of Canada. That is what a federation proper entails, not the Cameroonian manipulation.

All the above requirements were just not the case with West Cameroon whose Constitution came only twenty-four days after 'federation' that had taken place on October 1, 1961.[40] This constitution, furthermore, even emanated not from the West Cameroon Legislative Assembly; it came all the way from Yaoundé where it was enacted. The confusing impression is given, from the appended version of this constitution to Enonchong's (1967: 267-286) book, that it is the Legislature of West Cameroon that enacted it. "BE IT ENACTED by the Legislature of West Cameroon as follows: ...." (*id.*: 267). But the constitution is in reality only a schedule to a federal law:

[39] I have to also draw attention to the objection by Southall (1974: 146 n.8) to the use of 'subordinate' in the definition of 'centralized' and 'peripheralized' federations by William H. Riker, *Federalism: Origin, Operation, Significance* (Boston: Little, Brown and Company 1964) at 12.

[40] See the West Cameroon Constitution of October 25, 1961, titled *A Law to Establish a Constitution for the Federated State of West Cameroon.*

"Subject to the provisions of this Law, the Constitution of the Federated State of West Cameroon set in the Schedule of this Law shall come into effect at the commencement of this Law" (*ibid*). Could the confusion involved in the whole Foumban Enterprise be actually what was confusing even the confusionists themselves and thus turned Cameroon's 'fascinating federalism' into 'a snare, a false façade and a parade, an instrument without any real effectiveness for true evolution,' as President Ahidjo told the *Union Camerounaise* Party Congress in Bafoussam in November 1965?

Whatever the controversy surrounding Cameroon's fascinating federalism-turned sour, there can be little doubt that Foumban was a One- (or, at the most, a one-and-one-quarter-) State federation. East Cameroonians were neither keen at all on maintaining a state government (how could they do so when an unconstitutional emperor had been 'intellectually' crowned in Foumban?) – seeming not to even know what federalism was all about. That region's prime minister (like the Cameroonian P.M. of today – see Chapter 4 below) was just in name from the outset and one would simply have astonished most East Cameroonians by telling them that they were subject to two levels of government. The points being made here are to point to the obvious derogation of the requirement of both levels of governments in a federation being "co-ordinate". In Cameroon, there was, and always has been, only one unit (the proper meaning of Unitary?).

I think the Foumban actors could be rightly called the "Fathers of Confusion-Federation" and/or be credited with having created a "Unitary federation". That is, a highly centralized and monolithic ('federal') unitary state: notwithstanding the claims of "Dr. Enonchong[, who] has without doubt spent a great deal of energy and time in research to present an analysis of the facts and information contained in []his book",[41] that Cameroon

> Federalism supplies the restraint between the Cameroon national and the federated state governments which are each sovereign within their own powers. It is in this principle that there is a striking similarity between the United States and Cameroon systems and a significant departure of the

[41] Dr. J.N. Foncha, "Foreword" in H.N.A. Enonchong, *Cameroon Constitutional Law – Federalism in a Mixed Common-Law and Civil-Law System* (Yaoundé: Centre d'Édition et de Production de Manuel et d'Auxiliares de l'Enseignement, 1967) at ii. Dr. J.N. Foncha was the leader of the West Cameroon side in Foumban, later becoming, in addition to that region's prime minister, federal vice president.

> latter from the [unitary] system in vogue in the territories of her former administering powers, Great Britain and France [Enonchong, 1967: 23].

This is the kind of theorizing on the Foumban Federation that I think ought to be dismantled. Just how can all this be when Enonchong himself has just indicated not long ago that 'Federal Law Governs Federated State Institutions'? Are the confusionists not getting confused trying to confuse? In commenting on some so-called federations in the former Soviet bloc (an entity which was particularly punctuated by the single party), de Smith (1964: 285) has declared that

> It is clearly unhelpful to formulate general propositions about federal constitutions if they have to be stretched to accommodate systems in which the political bases on which the federal and regional governments rest their support are invariably the same because diversity would not be tolerated.

That is precisely what the FRC was/is all about. The Foumban federation, to Stark (1976: 423), was in fact "more shadow than reality" because Johnson (1970: 190) says it instead "centralized powers not only more than desired by Foncha and others, but more than had the structures of the first Cameroon Republic, structures about which there had already developed a lively controversy." Stark (1976: 427) would dispute that this was not Foncha's desire because he has found that, even before Foumban, "Foncha was already speaking of a more complete union than he himself realized." It is also clearly known from Le Vine and Nye (1964: 31, emphasis added) that "In effect, the 1972 [Cameroonian] Constitution restores *the unitary regime created in 1961* but with strengthened Presidential powers."[42] Le Vine and Nye's (1964: 31) also refer to Cameroon's 1972 Unitary Constitution as "[t]he country's third basic document since 1960...[which] radically altered the structure of power and government."[43] This is a very

---

[42] See also Anyangwe (1987: 129-131: "Federation *à la Camerounaise*"); Stark (1976: 423 – "highly centralized federalism"); and P.F. Gondec, "Les institutions politiques de la République Fédérale du Cameroun" 11:4 *Civilisations* (1961), 370-95.

[43] The Foumban Constitution achieved all this by not only eliminating the pre-Foumban Republic of Cameroun's bicephalic executive (with prime minister and president),

important statement because, had there been a federation at all, the Constitution of 1972 can then not be the "new" federal Cameroon's third (but second) constitution. In addition, the year 1960 will not also be the beginning date. Does this not also justify Ahidjo's automatic presidency of the federation "until the end of his present term of office" in article 51?

But why do Africa's "intellectuals in politics" still fear the truth (*avoir horreur de la vérité*) when they see Foumban as it is and yet present something else? The attitude of confusing in order to bury the issues is most visible especially with the intellectuals who are out to cover up the Foumban federation (the FRC) which, unlike most others in history (with the possible exception of the Austro-Hungarian Empire of 1867, and Bryce's "Federal Monarchy" in Germany between 1871-1918[44]), was "no loose framework, superimposed on existing patterns of social, political and economic organisation, but a solid foundation for their amalgamation into a single unit" (Rubin (1971: 143). A Unitary 'federation', as I have indicated before. Enonchong (who has all through been equating the FRC with the USA and Canada) seems to now reluctantly agree with all this and would appear to have some possible explanations for this Unitary Foumban federation. As Enonchong, (1967: xi) has noted, federalism,

> attractive and, indeed, workable and realistic as the new concept was to its proponents [in Cameroon], the various jurisprudential issues involved seemed rather illusive and sometimes nebulous... mainly because neither Great Britain nor France had practiced federalism and Cameroonians could not help but think in terms of the unitary constitutional systems to which they had been conditioned under the former administering authorities.

According to Enonchong's (1967: xi) findings, this way of thinking is the more especially so since, "the [preceding] German [federal?] administration had left little or no impact on the legal thinking of the Cameroon People."

These explanations, to my mind, are quite inadequate and laughable. Three reasons especially account for the inadequacy. First, was (federal)

---

but also drastically reducing the role of parliament, and *making the judiciary less independent and civil liberties less secure.* Johnson (1970: 191, emphasis added).

[44] For the descriptions of these two unions, see Wheare (1963: 5-6); and Kommers (1985: 195).

Nigeria next door colonized by Britain or not? Again, one realizes that Australia and Canada which are still constitutionally linked to the British Crown are both federal. Williams and Macintyre (2008: 9) tell us that the Constitution of the Commonwealth of Australia came into force on 1 January 1901; being the creation of "one indissoluble Federal Commonwealth under the Crown of the United Kingdom of Great Britain and Ireland" which was the result of protracted negotiations throughout the 1890s between the framers of the Constitution, the colonial parliaments, the people, and, ultimately, the Imperial Parliament.

All this will only be the natural result of, say, Canada's rejection of the unitary state when it could not possibly meet its needs. The drafters of the *British North America Act*, Newman (1968: 299) narrates, conceived a new kind of nation (Canada) which is neither a kingdom nor a republic; it is simply a self-governing dominion with constitutional ties to the British Crown and combines the British principles of responsible government (in which the executive is responsible to the legislature) with the American system of federal organization (in which sovereign powers are divided between central and local administrations). All the powers not specifically granted to the provinces, Newman concludes, are left with the federal authority – "exactly the reverse of the United States constitution." Canada did all this in spite of its traditional and persisting relationship with unitary United Kingdom (most probably because the latter granted the degree of independence they requested rather than the shadow of it?) and notwithstanding the great amount of insecurity emanating from its rebellious southern neighbour. Again, even in the business of adopting federalism, Canada did not copy *mot-à-mot* from down south where revolution, unlike bargaining, had brought independence. Revolution and the fear of a counter-revolution did not, however, also provide any excuse for polyethnic-melting-pot United States going down the unitary road. Why must it be different in the Cameroons particularly and Africa generally?

The second laughable reason for the thesis is that the same author holds that the Cameroonian constitution in question drew heavily from those of Canada and the United States and departed significantly from those of former colonial powers (Enonchong, 1967: 23). Finally, can the German Imperial Federal Monarchy have actually left nothing in the thinking of Cameroonians? If the answer is yes, then it is impossible to justify the concept of brotherhood, capped by the *Kamerun Idea*, that has too often been used (especially by Enonchong himself – see Chapter 2 below) to explicate the strange West Cameroonian mode of thinking before/at Foumban in July 1961.

Whether or not Germans influenced the FRC can also be seen in an examination of how this FRC resembles the Austro-Hungarian Empire and the German "Federal Monarchy". The FRC is slightly different from the Austro-Hungarian Empire. The Empire's general government was subordinate to the Austrian and Hungarian Parliaments unlike the FRC's amalgamation of Southern Cameroons: with "federal" being just whatever the PFR (not even the FNA) would make of it. Yet, in this same sense, the president of the FRC is similar to the Austro-Hungarian Empire where the Emperor-king's supreme executive power made both levels of government (unlike the American and Canadian ones) not independent governments. This then leads to Wheare's (1963: 6) finding that the "Austro-Hungarian Empire was at once a league and a unitary state." The FRC was/is only a highly centralized unitary state.

Can the FRC also be properly equated with the German "Federal Monarchy"? That is, have they some important distinguishing features, even though much more alike overall? Pure equation, it appears to me, will be wrong for a number of reasons, the most important of which relates to one-State dominance; the others revolve around legislation-making that I have already discussed above. The governing German Council (of the Federal Monarchy) depended upon state governments, especially that of dominant Prussia whose king and prime minister were, respectively, also the German Emperor, and Chancellor & President of the Council of Confederation. This made no room for the independence of general from regional governments, which is characteristic of other federations such as the United States – considered by Wheare (1963: 1) to be "the most important and the most successful example" of a federation. To this extent, the Monarchy greatly resembles the FRC because East Cameroonians especially knew no distinction between their state government (which never even existed but in name and in the astronomical numbers of ministers and deputies) and that of the Federation. This curious feature, as I have noted before, must have been greatly fortified by the lack of established institutions at and before Foumban on the part of the English-speaking entity. There is therefore no need trying to paint it otherwise (as most of the "intellectuals in politics" have been doing) because lies cannot be consistent, especially in regard of a 'democratic federalism' which is punctuated by open-ended emergency powers in the hands of the president of the 'federal' *République du Cameroun.*

Open-Ended Emergency Powers In The PFR's Hands

Cameroonian presidents, I think, could have still done whatever they did (and are still doing) without even passing through the much heralded amending formula in Federal article 47. And they will all still be within the spirit of the constitutions they are being accused of having violated. Also falling flat to the ground is the claim that the 'sovereign people of Cameroon' (if they are sovereign at all) have any say in the making and destruction of the country's "Solid Constitutions and Edifices". All this holds true because of Federal article 15 which (without the useless condition of the PFR consulting the state prime ministers – his personal appointees) has simply become the 1996 Constitution's article 9 that states:

> (1) The President of the Republic may, where circumstances [which are not defined anywhere in those constitutions] so warrant, declare by decree a state of emergency which shall confer upon him such special powers [how special too, nothing is said] as may be provided for by law [that is, his own decree].
>
> (2) In the event of a serious threat [as to what amounts to this, nothing is said] to the nation's territorial integrity or to its existence, its independence or institutions, the President of the Republic may declare a state of siege by decree and take any measures as *he* may deem necessary. He shall inform the Nation of his decision by message [emphasis added].

Was Ahidjo on 6 May 1972 not simply 'informing the Nation of his decision' through the FNA of what 'he deemed necessary' 'under the circumstances'? I have already indicated within this provision, in square parenthesis, some of the grave faults with the provision that accords the president open-ended powers. But I think it is still important here to invite the experts to further stress the point for us. Fombad (2004: 80) and Hogg (1996: 404-413) have posited that it is both common and desirable for modern states, even democratic ones, to adopt legislation that empowers the government to take swift and effective action in times of crisis, with this unavoidably resulting in some form of dictatorial powers. The constitutional entrenchment of emergency powers with adequate controls to guard against abuse, according to Fombad, is what makes such a dictatorship constitutional. On the other hand, he submits, where there are inadequate or no controls to prevent any abuse of these emergency powers (as is the case here in Cameroon), this basically gives rise to unrestrained and arguably unconstitutional dictatorship. Like Ondoa (1996: 14) before him, Fombad (2004: 80) has therefore "contended that Cameroon's emergency legislation, taken as a whole, confers enough extraordinary powers to enable the President of the Republic to rule without reference to any constitutional or legal process and oversight." That is the meaning of *pleins pouvoirs*, I guess.

Daniel Kemajou (an opposition parliamentarian in East Cameroon) had very accurately predicted all this as the reprehensible designs of the *pleins pouvoirs* law passed in French Cameroun in 1959. Unlike many of the agitprop politicians at the time, Kemajou did not fail to see the blameworthy designs of the *pleins pouvoirs* law when he had turned on Deputy Jean Akassou (a government supporter) in these thought-provoking words (cited in Le Vine, 1964: 186):

> Monsieur Akassou, you, do you know what *pleins pouvoirs* signify? They mean the suppression of liberty, they mean dictatorship!... How can you ask for *pleins pouvoirs* under such conditions? You who belong to the Government, don't you know what an electoral law is? If tomorrow the Prime Minister disagrees with you, he can make a law specifically directed against you, he can talk of inconsistency, he can redraw the electoral districts as it suits him, he can suppress anything he wishes by decree. And you Monsieur Arouna [then Minister of Health], you who suffered for this country, will you countenance the continued suffering of Cameroonians? Is it possible that you, Monsieur Arouna, participated in the ministers' meeting that adopted this criminal law, this despicable law?

The East Cameroon political chameleons he was dealing with never took him seriously but history has vindicated him. Ruling without any control is exactly what Ahidjo did in 1972 and it is exactly what Biya has been and is still doing, all thanks to the Foumban FRC that wantonly extended *pleins pouvoirs'* scope and field of application. Dr. E.M.L. Endeley (Dr. Foncha's opponent in West Cameroon) who had opposed the Foumban union that meant "East Cameroon-Francophone, oppressive laws and immanency laws were [to be] extended and applied in West Cameroon" (Ngwana, 2009) is described by Fonkeng as one of the great men who could see "ahead in time the viper that hid underneath this tall grass of so-called brotherhood."[45] The West Cameroon "intellectuals in politics" refused to heed to his warning. Has history also proven him correct? Are the intellectuals in politics today simply refusing to openly acknowledge it?

Thus, while Chapter 2 below will generally elaborate on the enigmatic and other blameworthy dealings, Fossungu (2013:29-32) has amply demonstrated that any talk of annexation then that has to be valid in Cameroon must have to be directed at the secretive dealings before and at Foumban, not to the 1972 and 1984 name-changing events. These later events were/are mere pieces of evidence of the annexationist act proper that had been born and baptized before, but confirmed in, Foumban in 1961 or a little before. The confirmation is in the nature of Foumban Constitution that President Ahidjo has been accused of having violated whereas it gave him a *carte blanche* (or authorized him) to do just anything he felt/feels like doing. I will only add that the assumption of emergency under article 15 of the Foumban Constitution was (1) "subject only to the conditions prescribed by federal law" and (2) that it be done "after consulting the Prime Ministers of the Federated States." I will take the consultation first.

Anyone who is claiming that President Ahidjo did not consult his appointees – the prime ministers (and especially that of West Cameroon, Solomon Tandeng Muna) – must have to prove that. Such a consultation would not even have made any difference (see Konings and Nyamnjoh, 1997: 210). But could someone in the capacity of West Cameroon P.M. and Federal Vice President have assumed the campaign manager function (see Fossungu, 2013:23-25) without having been "consulted"? An affirmative here would be just as astonishing as saying Ahidjo himself actually enacted legislation limiting his unlimited powers.

As to the subjecting legislation, one can be sure that none of such subjecting federal law had been enacted. President Ahidjo, by the same constitution, was responsible for all laws and the notorious 1961 anti-federation law can consolidate this point. As Gorji-Dinka (1996) tells us very clearly, "In 1961, Foncha was sitting down there when Ahidjo issued a law which empowered him (Ahidjo) to dismiss a government in Buea and

[45] E.F. Fonkeng, *The Captive* (Ottawa: Bhakti Press, 1990) at 25.

appoint another one. From that time till today, we have never been under constitutional rule." Note should also be taken of Decree 61-DF-15 of 20 December 1961 which Konings (1999: 302) says specified that the whole federation should be divided into administrative regions under the authority of Federal Inspectors of Administration, who were to be directly responsible to Ahidjo. Why was Foncha still 'sitting down there' then only to resign in June 1990 because, as Konings (1999: 307) quotes him for justifying, "the rule of the gun replaced the dialogue which the Anglophones cherish very much"? As President Ahidjo was responsible for all laws, it is simply ridiculous to imagine that he actually enacted any of such laws limiting his unconstrained powers and discretion.

Rubin (1971: 141) has even indicated that the federal legislature had the power to enact necessary legislation to protect human rights but it never did so. As I see it, there was simply no such power because Mirkine-Guetzévitch and Prélot (1950: xi) say power cannot be divorced from the ability to act and from its environment.[46] I hold that no such power existed: assuming, of course, that to have power is to have the ability and the willingness to control others or "to have the ability to take action, to make decisions, to be effective. In short ...to have power...is simply the ability to act."[47] Or better still in the words of Newman, for those federal parliamentarians or legislators to be said to have power must require them to "possess the ability to compel obedience, to shape events and trends – political and cultural as well as economic – in their favour."[48] Assuming further that the Cameroonian legislature even had that *power* (which Bertrand Russell considers to be 'the production of intended effects'), the simple reason why it could not exercise it is that the (almighty) PFR did not want it. How then could the PFR have enacted legislation restraining the PFR (himself) when no one else could? And could anyone have successfully challenged his (non-)exercise of powers in court when this court has never been independent of the chief executive?

---

[46] "*La notion de pouvoir ne peut être détachée des aspects qu'elle prend. Comme l'Esthétique est la science de la structure et la vie des formes belles, la Politique est celle des formes civiques.*"

[47] Bert Derveaux, with Kaye Derveaux, "The Enemies within Community Development" in James A. Draper, ed., *Citizen Participation: Canada* (Toronto: New Press, 1971), 93 at 104. See also Couloumbis and Wolfe (1986: 7); and Ian Robertson, *Sociology* 3rd ed. (New York: Worth Publishers, 1987) at 479-82.

[48] Peter C. Newman, *The Canadian Establishment* Volume 1 (Toronto: McClelland and Stewart Limited, 1975) at 387.

Closing Remarks

Federalism proper will propel development in Cameroon. But the federation has to be created now, from scratch, with emulation being sought from countries like Belgium, Switzerland and Canada. If properly instituted and followed, federalism is also an appropriate medium for properly instituting equality, justice and freedom in governance in African countries. All this cannot be done in Cameroon through the ceaseless calls for a return to the 1961 Federal arrangement. As I have shown here, there was no federation created in 1961 in Foumban and therefore there is none for now returning to. A federation does not exist simply because 'federal' is affixed to the name of a unitary centralized country. If it were to be so, then, by the same Foumban logic, the USA would not be federal because of the word 'united' in its name.

In 1961 the concept of federalism was largely used by some individuals only as a bargaining medium for personal favours from the President of the "Federal" *République du Cameroun* who, on his part, employed the concept solely as a tool, first, for the annexation of British Southern Cameroons and, second, for the ruthless crushing of the 'stormy and heady' opposition in East Cameroun. For example, to be able to easily achieve their ulterior goals, dealings between the two parties (Ahidjo's *Union Camerounaise* & Foncha's KNDP – Kamerun National Democratic Party) that 'created the federation' were shrouded in top secrecy, contrary to what some 'intellectuals in politics' such as Enonchong (1967: 83-84) do present. The parties to the secret pre- and post-Foumban dealings (not without the translator) did sufficiently reap their fruits of the secrecy. For instance, 'the secretive Foumban Constitution' required in article 53 that, until 1964, deputies to the FNA be nominated by the respective legislative assemblies of the two federated states. This questionable requirement, according to Benjamin (1972: 21), especially enabled President Ahidjo (whose *Union Camerounaise* party then controlled the Eastern Assembly) to muzzle the Opposition in East Cameroon and keep them out of the national or 'federal' level (and, what other level was there?). This equally applies to the Western Legislative Assembly which was dominated by Prime Minister/Vice President John Ngu Foncha's KNDP, thus also excluding Endeley's KNC (Kamerun National Congress) opposition party from the 'federal' level.

All this could simply not have been the case if those federal deputies were elected directly. That is, if the provision that specified the principle of representation (80,000 inhabitants per deputy) took effect from 1961. Deputies from the southern part of the country should then not have necessarily been persons favouring Ahidjo's measures and policies; an apt example buttressing the point here being Deputy Daniel Kemajou who, in his valiant opposition to the acquisition of *pleins pouvoirs* in 1959 by Premier Ahidjo, affirmed: "No and again No! Better to die in dignity than live in slavery and dishonour."[49] The Foumban Conference and Constitution, in a nutshell, transformed a parliamentary system into a presidentialist one by combining the position of head of state with those of head of government and of chief justice, and also making the president the sole judge of what the unity of the country entails, as well as how to run the affairs of the state. This act of transformation was to Johnson (1970: 191) the "most important consequence of federal union for Easterners [i.e. East Cameroonians]" because Bjornson (1991: 112) says it effectively "assured that the will of the governing elites could be imposed upon the people." That is precisely what Ahidjo did in 1961 and 1972, what Biya did in 1984 and continues to date doing. It is then clearly unhelpful to be claiming that "the sovereign people of Cameroon" counted in the making and destruction of the Solid Federal Edifice.

---

[49] See *Journal Officiel des Débats, Année Legislative* 1959-1960, First annual ordinary session, plenary meeting of 23 October 1959 at 29.

Chapter 2

Confusion, Manipulation, and the Invisible Hand of Federalism in Africa: Lessons in Patriotism, Sincerity, and Brotherhood in Cameroon

> For 34 years in some of the highest offices in this land, 13 [now 31] at the helm of state, and for all the experience usually – and often wrongly – associated with longevity of service, for all his claim to patriotism for his people, Mr. Biya's dreams and aspirations for his people, his most precious gift to them, have been summarised in the 60 articles of the draft constitution tabled before parliament last week [which, of course, became the 69-article 1996 Constitution barely one month later]. [Fohtung, 1995]

On The Invisible Hand of Federalism

Trager (1968: x) has posed some important questions that, inter alia, would help in deciphering the invisible hand of federalism. What is federalism, and why do federations form and fail? In other words, what are the prerequisites, if any, for a successful federation? Can one discern factors that make for success or failure? What role, for example, is played by the constitution itself, its formula for dividing power between the centre and the units? What relative importance should be attached to the non constitutional factors? Most of these issues have already been touched in the previous Chapter; this Chapter being devoted mostly to the forces pushing for and against federalism. There are some six factors that almost every writer on federalism has cited as being responsible for entities federating. These factors, constituting the bases of successful federations as set out by Wheare (1963) and cited by Southall (1974: 138) and Eleazu (1977: 17) are:

> A sense of military insecurity and the consequent need for common defence, a desire to be independent of foreign powers, and a realization that only through union could independence be secured; a hope of economic advantage from union; some political association of the

communities concerned prior to their federal union; geographical neighbourhood; and similarity of political institutions….

How many of these factors (if any) do apply to Cameroon's experience? Stevenson (1989: 13) has opined that it may be that no single factor can explain every instance of the formation of a federal union, and even in a particular case, as the Cameroonian here, a variety of factors may contribute. A critically balanced analysis of the FRC and other current proposals for federalism provides ample evidence that both the West and East Cameroonian political elites involved used the 1961 Foumban Conference merely as a means to something else and not for the sake of what federalism is usually adopted to achieve: special human rights protection. Thus, the invisible hand of federalism in Cameroon would come nowhere near those of other federations, explaining in part or in full what Fossungu (2013) sees as its funny multiculturalism and definition of culture that does not encapsulate history. It also explicates the insecurity (rather than security) that the people were dragged into.

Federating For Security?

The search or desire for security has certainly also played an enormous role in the formation of many great federations. H.W. Springer, according to Stevenson (1989: 13), has categorized all the security factors into two main groups of "predisposing conditions" and "inducements". Discussing R.D. Dikshit's *The Political Geography of Federalism* (1975), Stevenson (1989: 13) points out that he has instead distinguished factors leading to union from those leading to the retention of some degree of regional autonomy; indicating that a preponderance of the first will lead to the formation of a unitary state, while a preponderance of the second will prevent any union from taking place. Only a balance between the two will lead to federalism and only if the balance is maintained. On the other hand, Trager (1968: xiv) has summarized everything and come out with two compelling forces pushing for federalism, namely, (1) affording the necessary force for aggregating territory, and (2) readiness against some impending military-diplomatic threat or opportunity. This factor would explain why the Canadian Fathers of Confederation indicated that they were federating in order to escape "our impending misfortune" (Newman, 1968: 299; Hogg,

1996: 100-101). It is thus very important that all of the federating entities perceive the problem; otherwise, there is a problem.

Security will thus not be a credible factor if some of the entities are not feeling insecure. This is clearly seen in the Caribbean Federation which de Smith (1964: 280) says hinged tremulously on, "about to be bereft of its most important members", largely because Castro's communist Cuba which might have fostered West Indian unity was not considered enough threat especially by the Jamaicans who constituted the most important entity. The impending misfortune (security reasons) in Canada can scarcely be captured by anything in the case of Cameroon, not even by the much sung Igbo factor, discussed later in the context of the 'Kamerun Idea'. This Igbo Factor cannot float and is thus to be conveniently discarded as not being common to both prospective federating entities in Foumban, since East Cameroonians were not under its impulse. As Stevenson (1989: 13) has tersely noted, security motives are somewhat harder to discern, although not entirely absent, in other cases, "such as those of Australia, post-war Germany, and Cameroun." So why is it necessary to call anything federation there (in Cameroun): except the calculated use of the word as a trap into insecurity or state terrorism? It must be noted with Eleazu (1977: 17) that most of the security factors now have relatively no meaning because of the changed international environment and technological advancement. Does such advancement also affect the geographical factor? And did geography and patriotism push for federalism in Cameroon?

Most probably not; and the mere act of "federating" then is to be largely decried because, before the window-dressing exercise in Foumban, the key figures of the delegations of both "federating" states (to be accurate, two political parties – see Johnson, 1970, chapter 7; Zang-Atangana2, 1989; and Benjamin, 1972: 147) knew pretty well that they were looking at the federation issue from different sides of what Denning (1955: 15) quotes Prime Minister Winston Churchill for aptly describing as "the deepest gulf between us and [them]." This alone should however not be taken as saying that the parties at both extremes of the state-form spectrum cannot federate. They perfectly can do so because we have learned from the experts that federalism is necessarily a compromise solution for the extremes of separatism and of the unitary form. What is rather being deplored here is the fact that "federation" is camouflaged even when no agreement of minds to achieve practical and reasonable ends has been reached, thus leaving us with only what has been castigated as a *Gleichschaltung* of minds.[50] Yet, the intellectuals have been presenting a different picture. The politics of academic discussion obviously does not constrain agreement from the participants but it does not also give the participants the right to deliberately confuse or confiscate the issues.

The Hope for Economic Advantage and Geography

Federalism's invisible hand factor of the hope for economic advantage is evident in Chapter 3, with the economic and other neglect of Southern Cameroons aspirations. The present Chapter will be handling those of geography and patriotism, and of independence, being spiced with the question of the similarity (or otherwise) of political institutions. Geography has certainly provided significant momentum to the creation of many federations such as Australia, Canada, and the United States. But its positive contribution must not be exaggerated because Flanz (1968: 106) has cautioned that geography has "From the very outset… [also] worked to divide the new Federation [of West Indies]." In the particular case of the West Indies, Flanz (1968: 104) has concluded, the geographic factor requires little elaboration because even a casual look at the map suggests that the distance between Jamaica and Trinidad is too great to be bridged effectively by inter-territorial associations. Did geography, patriotism, and independence then play the role in Cameroon they often play in other federations? An answer will be attempted as I study some important lessons in patriotism, sincerity, and brotherhood.

Patriotism has been defined by Simpson and Weiner as "The character or passion of a patriot; love of or zealous devotion to one's country." A patriot, if the first sense of the definition has to be adopted, they say means "One who disinterestedly or self-sacrificingly exerts himself [or herself] to promote the well-being of his [or her] country; 'one whose ruling passion is the love of his [or her] country' (J); one who maintains and defends his [or her] country's freedom or rights."[51] These lessons on patriotism are actually some of the factors of federalism's invisible hand. It has been said that Southern Cameroons had to reunite with the Republic of Cameroun in 1961so as to

[50] Mieczyslaw Maneli, *Perelman's New Rhetoric as Philosophy and Methodology for the Next Century* (Dordrecht: kluwer Academic Publishers, 1994) at 32.

[51] J.A. Simpson and E.S.C. Weiner, eds., *The Oxford Dictionary* Vol. XI, 2nd ed. (Oxford: Clarendon Press, 1989) at 349.

achieve independence. This does not only beg the question but also would lead us to other questions. Southern Cameroons was reuniting to gain independence from whom (Nigeria or Britain)? Could that same independence not have been 'gained' without reuniting? Why could the Southern Cameroons political elites not present a common front at Foumban? Why have they still not done so until now? Who was running away from whom? And did they succeed in the race to hell/heaven? Who won and who lost? Did East Cameroon or the Republic of Cameroun also go to Foumban in 1961 in order to acquire 'real' freedom from France?

The crux of the matter indeed, as I see it here, revolves around the principle issue (largely overlooked by the theses being criticized) of whether the FRC of 1961 was 'a true federation' to be able to encapsulate all what it is said to have achieved for the English-speaking in particular (internal self-government) and Cameroonians generally (independence and advancement); a fact that must have provoked the youths' questioning, especially in the Introduction of this book. Rather than provide straightforward responses to the youths of the African continent, the "intellectuals in politics" and other politicians (bellyticians, to be accurate) have instead devised innumerable confusing theories on independence in Cameroon. The confusion and manipulation in regard of the issue of federating in Cameroon for independence and geography (aggregation of territory) will be exposed by an examination of some of the numerous independence theses on both Cameroon's independence from France and "Anglophone independence" from Cameroon. I will thus attempt answers through the patriotism-sincerity-brotherhood lessons which would take four main forms, namely, (1) the Yes-No Patriotic and Sincere Appeal to Nationalists, (2) the Independence from Reunification Postulate, (3) The Kamerun Idea and the West Cameroon Proposals, and (4) Translating in the Martian-Venusian Dialogue.

The Yes-No Patriotic and Sincere Appeal To Nationalists

Francophone Africa (in particular) is either independent or dependent; and it is not so difficult to tell the African people what the truth is without the confusion or what Fossungu has described as "double talking *meilleurism* in West-Central Africa".[52] People (including "Many Cameroonians [who

52 See Peter Ateh-Afac Fossungu, "Double-Talking *Meilleurism* in West-Central

Biya, 1986: 132 says] do not know their country") must all have to know that independence can simply not exist where there is none just because someone in the government (or the administration, to be correct[53]) patriotically says so. A better understanding of the issues will be enhanced by first having the appeal before the proof of its patriotism and sincerity, capped by the truth-telling offence.

Appealing For What And Why?

While "making this sincere and patriotic appeal" to all Cameroonians to join in the struggle "with a view to acquiring real freedom for…Cameroon…" (Biya, 1986: 140), the current President of the Republic (POR) of Cameroon (who has already been in power for thirty-one years, with a further endless seven-year term registered in November 2011) would at the same time be poignantly reminding Africans that there is no need for the struggle. As Biya (1986: 139) declares to them, "I want to remind you that the history of Cameroon did not begin in 1960, with our independence." Since Cameroonians, for example, already have this independence, against whom or what are the authorities then inviting them to struggle, and why? Perhaps the authorities do realize that the dubious manner of "achieving" what Cameroonians currently have does not make it the real thing?

The regime leaders would seem to be reading the experts' perplexity when Biya (1986: 139) immediately and rhetorically asked this very important question, the correct, non-manipulative, and straightforward answer to which, I would want to think, belies the entire confusion and manipulation in Francophone Africa generally but in Cameroon particularly: "How was this independence acquired?" The experts would then still be trying to divine the answer to the graphical question when they would be quickly interrupted by the confusing position of the Cameroon administration. This independence, Biya (1986: 139) has posited, "was neither 'given' nor 'granted' to Cameroonians. The independence of our country was hard won by many worthy children of the land." The POR's 1996 Constitution in its Preamble

Africa" *The Herald* N° 644 (10-11 August 1998), 10.

53 Some critics do, perhaps rightly so, hotly dispute the use of 'government' with regard to Cameroon, instead preferring 'administration'. According to Maître Yondo Mandengue Black, for example, Cameroon is only administered, not governed ("*Le Cameroun est administré mais non gouverné*"). See "Un peuple qui ne renouvelle pas ses cadres est un peuple sans avenir" *Le Messager* (23 mai 1996), 6-7 at 6. Yondo Black's thesis is heavily tied to the dependent status of the neo-colony.

(2nd paragraph) would also be talking of "*Jaloux de l'indépendence de la Patrie camerounaise chèrement acquise et résolu à préserver cette indépendence....*" The confusion on independence (also derived from federalism) in Cameroon is only starting.

Some 'obstinate' teachers such as Lantum (1991: 20) have disagreed with the tactics and have been talking to students about "the Republic of Cameroon which had been awarded independence by France on 1st January 1960." Lantum is obviously right as the discussion below on the *Kamerun Idea* would also show. But the Cameroonian administrators are certainly not happy about this kind of education that suggests to students that Cameroon's independence is not *real.* Biya (1986: 75) would thus be found decreeing the type of "Education [that] will, therefore, aim at giving Cameroonians the required knowledge as well as making them fully aware that their country is sovereign and that within their country they are masters of their own destiny." It has to be necessarily stressed that being sovereign and masters of their own destiny must properly entail that Africans (and not France) would effectively decide, for instance, who is to be their POR or prime minister (as the case may be). But this is clearly not the case because (like others[54]) Gorji-Dinka (1996) affirms that "The SDF does not know that Biya needs its agenda of putting an Anglophone in Etoudi [the presidency] in order to get the French to stand behind him – Paul Biya. The SDF does not know that they are the people keeping Biya in power. When they insist that Fru Ndi must enter Etoudi Paul Biya turns around and says: 'you see they want to put an Anglophone into this place?' They (the French) say no, over our dead bodies and stand behind Paul Biya." And, of course, Biya, in return, does whatever the French would demand of him, even if it means exterminating every Cameroonian and remaining president of just himself, Biya.

The confusion and emasculation of historical facts that are involved in this country would largely be responsible for the public ignorance in the Hinge of Africa. This emasculation can be seen here in one truth about Cameroon that the present author will certainly be 'guilty' of, namely, that this is an African country where saying, for example, that "You are pardoned" is not actually that you are excused. That is the bitter truth about

---

54 See also Delancey (1989: 1); Gros (1996); Bonny Kfua, "The Impossibility of Fru Ndi's Presidency" *The Herald* N° 551 (24-28 December 1997), 4; and Cameroon Post Editorial, "France's Stranglehold and Cameroon's Sovereignty" *Cameroon Post* (20-26 August 1996), 2.

presidential pardons in Cameroon. Or is the presidential pardon actually patriotic and sincere? A good response to this query must carry us to Bafoussam (the capital of Bamboutouszone[55]) where the proof of sincerity and patriotism is located and publicly hidden.

President Ahidjo had obtained *pleins pouvoirs* in 1959 (with French connivance and active backing) solely for what a constitutional historian (Awasom, 2002: 3) decries as "the uphill task of exterminating anti-French Cameroonians [mostly the *upecites*]." But the current Biya administration does claim to be patriotically and sincerely reintegrating those *upecites* that had not been slaughtered by President Ahidjo's 'First Republic'. It is however highly doubtful that there can indeed be sincerity and patriotism where a person clearly sees X but would continue to insistently say it is Z; as well as keep saying 'Yes-No' to important human rights questions and instruments. In such a situation one is bound to expose what one is attempting to conceal, no matter how much one tries to cover it up. Thus, Cameroon is eventually seen even by the authorities (though in their normal disguised manner) as being the unambiguous neo-colony about which their woolly sincere and patriotic appeal is being made.

Biya (1986: 140) thus states that "Even if, today, a good number of these freedom fighters are gone forever, some of them are still alive and they continue to be interested in the life and destiny of their Fatherland. It is to these people that I am making this sincere and patriotic appeal for them to

---

[55] I would henceforth use the more meaningful names for the ten provinces/regions/states of Cameroon that have been proposed by Fossungu (2013: 4) whose Table I is reproduced here for the reader's reference and convenience:

Proposed Cameroon State & Federal Capital Names

Proposed Name	Abbreviation/Capital		Former/Current Name
Adamawazone	ADZ	Ngaoundéré	Adamawa Region
Bamboutouszone	BBZ	Bafoussam	West Region
Benouezone	BNZ	Garoua	North Region
Debundschazone	DBZ	Buea	South West Region
Guinean-Savannazone	GSZ	Bertoua	East Region
Logonezone	LGZ	Maroua	Extreme North Region
Nyongzone	NYZ	Ebolowa	South Region
Sanagazone	SNZ	Akonolinga	Centre Region
Savannazone	SVZ	Bamenda	North West Region
Wourizone	WRZ	Douala	Littoral Region
Yaoundé City Zone	YCZ	Yaoundé	Yaoundé

Source: Fossungu (2013: 4)

join us in the ongoing struggle against neo-colonialism, with a view to acquiring real freedom for all Cameroonians." So it has taken this long to say just this? Like Fossungu,[56] Appiagyei-Atua (1999: xvi) seems to have the matter under control when he posits that "The[ir] cry against neo-colonialism was supposedly a cry for a better deal for African peoples, but in reality it was a complaint lodged by Africa's leaders to obtain a 'fairer share' in their collaborative-competitive relationship with Western capitalist interests [because] These leaders were involved in the very neo-colonialism they were condemning." That could explain why it has taken this long to say it; and is the appeal then both sincere and patriotic?

Bafoussam and the Proof of Sincerity and Patriotism

To prove the sincerity and patriotism in their appeal, the POR has brought forth some very controversial laws/decrees that have had to further inflate the "jumble of pieces", as a Supreme Court justice has aptly described Cameroon's confusion under the cover of legislation.[57] The unilingual laws and decrees (in a so-called bilingual Cameroon) in question are (1) *Loi N° 91/002 du 23 avril 1991 portant amnistie des infractions et condamnations politiques*; (2) *Loi N° 91/022 du 16 décembre 1991 portant réhabilitation de certaines figures de l'histoire du Cameroun*; and (3) *Décrets N° 92/091 et N° 92/092 du 4 mai 1992 portant modalités d'application de la loi d'amnistie N° 91/022 du 23 avril 1991*. While the first of these two decrees fixes the methods through which they can be reintegrated into the civil service (*"les modalités de réintégration dans les emplois publics des personnes bénéficiares de la loi d'amnistie..."*), the second deals with the manner of restoring whatever had been seized from the beneficiaries (*"les modalités de restitution des biens confisqués aux personnes bénéficiares"*) of the said Amnesty Law. Christine Youengo (a lecturer of l'Université de Yaoundé II) has commented incisively on the first law;[58] while another instructive comment on the second is provided by François Anoukaha of the same University.[59] As for the third, the two application decrees, there is also an

---

[56] See Peter Ateh-Afac Fossungu, "The Convicts and the Prison Guard" *The Herald* N° 592 (3-5 April 1998), 10.

[57] See Nyo'Wakai, "Foreword II" in Carlson Anyangwe, *The Magistracy and the Bar in Cameroon* (Yaoundé: PANAG-CEPER, 1989), xix.

[58] See 7 *Juridis Info (Revue de Législation et de Jurisprudence Camerounaise)* (1991), 5-9.

[59] See 9 *Juridis Info (Revue de Législation et de Jurisprudence Camerounaise)* (1992), 5-9.

interesting critical commentary by Anoukaha.[60] These two University of Yaoundé II professors have ably made my plunging here into the fine points of the controversy raised by these pieces of legislation unnecessary; thus giving me much needed time and space to take care of the pressing business of sincerity and of patriotism.

The cruel *Code Pénal Camerounais1965-67*[61] has been found by Clarence Smith to be good to "serve as a basis for a common African Penal Code."[62] The African continent must then actually be the dungeon that it is said to be? Doomed, according to Monsieur Dumont?[63] I must have to indicate here that in the presence of the sincere and patriotic appeal, the harsh provisions of this *Code Pénal* on federalism/self-determination/secession (discussed in Chapter 3 below) must then have to be scrapped. It could perhaps be argued that the brutal stance on federalism/secession by Cameroon's 'Model Penal Code for Africa' could have been justified in the sixties when Cameroon is said to have been under a huge threat of disintegration. If that argument stood then (because of the UPC 'terrorist' acts meant to acquire Cameroon's real independence), can it still be justified today, especially with the negative fortification of that 'Model Penal Code for Africa'? I do not think so and there are two main reasons for my position: (1) the claim of patriotism, sincerity and forgiveness that I have already explored at length and (2) changed conditions.

In the true spirit of liberalizing and sincerely pardoning fellow citizens (condemned without a real offence), torture and other forms of degrading and inhuman treatment have to be scrapped where they existed before and

---

60 See 10 *Juridis Info (Revue de Législation et de Jurisprudence Camerounaise)* (1992), 9-13.

61 Hereinafter CPC: being both *Loi N° 65-LF-24 du 12 novembre 1965* & *Loi N° 67-LF-1 du 12 juin 1967.*

62 J.A. Clarence Smith, "The Cameroon Penal Code: Practical Comparative Law" 17 *International and Comparative Law Quarterly* (1968), 651 at 671.

63 See R. Dumont, *L'Afrique Noire est mal partie* (Paris: Édition revue et corrigée Du Seuil, 1973), as discussed in David Fongang, "Les P.M.E. dans l'industrialisation de l'Afrique: Reflexion sur un modèle d'intégration économique" 9 *Juridis Info* (*Revue de Legislation et de Jurisprudence Camerounaises*) (1992), 29-32. The declaration that 'Black Africa is doomed '(*"l'Afrique Noire est mal partie"*) has already been condemned by Fongang as a means of discouraging Africans from retracing their steps and pursuing development strategies that synchronize with their own culture and realities; and by Azebaze (1997) as 'a kind of the many anti-democratic strategies that some foreign powers use to prop up African dictatorships that they have installed on the continent' ("*un sorte de charlatanisme au service des obstructions anti-démocratiques du régime en place*").

prevented from existing where they did not. That is not the case in Cameroon however because, while recent international conventions[64] (that have become national laws through due ratification and domestication, as lengthily demonstrated below in Chapter 3) are against them, the 'sincere and patriotic and pardoning' Cameroonian authorities have instead been reinforcing the CPC with laws that promote and protect perpetrators of inhuman treatment, genocide and torture. One of these laws enacted in 1997 (precisely *Loi N° 97/009 du 10 janvier 1997 modifiant et complétant certaines dispositions du Code Pénal*, article 132 *bis* (5) (c)) has now redefined torture in such a way that the state (the executive branch in particular) which is most often the torturer, is not only party and judge but has also been cleared from ever being accused of torturing because torture by the state is now not torture. What would international human rights law and practice be saying or doing about all this?

Changed conditions that have been largely discussed by Fossungu (2013: 236-237) would mean review of the emergency laws is absolutely necessary and called for, as has also been advocated by Anyangwe (1989: chapter 17 – 'Law Reform in Cameroon'). The repeated human rights and other abuses committed during the recurrent and prolonged periods of emergency rule in Cameroon, in the words of Fombad (2004: 81), are a reminder of the danger of open-ended and unchecked powers given to the POR with practically no controls. Fombad therefore has also suggested a review of the present emergency legislation, with the introduction of effective legislative oversight and control and judicial review on the one hand, and the removal of the present undefined residuum of power vested in the POR on the other hand,

---

[64] See, e.g., *Universal Declaration of Human Rights*, signed December 10, 1948, G.A. Res. 217 A (III), UN Doc. A/810, at 71 (1948), reprinted in [1948] U.N.Y.B. 465; *Charter of the United Nations*, 26 June 1945, Can. T.S. 1945 N° 7, 59 Stat. 1031, 145 U.K. F.S. 805; *Optional Protocol to the International Covenant on Civil and Political Rights*, (1976) 999 U.N.T.S. 171; *International Covenant on Economic, Social and Cultural Rights*, (1976) 993 U.N.T.S. 3; and *African Charter on Human and People's Rights* which was adopted on 27 June 1981 (OAU Doc. CAB/LEG/67/3, rev.5) and entered into force on 21 October 1986, and is reprinted in 21 I.L.M. (1982). But see, in particular, *Loi N° 97/007 du 10 janvier 1997 autorisant le Président de la République à ratifier la Convention des Nations Unies du 10 décembre 1984 contre la torture et autres peines ou traitements cruels, inhumains ou dégradants.* For further discussion of this international convention, see A. An-Na'im, "Towards a Cross-Cultural Approach to Defining International Standards of Human Rights. The Meaning of Cruel, Inhuman and Degrading Treatment or Punishment" in Abdullahi An-Na'im, ed., *Human Rights in Cross-Cultural Perspectives: A Quest for Consensus* (Philadelphia: University of Pennsylvania Press, 1992), 19.

as one of the many urgent constitutional reforms that are needed to put Cameroon's transition from authoritarianism to constitutional democracy back on track. These requisite reforms have to necessarily be effected; otherwise, it would only give credibility to the critics who question the sincerity and patriotism of the whole mystifying exercise; baffling, in addition, because in Cameroon no difference can be correctly made between amnesty in CPC section 73 and presidential pardon in CPC section 66 since all laws in their regard emanate from the Unity Palace in Etoudi.

There is even a lengthy and general demonstration from Barcroft (1993: 381) of the presidential pardon "as a mere hand-washing exercise." Although an individual-oriented means of redress whose raison d'être is to safeguard the individual from the more extreme side-effects of law enforcement, Barcroft (1993: 382) thinks its use can be, and has often been, abused. As Barcroft has tersely indicated at page 381, the contemporary employment of this executive decree is viewed by many as equally, if not more, reprehensible than the granting of an amnesty. In addition to the popular resentment generated by a decree of pardon, such a decree is thought to have more dubious constitutional credentials than its above-mentioned next-of-kin. The main source of controversy, he concludes, has been the inclination of the Executive branch to adopt an overly expansionist approach in its utilization of this power; in so doing it has intruded on areas of the law traditionally reserved for the other branches of government. That is exactly what has been done in Cameroon by the various laws and decrees in question as aptly demonstrated by the commentaries on them. In particular, Anoukaha thinks (at page 6 of his above-cited commentary) that the strange "*nouveau type de rehabilitation, la loi N° 91/022 retire ce pouvoir au juge.*" The condemned "mere hand-washing exercise" of these mechanisms is the more especially so in Cameroon where the president is the sole and final judge of when and how to grant or not to grant this pardon and/or amnesty, as has been proudly explained by the then Justice Minister, Laurent Esso.[65]

Specifically about the pardon of the *upécistes* under discussion, some critics have chiefly corroborated Barcroft's hand-washing thesis with some events in Bafoussam – why is it always in Bafoussam, one may ask?

[65] "*Le président de la République est le seul juge de l'opportunité. Il exerce ce droit quand il veut, comme il veut….Et n'a de compte à rendre à personne…, ni à ceux qui disent qu'ils n'ont rien demandé…, et encore moins aux 'mouches du coche'.*" See "Le Dossier du Jour: Comment le Président gracie un condamné" *Cameroun Tribune* (19 octobre 1998), 8-9 at 8.

Bafoussam is the capital of Bamboutouszone, the home of the Bamileke who, as lengthily shown by Fossungu (2013: 73-78), are important to any analysis of the Cameroon Federation because of their tight connection to the UPC and authentic independence. It is therefore only logical that, for special effects, all anti-federalism (we saw President Ahidjo's in Chapter 1, as well as to be further seen in the next Chapter) and anti-democracy (and, therefore, anti-real independence) speeches be dished out to Cameroonians from Bafoussam. Hence, during his anti-multipartism tour of the country on 12 September 1991 in Bafoussam (just a few months after the pardoning laws and decrees in question), the same Cameroonian President Biya pardoning them was still condemning the same *upécistes* 'for their intransigent stand on Cameroon's independence' (*"pour leurs choix intransigeants"*) which, to Wang Sonne, can only mean that these UPC freedom fighters were wrong in Mr. Biya's opinion in fighting for the independence and dignity of Cameroon.[66] Wang Sonne's thesis would explain the free inhuman treatment being dished out in Africa (even in the twenty-first century) to anyone (*upécistes* or not) who advocates human rights and dignity there; truth-telling thus becoming a very serious crime.

A Truth-Telling Offence in Cameroon?

The response to the question is yes; deriving from the fact that certain provisions of the CPC (notably section 111 on secession, as fully discussed below in Chapter 3) would heavily come down on any other person who (though not even 'infringing' the territorial integrity of Cameroon like the President of the Republic does so often) demands that the dictatorship be terminated. It is precisely in view of this CPC provision that 59 people were arrested across Savannazone (North West Region) for agitating in favour of federalism and democracy and detained "for life" since March 1997 at the Kondengui Prison in Yaoundé in Sanagazone (Centre Region). According to Andu's report, in early 1998 Barrister Charles Achaleke Taku who is a leading human rights crusader, represented the 59 detainees and invoked, to no avail, sections 7 and 8 of the "much-regulated" Ordinance regulating the Supreme Court (Fossungu, 2013: 136-137), unsuccessfully urging that un-apex Court to transfer the applicants and any case that may be pending against them to

---

66 *"ces combattants upécistes ont... eu tort de revendiquer la dignité de leur pays, aux yeux de M. Biya."* Wang Sonne, "U.P.C.: 1955-1996: 41 ans de musellement et de divisions" Le *Messager* N° 542 (12 septembre 1996), 6-7 at 7.

their respective 'common law jurisdiction' in Savannazone.[67]

What the *North-West Terrorism Detainees* are saying here about their jurisdiction for trial is aptly capturing the neglect or denial of their culture/history. As will be seen in the next Part of this Chapter, the SDF four-state federation project even carries this denial to unprecedented heights, as well as its implicitly espousing the federation-is-secession theory. The Anglo-Saxon heritage was not protected at all in Foumban where its eventual systematic destruction was no secret to 'inner circle' Anglophones who pretty well knew of the Cameroon Republic's *political master plan of assimilation* and still went ahead to 'duly sell' the English-speaking people by joyfully baptizing and confirming the plan (see especially 'Translating in the Martian-Venusian Dialogue' below). Otherwise, why then is federalism still being sought today, with all the untold injuries to, and enslavement of, "their people"? It is thus still because of the same CPC section 111 that Justice Ebong Frederick Alobwede and Five Others (with whom he made the Independence Proclamation[68]) had, since 11 January 2000, become "for life" tenants of the inhuman underground cells of Yaoundé, never to see natural light, just for refusing to remain 'slaves bought with nothing' in the Republic of Cameroon. (According to Ngwana (2009), they were only released in 2008.) That is precisely the slavery and dishonour Deputy Daniel Kemajou categorically refused to live with as far back as 1959 when he valiantly opposed the acquisition of *pleins pouvoirs* by Premier Ahidjo; powers that are *so full* that they obviously and easily turn truth-telling into an offence.

What is even more alarming is the fact that anyone who would simply indicate (like the author of this book) how barbaric all the wanton arrest and detention of innocent citizens are, would also be guilty not only of 'the offence of spreading falsehood' but also of the other one called 'Contempt of President' in CPC section 153(1) *(outrage au Président de la République)*. Regarding this 'crime', the *Model Penal Code for Africa* ordains in section 153(3) that 'the truth of the supposedly defamatory matter can never be proven

---

[67] See Ezieh Christopher Andu, "Terrorism in NW: Detainees File Motion at Supreme Court, Say They Won't Have Fair Trial in Yaounde But in Bamenda" *The Herald* N° 553 (31 December-4 January 1998), 1 & 2.

[68] See the Proclamation of the Restoration of the Sovereignty and Independence of the Southern Cameroons, Buea, Southern Cameroons, December 30, 1999, available at <http://www.southerncameroons.org/index3.htm> (last visited in July 2011) [hereinafter Independence Proclamation].

whatsoever'. You can now begin to see why most intellectuals in this stupid, dishonest, and ridiculous democracy have simply learned to engage in telling lies. It appears to be the 'profitable' thing to do since today in Cameroon, as Eko (2003: 86) further explains, libel is a criminal offence and journalists who are too critical of the president or government ministers have been charged with breaking laws against propagating false information and insulting the authorities. "*Advanced democracy*, as stupid, dishonest and ridiculous as this *new deal* concept is, barely stops short of entrenching the canning of journalists and writers in the constitution."[69] And these are the same professionals the same POR has openly invited to teach Cameroonians about their most basic rights (as seen below in Chapter 3)? In an a*dvanced* democracy people are simply guilty for telling the truth. That explains why a journalist like Pius Njawé who merely states the truth about the POR's health must be languishing in jail despite all the clarion calls from Cameroonians and foreigners alike for his release.

Once more, it is my strong belief that a state must be seen to ensure that its laws and practices accord with its international commitments in order not to lengthen the documented list of its human rights violations to an extent unlike anything the world has ever known. Most African states would easily ratify most of the international human rights treaties and conventions but that is about as far as the matter goes because all the pleas against and condemnation of state terrorism from both Africans and some concerned members of the international community must simply be like throwing water on the back of a duck. It just does not sink in. For instance, if the case of the *North-West Terrorism Detainees* is not state terrorism, how, for instance, does a case from a province even get to the Supreme Court in Yaoundé (Cameroon) without having passed through lower courts and the Court of Appeal of the province concerned? Where are the much-talked of decentralization and

[69] Ndi Chia (1995a). See also Femi Osofisan, "Warriors of a Failed Utopia? – West African Writers Since the '70s" (being a lecture delivered at The Second Annual African Studies Lecture given at the University of Leeds on the 24th April 1996) *Leeds African Studies Bulletin* N° 61 (1996), 11. For further discussion of the Njawe case that makes the point so well, see, e.g., Melvin Akam, "Droit de dire et devoir de taire: Njawé paye le tribut de la liberté de la presse" *Le Messager* N° 707 (26 décembre 1997), 5; Philip Njaru, "President Biya, Reconsider Jailing Njawe" *The Herald* N° 559 (16-18 January 1998), 4; Gervais Nitcheu Totalé, "La justice sanctionne Pius Njawé le patron du Messager: deux ans de prison ferme" *L'Effort Camerounais* N° 94 (15-21 janvier 1998), 4; and Thomas Eyoum'a Ntoh, "Affaire Njawé: Charabia politico-judiciare" *Le Messager* N° 716 (16 janvier 1998), 5.

federalism in Cameroon? Isn't the stark refusal of federalism (self-determination *within* the state) responsible for secession (self-determination *without* the oppressing state)? That is what is threatening the integrity of Cameroon; a nation at the heart of whose confusing independence theories is the Southern Cameroons' vexed autonomy that (although still being sought now) is said to have been acquired through reunification by way of federalism in 1961.

The Independence from Reunification Postulates

Awasom (2000: 92) has posited that Cameroon's "Anglophones unilaterally opted to achieve independence by joining the Cameroon Republic. Reunification was not an imposition from Francophones." It might be true that it was not imposed by Froncophones but it is now an open secret that "federation", the mode of that reunification, was a deception that emanated from both the Francophone leadership and 'inner circle' Anglophones. The assertion of the constitutional historian is however important in its indication of the desire for independence as being the sole goal of reunification. Chief Justice Endeley (described by Anyangwe, 1989: xv, as one of "two of Cameroon's ablest and finest judges") has also made the desire of reuniting or federating for independence. "When in 1961 the former Southern Cameroons [still] under United Kingdom trusteeship gained independence by reuniting with her East Cameroon sister state which had earlier gained independence from France [in 1960], the resulting political unit was the Federal Republic of Cameroon whose components were the Federated States of East Cameroon and West Cameroon."[70] Some questions have been raised regarding how and why the 'intellectuals in politics' of the dependent Southern Cameroons should have been thinking that they could have had independence by re-uniting, before it, with an already 'independent' and more populous territory. A sound grasp of the significance of the question would call for a brief discussion of some forms of federalism – integrative and devolutionary. Neither of these two forms of federalism would *appear* to be feasible in the case of the Cameroons (1961-72), if one has to stick to some experts' definitions of these concepts.

---

[70] S.M.L. Endeley, "Foreword I" in Carlson Anyangwe, *The Magistracy and the Bar in Cameroon* (Yaoundé: PANAG-CEPER, 1989) at xvii.

Integrative Federalism In Foumban?

Integrative federalism (which opposes the devolutionary type which I discuss below through the SDF project) has been defined by Lenaerts (1990: 205) as a constitutional order that strives at unity in diversity among previously independent or confederally related component entities. Citing *The Oxford English Dictionary*, Stevenson (1989: 3) has said that such a *federation* is the formation of a political unity out of a number of separate states, provinces or colonies, so that each retains the management of its internal affairs. As this specialist has proceeded to explain on the same page, in the definition of 'federation' a new and different basis of distinction (as compared to that of *federalism* by the same *Dictionary*) appears because it is explicitly stated that the components of the federation, whether states, provinces, or colonies, previously enjoyed a separate existence.[71] As Southern Cameroons enjoyed virtually none of these attributes, could the 'integrative' model of federalism have been instituted at Foumban? Could this model have been feasible even if those arranging it from *dependent* Southern Cameroons were tough and business-like rather than suppliant as they overly were?

There is hardly general agreement here; with some critics of UN and British performance in the Cameroons not thinking so because either way (joining Nigeria or the Republic of Cameroon) tiny Southern Cameroons had to be dealing with a more populous and already independent state. Konings and Nyamnjoh (1997: 209) have indicated that during negotiations on the constitution, particularly at the Foumban conference in July 1961, the bargaining strength of the francophone delegation reflected the fact that the size and population of the Anglophone region was small, comprising only nine per cent of the total area and about a quarter of the total population. And even more important, by the time of these negotiations, the Southern Cameroons had still to achieve its independence by *joining* the sovereign Republic of Cameroon, whose President, Ahmadou Ahidjo, as leader of the francophone delegation, was able to dictate the terms for federation by

[71] For further development in the distinction between federation and federalism, see generally Preston T. King, *Federalism and Federation* (Baltimore, MD: John Hopkins University Press, 1982).

capitalising on his territory's 'senior' status. And this senior status is seen reflected in some of the very first decisions to be taken in the early 1960s.[72]

One of the most fatal reasons why Southern Cameroons could not "secure far-reaching concessions," Anyangwe (1987: 128) thinks, "is the hard reality that the Southern Cameroons though with virtually all the attributes of a sovereign state was still under British trusteeship whereas the Cameroon Republic was already a sovereign state. Under these circumstances, defeat was inevitable." Eko (2003: 82) attributes this weakened position to the British neglect of the territory. Some others think that the United Nations, in leaving Southern Cameroons no choice of the third option of staying on their own, made such defeat inevitable either way. As Stark (1976: 427) puts it,

> The Southern Cameroons would have to join a country – Nigeria or Cameroon – that was already independent. Not only would its small size and population stand against equality in such a relationship, but the two parts of the federation – if federation was to be the link – would be unequal in terms of sovereignty at the beginning of the relationship. The U.N. had taken away Foncha's bargaining position. He was forced to join the country which the voters favoured without being able to use future withdrawal as a lever.

I have to draw attention to the fact that the Foncha camp was not 'forced by voters' because they had already had their 'country' of choice even before the 'voters' favoured any. Foncha's speech that is cited and discussed by Fossungu (2013: 29-30) not only 'sleeps and dreams on brotherhood' but also carries the fallacy of the gaining of independence by reuniting or federating with French Cameroun. The attempt to also hide behind the dependent status of the territory might be hard to sell. This is especially so because the British and United Nations actions in Cameroon cannot have answered a lot of other questions surrounding the Foumban Enterprise. For instance, the dependent status of Southern Cameroons at Foumban could not have been exclusively decisive in the achievement of what was there

[72] Such as in 1961 regarding the side of the road (left or right) on which to drive, on which issue "The majority [simply] carried the day and all Cameroonians now drive on the right side of the road" (Eko, 2003: 83); and the legal tender in 1962 and metric system in 1964 (Konings, 1999: 303).

attained. Some experts like Stevenson (1989: 3-4) have even cautioned against the strict requirement of previous separate existence for the federating entities, stressing "that only some of the subnational units need to have enjoyed a previous separate existence." Genuine intellectuals *in* politics, of course, must surely recognize this plain fact. Because they woefully failed to think about the general good, instead being preoccupied with temporary personal favours, there is still Southern Cameroons' vexed autonomy that is said to have been acquired through reunification and/or federalism in 1961 although it is still being sought now – leading us into another clear example of camouflaging sublimation for federalism from the SDF.

Devolutionary Federalism In The SDF Four-State Federation?

As Southern Cameroonsians (or English-speaking Cameroonians) intensify their demands for federalism that can assure the survival of their inherited culture, it would appear that the Biya administration (that seems capable of buying off just anyone, even the Commonwealth – see Fossungu (2013: 34) – has bought and brought in the main opposition party to coolly and unnoticeably do its nasty sublimation job. Topmost in the general matter of confusing and oppressing in Africa must also be included the main Cameroon opposition party, Anglophone-led SDF. Rather than reject it outright like the Biya regime, this political party has suggested the federal structure for Cameroon. But I would venture to say here that their federalism is more poisonous than the current government's *le fédéralisme est sans objet* stance, which is equally unacceptable. It is not really whether, but only how, federalism should be the rule in Cameroon. But when one keenly looks at their *how* federalism should be that rule, the SDF envisaged federation quickly turns sour because of its reckless confusion and manipulation, smeared especially by the deplorable trend of Cameroon's English-speaking always rushing to find (personal) favours with the French-speaking, even at the expense of the survival of the cultural community. This appalling inclination dates as far back as the late 50s (see Konings, 1999: 302-303) and is largely responsible for the unsettling Cameroon human rights climate.

The false impression given to the wider public is that the SDF federation is geared toward devolving powers to the benefit of multiculturalism and separation of powers. Devolutionary federalism (for previously unitary states, on which Belgium is well known) is a constitutional order that redistributes the powers of a previously unitary State like Cameroon among its component entities, with these entities obtaining an autonomous status within their fields of responsibility (Lenaerts, 1990: 205). This is what might also have happened to the United Province of Canada (current Ontario and Quebec) on the establishment of Confederation. The Belgians, as just noted, are invaluable instructors in this business, having successfully moved, as ably shown by Shapiro (1995: 57-87) and Dumont *et al* (2008: 36-37), "From a Unitary Belgium to a Federal Belgium". This form of federalism is clearly what Cameroonians now have open to them although it was excluded from (or not feasible during?) the Foumban Experiment in 1961. As complex as the Belgian experiment is, Dumont *et al* (2008: 35) in their chapter of the book, "attempt to describe the distribution of powers in Belgium as briefly as we can, without doing violence to its richness and complexity – concentrating on major characteristics rather than on an exhaustive inventory of rules." 'From a Unitary Cameroon to a Federal Cameroon' is however not what the SDF four-state project aims at but only the sublimation of the English-speaking community; a strategy which is worse than what is currently in place. I will show how this is so by examining (1) the contents of the federation and (2) its flawed assumptions and forces behind it.

On The Contents of the SDF Federation Project

If federalism is being now pursued as a means of protecting human rights and preserving and promoting cultural diversity in Cameroon, it is argued here that the SDF envisaged federation is instead geared towards achieving the opposite results, but even more covertly and more devastatingly. It would instead worsen the situation for self-determination especially for the English-speaking people. The SDF four-state model is one of the many proposals for federalism but (quite apart from "This [equally confusioncratic Anglophone] federal draft constitution [which] was never seriously discussed by the Technical Committee for the Revision of the Constitution" – Konings, 1999: 316) it seems to be the only one that has gone as far as touching on the exact number of entities and *their exact contents*. By the terms of article 61(1) of the 1996 Constitution of Cameroon, East or French Cameroon in the 1961-72 federation constituted eight of the current ten provinces or regions, with the exception of the two 'Anglophone' regions of North-West (Savannazone) and South-West (Debundschazone). According to Endali's (1996) incisive report on Political Confusion in Cameroon, the SDF projected four states –

with the existing provinces constituting them in brackets – will be the Sawa State (South West/Littoral), the Grassfield State (North West/West), the Beti State (Centre, South, and East) and the Magida State (Adamawa, North, and Far North).

With a clear picture now of the SDF combination of the existing provinces into their federation's four states, one must be wondering if the SDF is really the *Sofa Don Finish* ('the end of slavery') as the common folks have been made to think the acronym of SDF actually means. The answer that is convincing has been provided by the critics who see in it only the usual strategy of (especially the Anglophone) 'intellectuals in politics' in Cameroon to let the masses think that they are being led to Heaven when in actual fact they are instead being sent to the dungeons.[73] The other important question has already been posed by the Alliance for Democracy and Development (ADD) president as to who even gave the SDF the right to carve out these states (see Fossungu, 2013: 78-79). I would only add that, if adopted, the SDF federation would make things even worse for the English-speaking minority. The contents of the SDF states are particularly disturbing as the federation is geared toward something else than federalism and I am still wondering if this is the same federation project Gros is alluding to. According to Gros (1996) who is University of Missouri professor of political science and public policy, Anglophone populist Fru Ndi of the SDF, as president of Cameroon, "would likely have favoured the establishment of a federated state with real powers for regional governments. Such an arrangement would have meant greater autonomy for the English-speaking provinces: North West and oil-rich South West. The prospect of such shifts upsets not only France but also most of the other parties in the largely French-speaking opposition, and partly accounts for the absence of 'interparty alliances'."

If this SDF four-state project, the contents of which have been laid out above, is actually what Gros has posited as providing "greater autonomy for the English-speaking provinces" (Debundschazone and Savannazone), then I would clearly differ with both the professor and the SDF. By submerging the two separate English-speaking regions (Debundschazone and Savannazone) into the two French-speaking regions of Wourizone and Bamboutouszone,

[73] See Peter Ateh-Afac Fossungu, "Paradoxes of Cameroon's Intellectuals" *The Herald* N° 559 (16-18 January 1998), 4.

respectively, the SDF federation would actually be destroying any semblance of 'multiculturalism' that is still manifesting itself in this country, in the face of the relentless official pressure to uniformize or assimilate. I would rather the English-speaking stay a minority in Cameroon but be, at least, masters of their respective regions (assuming that they are so very different that they cannot work together in a single English-speaking state) than the double-minority jeopardy the SDF is creating for them. This looks like Foumban repeating itself on a grander and more devastating scale. Henceforth, by the SDF federal state, the English-speaking would not only be a minority in Cameroon but, first and worst of all, an insignificant minority in their respective SDF-states (Sawa and Grassfield). It amounts to their fighting minoritarianism on two levels (rather than one).

According to reports (Fossungu, 2013: 87), the 19.4 million given as Cameroon's current population is distributed in the ten states as follows: Adamawazone, 1,015,622; Bamboutouszone (West), 1,785,285; Benouezone (North), 2,050,229; Debundschazone (South West), 1,384,286; Guinean-Savannazone (East), 801,968; Logonezone (Far North), 3,480,414; Nyongzone (South), 692,142; Sanagazone (Centre), 3,525,664; Savannazone (North West), 1,804,695; and Wourizone (Littoral), 2,865,795. In the SDF's Grassfield State, North Westerners (Savannazonians) are slightly not a minority but South Westerners (Debundschazonians) are significantly one in their Sawa State. What, by the way, is the advantage for North Westerners being an insignificant majority in one of the four states of what Konings and Nyamnjoh (1997: 208, 213, & passim) aptly describe as "the francophone-dominated state"? Sublimation, sublimation, sublimation, is the goal; and this (it must be indicated in bold black and white) is actually the reason why the SDF proposal is very much favoured by most French-speaking Cameroonians who have traditionally considered anything federal to be heresy.[74] "Many Francophones," Endali (1996) also clearly states in his report on Political Confusion, "tend to favour the SDF option of a four-state federation." The same ideology would be found lurking behind "the major reasons why many Francophone supporters of the SDF in the Littoral and West Provinces proposed a federation of states based on two differently

[74] Konings (1999: 291) makes the point clear when he opines that "There is ample evidence that the government's stand on the 'Anglophone problem' is supported by the majority of the Francophone elite and by a section of the Anglophone elite closely allied to the regime in power."

constituted entities: the two Anglophone provinces and the Francophone West and Littoral Provinces together as one state, and the remainder of Francophone Cameroon as the other" (Konings, 1999: 318). If my complete-annihilation thesis were to be wrong, then why do many of these Francophones not tend to also support the other options of a ten-state multicultural federation?

Could one not also sympathize with the majority of Cameroon's French-speaking majority in now suspecting that federalism is being sought especially by the English-speaking minority only as a means to secede? This suspicion is particularly fortified in light of the persistent and somewhat unhelpful calls for a "return to the 1961 Foumban two-state Federation" (advocated, e.g. by Gorji-Dinka, 1991) rather than something in the nature of Etinge's (1991) more enlightened bicultural 10-state model. Apart from the external French factor (see Gros, 1996; and Azebaze, 1997), the suspicion of the majority of the Francophone majority could be buttressed by two factors. The first is the fact that the same Anglophones (as British Southern Cameroonsians) used 'federalism' through reunification in 1961 simply to get away from the Federation of Nigeria.[75] So, the argument could run, if they were real federalists, why would they be leaving a federation in 1961 to enter into something that was everything but a federation? The second has to do with the favourable Francophone reaction to the SDF four-state federation that is geared toward completely obliterating their separate identity and territory, and thus putting out any future prospects of self-determination for them. This SDF strategy is not just annexation that had already occurred before and in 1961 but complete sublimation.

On the Federation's Flawed Assumptions and Invisible Hands

By their federal project, the SDF would seem to be only interested in pleasing the Francophone majority in order to grab power, and not in seeing to it that human rights generally and especially minority cultural rights are protected and respected. For this confusion and manipulation (confusioncracy) they would be trying to hide behind 'national unity' just like the Biya regime does every day and minute. While the SDF attractively calls it

[75] "It was Southern Cameroons which voted in the 1961 United Nations plebiscite for reunification with French Cameroun rather than for integration into Nigeria." Konings and Nyamnjoh (1997: 209).

four-state federalism, Biya's Cameroon People Democratic Movement (CPDM) glorifies it as the "Perfect Nation" (see Fossungu, 2013: 30-31). Both the SDF opposition and the CPDM government are thus claiming the respect for human rights in Africa *only after* the attainment of development or national unity – their camouflaged name for assimilation and sublimation. Books upon books can be and have already been written on/about this up-side-down view. Appiagyei-Atua (1999: xvii) has castigated it as an

> Approach [that] would not only numb the [African] people's resistance to oppression and suppression but also dissuade then from proposing an alternative bill of rights that speaks directly to their past and present experiences. This attitude of African leaders, with the influence and active collaboration of Western capitalist interests sets the tone for the analysis of this work… [which] rests on the key issue: whether rights should be taken as a foundation to development or whether they should take a back-seat and only become relevant after development is attained.

Is there even any other reason, other than that of confusion and oppression, for using 'Democratic' in the names of political parties that do not tolerate dissent or change in their direction? The SDF opposition is just as guilty of the lack of the democratic spirit (a condition sine qua non for federalism) as is the CPDM party currently in power because "I [Newfoundland Premier Wells] have always held the view that 10 years is more than long enough to hold the responsibility of leader of a major party, either as leader of the opposition or leader of the government."[76] This important democracy statement is coming from a provincial premier in a country using a system of government (parliamentary) that puts no limit on the duration and number of terms a leader can have. In Cameroon (before the 2008 amendment) the 1996 Constitution in article 6(2) apparently 'limited' executive terms of office to two – making 14 years in total (to leave out all the other manipulative and confusing laws[77]). Yet, Mr. Biya of the CPDM has been in power for more than thirty years and still endlessly running, while Ni John Fru Ndi is still the Chairman or leader of the

[76] Cited in "Tobin Touted to Lead Nfld" *Montreal Gazette* (20 December 1995), A8.

[77] This issue's uncertainty and ambiguity have been explored by Peter Ateh-Afac Fossungu, "War of Laws and Executive Term [of] Office in Cameroon" *The Herald* (28-29 September 1998),10.

opposing SDF and has been since the party's inception in the early 1990s.[78] It is thus something else that the SDF is after, not federalism because undemocratic people cannot genuinely be talking of federalism.

This thesis applies as well to the African Union that the undemocratic and un-African (neoclonial) heads of states and of governments have pre-emptively created to stifle the African peoples's attempts to come together. Tell me, for example, how these people being called African leaders can truly be desirious of African unity when they have made one of the AU's conspicuous visions to be "To defend the sovereignty, territorial integrity and independence of its Member States"? Genuine African unity even does not necessarily have to begin with all of this continent's states on board. Again, what even would be the 'sovereignty' and 'independence' that the Francophone members of this AU are actually talking of/about? My straightforward take is that, until these African states are individually democratic (and, therefore, independent of neoclonialism), the gathering of their heads (constituting the AU's "supreme organ" to whom all its other organs are "responsible") anywhere to talk 'African unity' is just as hypocritical and useless as is the SDF and CPDM democratic nonsense in Cameroon (see Chapter 3 below for more). And the proof about my theory on the SDF is amply there: first, is what Konings and Nyamnjoh (1997: 216) have castigated as "its half-hearted stand as regards the `anglophone problem"'; and, second, a true federal union must not involve the act of one of the entities 'annexing' or 'subliming' the other(s).

The English-speaking people of this country in particular have for so long been resisting being completely turned into President Biya's outmoded 'Perfect Nation'. The ball has therefore been conveniently handed over to the Anglophone-led SDF to do the clean-up or assimilation, Foumban-style, since it is well known (from Foumban) that the real enemy of the English-speaking in Cameroon is the English-speaking (see Fossungu, 2013: 30-31);

---

[78] For more details or studies on the undemocratic nature of the SDF, the following early literature would be very useful: Marc Yared, "Bernard Muna-John Fru Ndi: le divorce" *Jeune Afrique* (8-14 Avril 1993), 22-23; Asong Ndifor, "SDF Discipline: A Source of Strength Yet A Cause for Concern" *The Herald* (9-10 December 1996), 7; Peterkins Manyong, "Conflict Within SDF Explodes: Secretary General to Face Trial" *The Herald* (18-19 March 1998), 1; Nkem-Nkafu Njikem, "Conflict Within the SDF" *The Herald* (30-31Match 1998), 10; Sam-Nuvela Fonkem, "How Free Is Liberty Spot?" *The Post* (8 May 1998), 7; and Edward Besong Achuo, "Becoming Another Victim of the North West Mafia?" *The Herald* (20-21 April 1998), 4.

and as well that Anglophone 'intellectuals in politics' are very good at leading their own people into the dungeon while giving them the contrary notion. That could be the truth behind the SDF project. Were it otherwise, what is the problem the SDF is trying to solve in the first place? The biting issues of governance and development in Cameroon today are largely mere inevitable consequences of the erratic 1961 Foumban arrangements. One would expect that the lessons should have been learned by now, more than fifty years after.

Providing empirical evidence on the extent to which inappropriate governing strategies are the main internal obstacle to development in Cameroon, John Bobuin Gemandze and Tangie Nsoh Fonchingong in their 2009 book (*Cameroon: The Stakes and Challenges of Governance and Development*) have argued for a departure from the inhibition by the adoption of good governance strategies that comprise, among others, "decentralizing administration to make for popular participation and ensure accountability; taking the necessary steps to fight corruption; and ensuring the enforcement of property and cultural rights."[79] The SDF project does not at all try to meet these conditions but merely assumes that there are more important things (regarding governance and development especially) that do bind an English-speaking Cameroonian from Savannazone to a French-speaking Cameroonian in Bamboutouszone than to a fellow English-speaking compatriot from Debundschazone and/or vice versa. Should that be the case, would there be any reason for the general bitterness today from the English-speaking people in Biya's 'Republic of Cameroon'?

The discussion below in the first Part of Chapter 3 is pellucid on the SDF Federation being highly flawed in projecting only the local ethnic factor, and in completely ignoring the most important factors (the English and French colonial styles and cultures) and their lasting effects on the local ethnic configuration. Use is therefore made of the Bangwa from Debundschazone (English-speaking) and the Bamileke from Bamboutouszone (French-speaking). As will be more elaborately seen in the next Chapter, both groups have the same ancestry (just like the Bakweri of Debundschazone and the Douala of Wourizone) but the Bangwa are now quite different people from the Bamileke solely because of the division of German Kamerun between the English and the French in 1916. One of the

79 *See* <http://www.langaa-rpcig.net/Cameroon-The-Stakes-and-Challenges.html>, visited on 8 June 2011.

principal, if not the only, reasons for the Bangwa now being different from the Bamileke is the different system of governance of the respective colonial powers.

Bangwa, Brain (1972: 9) has made clear, "is not a term for a tribe or any kind of political unit, and is used specifically for those nine Bamileke chiefdoms accidentally caught on the British side of the French-British trusteeship boundaries, after the defeat of the Germans in the 1914-18 war. Although artificial, the boundary has had important effects, the anglophone Bamileke of West Cameroun being quite a different cultural product from the francophone Bamileke of East Cameroun." In view of the concise historical, cultural and sociological survey that undeniably distinguishes the Bangwa of Debundschazone from the Bamileke of Bamboutouszone, it would be hard to deny that the SDF four-state suggestion, especially in its contents, is solely myopic: being seemingly influenced principally by the urgent need to please the French-speaking majority and get elected, smeared by the rubbish in this country called the North West/South West Divide[80] whose name couples well with the discussion this far to tell the reader what it is all about – myopia, mixed with high doses of manipulation and confusion – confusioncracy is what I call this system of governance or leadership.

You will also find this nonsense being "stirred up from time to time by ethnic political entrepreneurs" (Konings, 1999: 305) such as the authors of the All Anglophone Conference draft federal constitution that has been discussed by Konings (*id.*: 311-316). To begin with, I give them the necessary credit for the effort of even tendering something we can start working with; which is why I am even talking about the attempt. Two of the members of the august drafting committee have been among the few of my UNIYAO lecturers that I hold in very high esteem for their academic integrity and honesty. What I really find obnoxious with the draft is its putting of people's ethnic affiliations before their competence in a democracy. It seems to me that over fifty years of dictatorship would have had such debilitating effects that most of us can simply not be able to move on without letting the divide-and-rule devices of the dictatorship to continue influencing everything we do. If what the committee proposes is really intended to be a constitutionalism-based democracy and federalism, rather than an 'ethnic-based-rotationary

[80] For a good analysis and grasp of this craze with the 'Anglophones' of Cameroon, see Konings and Nyamnjoh (1997: 227-28, 224-25, & 211-213).

federalism', I do not see any reason for the too much stress on the ethnicity of who succeeds who; as well as their lengthy arguments "that such a detailed constitution was absolutely necessary in the specific Cameroonian context characterised by 'the Anglophone-Francophone divide, inter-ethnic suspicions and rivalries, bad governance, unequal distribution of the 'national cake' and arbitrary and despotic government since independence and reunification" (Konings, 1999: 311).

My criticisms of the Biya-Ahidjo stance on federalism and democracy in Chapter 3 apply here as well. In addition, I think the drafters clearly seem to have all their eyes on the "national cake" rather than on fashioning clear-cut rules for getting to or eating it. My critiques on the a priori personification of public debates (especially in this Chapter 2) also come in here. But Anyefru (2010: 85) seems to have grasped the matter well when he posits that "its [Anglophone Problem's] intensification following the wave of democratisation in Africa since the early 1990s has seen an increased rather decreased extent of ethnic politics and conflicts in that it has reshaped the struggle among elites seeking to defend or challenge the distribution of state power and resources....The introduction of some degree of political liberalisation triggered renewed claims to rights in Anglophone Cameroon." If liberalism can only lead to this, what is the need for condemning the dictatorship then? What else is their justification that "The governor could not be then succeeded by a member of the same ethnic group or municipality" (Konings, 1999: 315)? The same applying to the prime minister, I simply do not see why Oben should be barred from showing his own skills as governor of Debundschazone simply because the out-going governor happens to be an Orock from Manyu or Victoria (his municipality of choice).

The constitution, for instance, does not need to spell out every toilet-going rule in it if the system is one clothed with an independent judiciary (which they have interestingly made room for) whose role it will be to interpret and uphold the *general* principles therein embedded. Principles can clearly not be of general application when people's ethnic groups have been put ahead of their competence and other abilities. What then is the difference with the current Biya-ethnically-based appointive system? Indeed, you will appreciate what I am saying here about an independent and competent arbiter if you consider, for instance, that the constitutional distribution of powers and responsibilities in the Australian federation has proved to be exceptionally flexible despite clear indication from the experts like Williams and Macintyre (2008: 9) that it was originally "conceived as a decentralized federation with the bulk of powers remaining in the hands of the states, in fact there has been a steady accretion of power to the Commonwealth government since shortly after federation in 1901." All that has been able to happen without any of the states or citizens crying for secession because the judiciary, to which anyone/state feeling aggrieved turns to, is independent and has upheld or dismissed complaints based on the court's interpretation of the founders' briefly stated intent. Just give us an independent and culturally-balanced judiciary that is jammed with persons of integrity (even if they are all from the same ethnic group or family!) and even the current 1996 unitary centralized constitution will become a formidable 'Federal' Constitution in their hands.[81]

Furthermore, are we looking for competent people for effective national leadership or mere tribal rotation? Let me use a very banal but real illustration here before you also get to further read this absurd ethnic requirement in the context of 'the mathematics of representation' in Chapter 4 below. Granted even that there should be constitutional provision for rotation between the two cultural groups,[82] why does the candidates' ethnic group have to come into play here? If the outgoing president, for instance, was a competent English-speaking Bameleke person, that means all competent French-speaking Bameleke people are automatically excluded from vying for the position. Yet, this is supposed to be a federal democracy? Also, any political party that has only competent Bameleke candidates for the position is therefore also excluded from fielding any candidates; etc. Let us get this clear and simple message: In a true federation those who cannot think anything but ethnic would still be entitled to limit themselves to the 'ethnic level' while those who think above 'ethnic', 'provincial', 'regional' lines would be entitled to vie for federal or national leadership positions. That is the main reason why a federal system is adopted in the first place: not

---

[81] According to Meekison (1986:75), "Some see the [1996] document as centralizing, others as decentralizing. [But] The reality is that both tendencies can be found." See also Joseph R.A. Ayee, "The Measurement of Decentralization: The Ghanaian Experience, 1988-92" 95 (378) *African Affairs* (January 1996), 31.

[82] I would rather we make the candidate's bilingualism (or tri-lingualism: English, French, & Njangawatok – see Fossungu, 2013:161-166) an important factor rather than mere rotation between Anglophones and Francophones. This requirement would seem to be more promotional of national unity and multiculturalism than the 'rotation stuff'.

to kill but to give forceful expression to those peculiarities without letting the same threaten the national entity, as they often do when we want to forcefully eliminate them through the NEG (see Fossungu, 2013: 206-235).

These ethnic political entrepreneurs simply cannot grasp even simple and straightforward (ten-state) federalism. They had better not even venture near "Belgium's double symmetry, which involves two different kinds of federating units that cut across, and overlap, each other" (Majeed, 2008: 3) because they just cannot handle it. As Dumont *et al* (2008: 35) would agree with me, "It is not easy to use simple [ethnic] language to describe something that is not simple, and Belgian federalism is far from simple [because,] Built without preconceived ideas or an overarching doctrine [like the North West/South West Divide], it accumulates original – sometimes labyrinthine – solutions as it goes along." In short, I would simply dub the 65-member Anglophone Standing (but actually 'sitting down there' like Foncha) Committee's proposed document as the anti-federalism "Ethnic Federal Draft Constitution" and place it alongside Fossungu's (2013: chapter 5) "Confusioncracy Passing for Balanced Development".

As can be seen, Cameroon's English-speaking community seems to be very good only at fighting themselves over belly-issues rather than scrutinizing and fighting against dictatorship and some of the numerous anomalies in the country generally but particularly those that endanger their cultural and other group rights. This attitude has been greatly encouraged by both the Ahidjo-Biya administration and the SDF opposition. My view is that multiculturalism has a better future in Cameroon under the ten-state federal model than under the two-state or the SDF four-state federation. Federalism traditionally has been adopted to solve the kind of ethnic, cultural and political problems that Cameroon and many other African states face. But this solution is being "proposed" by many in Cameroon not because they actually understand and believe in it; but solely as a political expedient means of replacing the current dictator with 'their own strongman' and thence tell everyone else that now is our time to do whatever we want with this country (*maintenant c'est notre tour de bouffer*). This is particularly true of the SDF and its four-state federation project. The NW-SW Divided that is exhibited and glorified in the SDF and other federation projects does effectively and enormously prevent the rise of the *Quebec Factor* in the Cameroon political scene (see Chapter 4 below for more of it). The emergence of such a factor should go a long way toward ensuring human rights respect not only for

English-speaking Cameroonians but for all in Cameroon. The refusal by the SDF to pay close attention to the (foreign) cultural factor can only be understood in the sense that the bridging of gulfs has never been the goal of their Four-State Federation Enterprise.

The SDF project is faulty but the mere fact that this main opposition party has suggested federalism is itself laudable in the sense that it is not a question of whether, but only how, federalism should be the rule in Cameroon. Federalism proper in this country is actually what Elazar and Ikeda would refer to as the 'Royal Road to Lasting Peace' there. [83] That is how the experts all think it is not very hard for the Cameroon state to protect the English-speaking minority and thus also safeguard Cameroon's integrity. But this cannot be done by simply affixing "federalism" while subliming cultural communities.

Any form of state (and/or system of government) in Cameroon that does not further respect for human rights, including group cultural rights, might only be a racket. This kind of "racket", exemplified by both the Foumban 'Federal' *République du Cameroun* (that some are now suggesting 'a return to') and the SDF four-state federation, ought to be quickly dismantled. This is what ought to be done because Peter J.H. Okondo in Chitepo (1964: 19-20) strongly thinks "That kind of [state] organization does not fit any definition of beneficial federation. Why do we federate? For the destruction of individual liberty? Or do we federate to improve the lot of mankind within the federal structure? A federation for the subjugation of the majority [or minority] of the people is not worth keeping. It is a kind of racket; it is a trick of the minority [or majority] to keep the majority [or minority] dominated, and it should be dismantled [and something acceptable put in its place]." This is what must be done since doing so is the sane way to remaking truth, patriotism and sincerity noble ideals in Africa, and not offences as it is currently the case – as embodied in the federalism-is-secession rhetoric; one of its subsets being this other clear case of independence doublespeak from those in power in the form of the Size-and-Numbers Independence Thesis.

---

[83] See Daisaku Ikeda, *A Lasting Peace* Vol. II (New York & Tokyo: Weatherhill, 1987) at 179-185; and David Judah Elazar, *Federalism and the Way to Peace* (Kingston: Queen's University, 1994).

The Size-And-Numbers Independence Thesis

As one learns from Mbinglo (1996), regarding the war of positions about the Southern Cameroons that is taking place on the pages of newspapers, another 'intellectual in politics' (Honourable N.N. Mbile of the ruling CPDM party, who is strongly opposed to Southern Cameroons independence from Cameroon) would begin by 'arguing' that "Southern Cameroons was [not] militarily capable of taking on *La République du Cameroun* in the bid to be free, given the latter's might in [land] area and numbers." (You should recall Ahidjo in Foumban, as seen above, also using a similar thesis to dictate his terms to Southern Cameroons.) But, before anyone even has the time to respond to him, Mbile, in his very next utterance, would be heaping praises on Cameroon's army in Bakassi (the disputed oil-rich territory between Cameroon and Nigeria[84]) in these lines given by Mbinglo (1996):

> Do we appreciate the great sense of patriotism and valour of our armed forces at Bakassi as they exchange blow for blow with an army much larger in numbers than they? Of course, the exploits and heroism of our boys are consistent with the truism that where a cause is just and right numbers are of little consequence and that in modern warfare, numbers alone do hardly determine the outcome.

There is hardly need for any further comment on this 'go-for-before-for-back' Size-and-Numbers thesis: except to indicate that either Monsieur Mbilé forgot his major premise or is plainly saying that the Southern Cameroonsian cause for human dignity is not just nor right. The best I can do here to better expose the confusion of personal for general interests in Africa is to place the Mbile-thesis alongside the other one from Lantum (1991: 20) that would be telling the questioning English-speaking youths of "the achieving [of] future self-government, independence and fuller freedom for his people [them]" in 1961 because of Dr. Fonlon's "brilliant show-up at the Foumban

---

[84] For more historical and socio-legal analysis on the dispute, see Piet Konings "The Anglophone Cameroon-Nigeria Boundary: Opportunities and Conflicts" 104 (415) *African Affairs* (2005), 275-301; Joe C. Irwin, "An Alternate Role for the International Court of Justice: Applied to Cameroon v. Nigeria" 26:4 *Denver Journal of International Law & Policy* (1998), 759; and Njinkeng Julius Bekong, "International Dispute Settlement: Land and Maritime Boundary between Cameroon and Nigeria – Origin of the Dispute and Provisional Measures" 9 *African Journal of International and Comparative Law* (1997), 287-310.

Constitutional Talks 17-21 July 1961 where he volunteered to serve as interpreter when communication between the negotiating parties was prov[ing] to be in[e]ffective." The Francophone leadership in Cameroon would seem to understand well that whenever their obtaining anything geared towards their political master plan of assimilation is proving ineffective they can rely a hundred percent on Anglophone "leaders" or "intellectuals in politics" to do away with that inefficiency; the FRC in Foumban initiated it, with a recent and handy case being Anglophone-led SDF, as exposed in the section before this. To further demonstrate all these, I will next lengthily and critically examine (1) the Kamerun Idea and the West Cameroon Package for union, and (2) the Role of Translation in the Foumban Enterprise.

The Kamerun Idea and the West Cameroon Package for Union

Was the *Kamerun Idea* (otherwise known as patriotism or brotherhood) really the force behind the dealings before and at Foumban? According to Newman (1968: xi), geography *per se* cannot be a decisive ingredient where the situation resembles that of pre-1968 "Canada, which had always been blessed with more geography than history." Unlike Canada, Cameroon would seem to have been blessed with more history than geography; with its little geography (territory) even appearing to have been diminishing over the years: contrary to the conspicuous claims couched in the *Kamerun Idea.* With the confirmation of the partition boundaries of 16 March 1916 (which surprisingly left Douala and Dschang to France[85]) by the London Declaration of 10 July 1919, Britain proceeded to attach its part of the Mandate to two Nigerian Regions. British Northern Cameroons (hereinafter BNC) was attached to Northern Nigeria while British Southern Cameroons (hereinafter BSC) – being the current two English-speaking North West and

85 "Surprisingly", Anyangwe (1987: 45) has written in lament, "Britain readily surrendered Douala to France. The latter had scored a diplomatic victory over Britain who thereby threw away another opportunity of acquiring Douala." The other opportunities include the many letters shown by Harry R. Rudin, *Germans in the Cameroons 1884-1914: A Case Study in Modern Imperialism* (Cambridge, Mass: Yale University Press, 1968) to have been written by the Douala Kings to "Dearest Madam" (the Queen of Britain), pleading with her to colonize their land before the Germans did. It is British forces that had chased out the Germans from the two strategic towns (Douala & Dschang), one in Bamboutouszone and the other in Wourizone.

South West – was incorporated into Eastern Nigeria, a region that is dominated by the Igbo. The *Kamerun Idea* is said to be largely tied to the Igbo Factor.

The Igbo people of Eastern Nigeria were left by Britain to administer and lord over the Southern Cameroonsians. The new sub-masters (the Igbo) considered and treated the newly incorporated "German-speaking" Southern Cameroonsians as second-class citizens (see Konings and Nyamnjoh, 1997: 209). This second-rate treatment is said to have greatly aided in nurturing the *Kamerun Idea* among Southern Cameroonsians. This *Kamerun Idea* embodies the desire to reconstitute the former German colony (or 'protectorate', as some prefer to refer to it) by reuniting its severed parts into one family,[86] and was not limited entirely to Southern Cameroonsians. Were the Igbo also after East Cameroonians, if the *Kamerun Idea* is tied to them? For instance, Benjamin (1972: 188 n.20) points out how Mr. Ahidjo (who was then Prime Minister of French Cameroun) categorically affirmed in his *discours d'investiture* on 18 October 1958 that it was pressing to begin dialogue with British Cameroons "*Pour la reconstitution du Cameroun arbitrairement divisé….*" Some authors have then used this *Kamerun Idea* in explicating and/or justifying the bizarre Southern Cameroonsian mode of thinking before and at Foumban. As Enonchong (1967: 83), for instance, has asserted,

> For a majority of Cameroonians, the aspiration to reunify, though repressed and uncertain at certain stages, had not yet evaporated. The use of 'Kamerun' [the German spelling] in the titles of all the first main political parties in the Territories, even those which later no longer pursued the goal of reunification, constituted an interesting echo of the yearning for the fulfilment of this one desired end. The general mental attachment to 'Kamerun' was a symbolic manifestation of the sense of **oneness** which had already crystallized in the Cameroonian before [the division of their country in] 1916 [bold is as in original].

---

[86] For further discussion of the *Kamerun Idea* and the plebiscites in British Cameroons, see E. Ardener, "The Kamerun Idea" *West Africa* (7-14 June 1958), 559; Awasom (2000) ; Victor T. Le Vine, "The Politics of Partition of Africa: The Cameroons and the Myth of Unification" 17 *Journal of International Affair* (1964) at 198-210; and Claude E. Welch, *Dream of Unity: Pan-Africanism and Political Unification in West Africa* (Cornell University Press, 1966) at 216-241.

This study on confusioncracy and human rights argues otherwise. If the said *Kamerun Idea* was so much the locomotive force for re-unification or federalism in the Cameroons, it is tainted with colossal failure in at least three respects: (1) the UN plebiscites, (2) the territories ceded by France, and (3) a negative on, and not passing, the federalism constituting tests.

Why Two Sets Of UN Plebiscites, And No Return Of Ceded Territories?

The *Idea* ought to have also properly prevented two sets of United Nations (UN) plebiscites in British Cameroons – a part of which was later known as West Cameroon. Elaborating on the UN plebiscites point will also throw some light on the issue of similarity (or otherwise) of political institutions of the federating entities at Foumban. Both 'federating' territories – East Cameroon by France and West Cameroon by Britain – were administered under mandate to the League of Nations until after World War II, when the Cameroons (both East and West) became trust territories of the UN under the same pre-UN administrations. As Peaslee (1974: 83) puts it, French Cameroun received internal autonomy through a decree of 16 April 1957 and on 12 November 1958 France requested the UN to grant them independence on 1 January 1960. West Cameroon never even gained such independence, real or fake. Moreover, as many constitutional historians have shown, the pre-independence constitutional development picture in East Cameroon was very unlike what was found in West Cameroon, and did greatly put its imprints on the reunification arrangements.

To begin with, one can point to the stark absence of established (constitutional) institutions in British Southern Cameroons (BSC), as already discussed in Chapter 1 above. Some active participants of the federal epoch like Gorji-Dinka (1996) will challenge my theory on the absence of established institutions by arguing that there was the Southern Cameroons' Constitutional Order-in-Council which mysteriously disappeared before Foumban. No doubt that there was in fact the allegedly disappeared Constitutional-Order-in-Council.[87] (Why it vanished, is still part of the confusioncracy, isn't it?) But my thesis on the absence of established institutions is still valid since the said Order-in -Council which was "*Made* [on] *12th September, 1960* [and] *Laid before* [the British] *Parliament* [on] *16th*

[87] See *The Southern Cameroons (Constitution) Order in Council, 1960* (Printed in England and published by Her Majesty's Stationary Office: 1960).

September, 1960" only came "*into Operation* [on] *1st October, 1960*" (*ibid*) – only one year before the Foumban Federal Constitution entered into force; a federal constitution that, paradoxically, came to further concentrate rather than separate powers.

On the other hand, the French portion of the Mandate-Trust was not attached to adjacent French colonies like British Cameroons was to two different Nigerian Regions; BNC to Northern Nigeria and BSC to Eastern Nigeria. Furthermore, by a decree of 23 March 1921, as Tixier (1974: 14-15) explains, French Cameroon enjoyed political and financial autonomy under the authority of a Colonial Governor. French Cameroon was already a self-governing colony so to speak. Like Awasom (2002), Enonchong (1967: 80-81) also indicates that from February 1959 to January 1, 1960, the machinery of government in the territory of East Cameroon functioned under a constitution of two legal texts, Ordinance N° 59-1373 and Law N° 59-2. In addition, Law N° 59-36 of October 31, 1959, had expressly delegated to the colonial Government the power to legislate by Ordinance and to draft a constitution to be submitted to the country for approval. It was in response to this provision that executive Ordinance N° 60-1 of January 1, 1960, was promulgated on the day of the territory's attainment of independence. The draft independence constitution, ratified by referendum in February 1960, was only later promulgated on March 4, 1960.

British Cameroons was not self-governing and, in addition, not administered as a single territory within Nigeria. The southern zone (BSC) was administered as part of Eastern Nigeria – becoming a separate region of Nigeria only from "1954, when it achieved a quasi-regional status and a limited degree of self-government within the Federation of Nigeria, where it attained full regional status in 1958" (Konings and Nyamnjoh, 1997: 208). Colonial laws in the 'grand colony' of Nigeria were merely extended to BSC in 1955 by the legislation known as *Southern Cameroons High Court Law, 1955*, the most relevant sections 11 and 15 of which have been legally dissected by both Atubah and Galega.[88] The northern zone (BNC) was made part of Northern Nigeria from 1920. Following both Nigeria's and the Republic of Cameroon's independence in 1960, the United Nations (then dominated by

[88] See Awutah Philip Atubah, "The Legal Implications of Sections 11 and 15 of the Southern Cameroons High Court Law 1955" *The Herald* N° 430 (10-11 March 1997), 4; and Samgena D. Galega, "Strict Liability for Defective Products in Cameroon? Some Illuminating Lessons from Abroad" 48 *Journal of African Law* (2004), 239-67.

Britain and France and their allies) decided to hold a plebiscite on 11 February 1961 in British Cameroons. The plebiscite required them (quite contrary to the overwhelming wishes of British Cameroonsians to stay on their own) to either join Nigeria or French Cameroun. There was no third option tolerated, leading some critics to legitimately wonder if this was actually choice or betrayal.[89]

Apparently, the British had pinned all hopes of having BSC also remain in Nigeria (like BNC) on the Phillipson Report.[90] In so doing, the British had grossly neglected the use that local politicians were making of both the Igbo and Bamileke factors that the British had somewhat (un)intentionally created. I am here referring to what can be expediently called '*The Endeley-Foncha Pendulum*'[91] that Johnson (1970: 120-121, citing *West Africa* of May 14, 1965) exposes. Before 1956, when Dr. E.M.L. Endeley (of the KNC) was committed to reunification, he pressed for the elimination or relaxation of naturalization requirements for "French" Cameroonians (mostly *upécistes*) residing in the Territory of BSC 'in order to have their votes'. But in 1957, Johnson's report pursues, when Endeley opposed full reunification, he pressured the Parliament to disenfranchise them. The pro-reunification forces, led by John Ngu Foncha's KNDP, pressed for their enfranchisement at that time, but later, during the plebiscite campaign in 1961, the pro-Nigerian forces led by Endeley and the pro-reunification forces of the KNDP switched positions again. The KNDP, according to Johnson's conclusion, thought that there were more Nigerian migrants (anti-reunificationists) in the Territory than French Cameroonians, and the KNDP's reunification cause was to be advanced by having both groups removed from the voting rolls. That is exactly the strategy that resulted to the

---

[89] See John Percival, *The 1961 Cameroon Plebiscite: Choice or Betrayal?* (Bamenda, Cameroon: Langaa RPCIG, 2008); B. Fondong, "Anglophone Independence: SCNC to Sue Britain" *The Herald* (31 July-1 August 1996) 1; and Peter Ateh-Afac Fossungu, "British and United Nations Nakedness in Cameroon" *The Herald* (25-26 January 1999) 10. For a lengthy critical exposition of the mandate-trust period, see Enonchong (1967: 53-82); Gardinier (1963); Le Vine (1964: 131-214); and Joseph-Marie Zang-Atangana, *Les forces politiques au Cameroun réunifié: Tome 3 – Les groups de pression* (Paris: L'Harmattan, 1989) at 47-60.

[90] See Sir Sydney Phillipson, *Financial, Economic, and Administrative Consequences to the Southern Cameroons of Separation from the Federation of Nigeria* (Lagos, 1959).

[91] For Endeley's curriculum vitae/biography, see Le Vine (1971: 22-23); and for Foncha's, see Benjamin (1972: 212). For the tussle between them, also see Konings and Nyamnjoh (1997: 211-212).

West Cameroonian song (Konings and Nyamnjoh, 1997: 212): `Foncha has walloped Endeley. Foncha has walloped Endeley. If Foncha hadn't been there, Endeley would have sold us. '

It can thus be seen that the BSC politicians were busy only fighting themselves on petty and selfish issues rather than demanding – as would be the case for people (such as the banned UPC party?) who are really interested in regaining or reconstituting German Kamerun – that both sectors of British Cameroons be treated as an entity. Much fatal to Cameroon's geography is the fact that, instead of a single plebiscite for the entire British Cameroons, two sets of them were held: one for each of the two portions. These two portions (BNC and BSC), for some reasons to be evoked shortly, went in opposite directions. As Tixier (1974: 16) puts it, "Nearly 60 per cent of the voters in the north opted for integration with Nigeria. In the south, a large majority pronounced itself in favour of union with the Eastern Cameroons." *A large majority* is obviously far greater than *nearly 60%* but this does not give us actual figures to work with arithmetically (the more so as I have to appropriately prepare you to *possibly* do *impossible mathematics* in Chapter 4 below). From Le Vine (1971: 16) as Table 1 of this book, we get actual figures for the purpose. Table 1 indicates that the total votes from both portions were 244,037 for Nigeria and 331,230 for the Cameroun Republic. The overall results do clearly indicate therefore that, had there been just one plebiscite, British Cameroons reunification with French Cameroun should have carried the day, and thus be realizing the *Kamerun Idea*, if that was actually the goal.

Table 1: UN Plebiscite Results in British Cameroons

Area	For Cameroon Republic	For Nigeria	Total Votes	Margins
Southern Cameroons	233,571	97,741	331,312	135,830
Northern Cameroons	97,659	146,296	243,955	48,637
Total	331,230	244,037	575,267	

Source: Le Vine (1971: 16)

The religious traditions in BNC and BSC, among other factors, can be instrumental in understanding why the two regions took opposite directions in the plebiscites. BNC was predominantly Moslem. No language problem might have been noticeable there because Islam might have conveniently provided a common language with Moslem Northern Nigeria. "Islam and the Arabic language," some studies such as Magstadt (1991: 16) have discovered, always "impart a cultural unity that sets the nations of the Arab world apart from other nations." Nelson *et al* (1974: 82-84) have further discussed the 'Effects of Islam' in Cameroon. There was thus no initial friction generated between German-speaking British Northern Cameroonsians and their newly-found English-speaking Nigerian sub-colonizers with whom they had already worked without major incidents for about forty years (before the UN plebiscites).

The Islam faith in BNC must have furnished easy identification with Northern Nigeria through its Arabic language. This language advantage coupled smoothly with "Fulani Social Structure" (for a detailed discussion of which, see Nelson *et al*, 1974: 80-82) which usually facilitates an easy rallying around a few leaders who speak for almost everyone. The rallying advantage being discussed here is well exemplified by the pre-1983 Northern Province of (East) Cameroon: until Southern and Christian President Paul Biya's new administrative division of 22 August 1983 that increased the number of provinces in Cameroon from seven to ten by cutting '*The Grand North*' of President Ahidjo into the current three regions (Adamawazone, Benouezone, and Logonezone) through Presidential Decree N° 83/390.[92] Until the 1983 administrative changes, Northern and Moslem President Ahmadou Ahidjo used to stand for the whole of '*The Grand North*'. Zang-Atangana paints the rallying picture extremely well when he discusses the intriguing history of President Ahidjo's ruling *Union Camerounaise*.[93]

The foregoing picture in Moslem BNC was very radically different from what was shaping up in the predominantly Christian BSC where, unfortunately, as Stark (1976: 434-435) has pointed out, the Endeley, Foncha and Muna self-centred "party splits and political fights would fill a small

---

[92] Note these administrative changes well because you will obviously need this information to better understand the meaning of 'whoever' & 'whatever manner' in the secession discussion in Chapter 3.

[93] See Joseph-Marie Zang-Atangana, *Les forces politiques au Cameroun réunifié: Tome 1 – Les partis politiques avant la reunification* (Paris : L'Harmattan, 1989) at 9-38.

volume." This was the same picture these BSC politicians carried to Foumban, thus making defeat a foregone conclusion. Some critics may be wondering why we should "always refer back to the Plebiscite days of Endeley, Foncha and Muna when Anglophone survival is at stake, but do nothing to avoid a repetition of this sad historic event… [Why don't we] make use of this history to reconstruct the present and guarantee a better future for our children"[94]? It is my belief that to be able to avoid a repetition of some of these sad historic events in Africa, we must, of necessity, first admit that the said events have that character and be able to know why. All this can simply not be the case with the rampant confusion and manipulation that are being littered around the whole place by a lot of African "intellectuals in politics" whose 'cow dung intellectualism' has been found by Ntenga (1997) to be largely perpetuating the infamous North-West/South-West Divide initiated by said personalities who were the principal protagonists in the UN 1961 plebiscite in BSC (today called "Anglophone Cameroon"). The first of them (Endeley who hails from Southwest) was head of the Opposition at the time and led the Join-Nigeria Option while the other two in Government at the time (with Foncha as Prime Minister) hail from Northwest – and championed the Reunification Option that carried the day.

The image that these BSC (then West Cameroon) politicians then presented (to give Canadians in particular a good glimpse of the roots of the craze in Cameroon today called the North West/South West Divide) can be likened to the following scenario. The *Parti Québécois* carries Québec through a YES win in a referendum for sovereignty and then secretly (and completely ignoring the Opposition: Quebec Liberals and *Action Démocratique du Québec* (ADQ)) negotiates with Ottawa on the terms of separation – simply because the Opposition had stood against sovereignty. Could a divided West Cameroon (or Quebec) in this scenario get a deal any better than what it would have gotten if openly present as a united front? Would it even be correct to describe the system at the time in BSC as 'Anglo-Saxon', let alone present it as having been as glorious as some commentators do claim it was? Can Stephen Harper, for instance, simply govern Canada without the Opposition? Like several others, Fohtung could not help declaring that "The

[94] Epanti, "Open Letter to All Anglophones: Bury Your Differences and Fight for Your Identity" *The Herald* N° 337 (31 July-1 August 1996), 4.

paradox, truly, is that Anglophones [in Cameroon] speak with pain and nostalgia about their beloved [A]nglo-[S]axon system of West Cameroon fame but strangely keep quiet about why such a solid system collapsed and melted so readily in the face of the Ahidjo-Biya system."[95] Viewing the manner the BSC political elites comported themselves, what kind of federation or governmental system could have been hammered out with the other side? And why is the so-called NW/SW Divide still perpetuating itself to date in Cameroon? And why was the return of Kamerun territories not also called for by the *Kamerun Idealists*?

It is surely the avoidance of straightforward answers to important questions from the youths of today that is trying to hide behind the *Kamerun Idea* which I find, in this particular instance, to be only a tool for confusion and manipulation of the issues. Otherwise, the supposed adherents of the *Idea* should have also called for and insisted on the unconditional return of all the other territories ceded to neighbouring French colonies since "Under the German regime (1884-1914) the territory, which we now call Cameroon and other parts [that were] ceded to Gabon and the [C]entral African Republic belonged to the German protectorate KAMERUN which they acquired by the Conference of Berlin in 1884."[96] More than one-third of Kamerun under French Trusteeship disappeared in this fashion to the profit of those neighbouring French colonies and their return would normally have been demanded if the *Kamerun Idea* was in fact the idea behind the federalism that it even negates.[97]

To stress it again, it is not wrong to suspect that if the reconstitution of German Kamerun (aggregation of territory) was so much the *Idea* in Foumban, then naturally these same 'patriotic' leaders (especially those from BSC) should have done at least two things: first, insist on there being just a

---

[95] Barry B. Fohtung, "Yaounde or the ACME of Anglophone Masturbation-I" *Cameroon Post* N° 0028 (8-14 October 1996), 8. See also Peter Ateh-Afac Fossungu, "West Cameroon Lost in Foumban" *The Herald* N° 701 (18-20 December 1998), 4.

[96] Lantum (1991: 20, capitals as in original). For a complete view of Kamerun before the fateful 1916 partition, see the instructive '*dossiers*' titled "Minorités, autochtones, allogènes et démocratie" *La Nouvelle Expression* (23 mai 1996), 1-28 at 2.

[97] Could this call be actually what the ADD is now advocating for when its president talks of Ahidjo's enlargement of the federation in 1972? This point is the most intriguing of anything I have so far encountered in regard of all the talk of federalism in Cameroon, as demonstrated in Fossungu (2013: 216, 130-31, & 134-36). Whatever the case, I will here concentrate on the *Kamerun Idea* and the Foumban Enterprise.

single plebiscite for the whole of British Cameroons (and not two sets as was actually the case); and second, also insist that the ceded territories to neighbouring French colonies be restored. In French initial thinking, they would still have reaped their fruits off Kamerun should the Trust/Mandate subsequently revert,[98] as is the usual thing to do, to the international body (first the League of Nations, then the UN) said to have *entrusted* the entire territory to France and Britain. It should be noted, of course, that these European countries had already shared the country among themselves in 1916, some three years before the League of Nations was even born. I could write volumes on the irregularities of the mandate and trusteeship system in the Cameroons but that is outside the scope of this Chapter which must continue scrutinizing the infamous *Kamerun Idea* that does not pass a lot of tests except the one in process manipulation.

Negating or Passing The Federalism Constituting Tests?

The *Kamerun Idea*, much more importantly, clearly negatives and simply does not pass the federalism constituting tests previously stated in chapter 1; also making the claim of patriotism contradictory. Although patriotism (or the love of one's country) is high up among the things that could later be nurtured as veritable factors to sustain a federal union,[99] it appears to have no place regarding its initial formation. It is even contradictory to be patriotic toward an unborn country, the being of which is also clearly indicative of the fact that federalism in Cameroon was not sought for the raison d'être that is its own.

The histories of federations seem to all point to the fact that patriotism has hardly found itself on top of the list of initial forces that constitute the 'peculiar circumstances' pushing for federation. As one is clearly told by Newman (1968: 298), the formation of several renowned federations "was no grand design conceived in a sudden burst of patriotism. It was [rather] a desperate gesture by the British North American colonies [for instance] to counter the mounting economic difficulties that were threatening the survival of them all. The problems of each colony reached crisis proportions at the

---

[98] The British were thinking the same (although having but Germany in mind) when they neglected spending on the territory and therefore left it entirely to Nigeria's hands. See Konings and Nyamnjoh (1997: 208 n. 4).

[99] For a lengthy discussion of the bulk of these federalism-sustaining factors, see Flanz (1968: 103-116); and Franck (1968a: 9-11).

same time, and only in the sharing of burdens did there appear to be hope of solutions." The concept of brotherhood, capped by the *Kamerun Idea*, that some experts use in explicating the demeanours of the Southern Cameroonsian political elites before/at/after Foumban is unconvincing and can simply not float; the floatable principle instead being that of the assimilation of Southern Cameroonsians into French Cameroon even before Foumban by the 'intellectuals in politics'.

The *Kamerun Idea* finds a parallel in PAFMECA in East Africa. It is this PAFMECA that later became the Organization of African (dis)Unity (OAU).[100] The resemblance is that both PAFMECA and the *Kamerun Idea* are built only on a highly personalized coincidence of the personal visions and ambitions of what Franck describes as a very small handful of leaders known for intriguing and twisting plain facts to serve their self-centeredness.[101] The demeanours of some OAU leaders would also aptly make the point. After narrating, for instance, how President Paul Biya of Cameroon (who was then assuming the leadership of the OAU in 1996) alerted Nigeria's General Sani Abacha of an assassination attempt, some critics[102] such as Gobata (1996) have questioned: "But why can the duo not also come together to stop the assassination of innocent ordinary people in this senseless Bakassi conflict? Is the answer not blowing in the wind? It is about time that ordinary people all over the world got up and co-operated and joined hands to protect their collective interests."

As I have said, in cases like those of the *Kamerun Idea* and the PAFMECA, what one is bound to have are *only* the Intellectuals in Process

---

[100] Waindim (1995: 4) has blamed African disunity on "African leaders who have rendered the OAU impotent and by so doing, have invited the wrath of history which will be their ultimate judge." See also Animbom Evarestus Animbom "Is the OUA Worth a Dime?" *The Herald* N° 597 (20-21 April 1998), 10; and Kofi Oteng Kufuor, "The Collapse of the Organization of African Unity: Lessons from Economics and History" 45 *Journal of African Law* (2005), 132-144.

[101] See Franck (1968a: 14-15 & 3-4). For the Cameroon case specifically, see Benjamin (1972: 146-147); and Johnson (1970: chapter 7). For the similar West Indian situation, see Flanz (1968: 111 & 113-116).

[102] See A.A. Nyangkwe, "War Looms in Bakassi as France Arms Cameroon and Nigeria" *The Herald* N° 590 (30-31 March 1998), 1; Pius Kwedi, "OAU Summit: Bakassi Shelved to Guarantee Abacha's Presence in Yaounde – Nigeria Flies in Security Cars" *The Herald* N° 327 (8-9 July 1996), 1; and *Décret N° 98/042 du 11 mars 1998 portant attribution de la médaille de la vaillance* (posthumously decorating soldiers killed in the Bakassi conflict between Cameroon and Nigeria).

Manipulation. What is actually exhibited by this category of intellectuals would very easily lend credence to Albert Einstein's thesis (cited in Pearson and Rochester, 1984: 2) that politics is more difficult than physics, mathematics, philosophy, theology, law, or medicine. When and where only personal interests are predominating, realities are always bent to fit certain forms rather certain forms bending to fit reality. The reality that remains in Africa, however, is that Foumban's principal actors employed "federalism" not for the sake of what it is usually meant to do. Federalism is thus not what was actually in mind and ample evidence to this effect can be gleaned from the speeches of/about Foumban's principal actors. Not even their claim of patriotism can save the case as the West Cameroon proposals for union can further prove.

Double Nationalities In The West Cameroon Proposals

The West Cameroon (or BSC) proposals for union would clearly negative the patriotism factor that is couched in the *Kamerun Idea* just discussed. I am not going to elaborately discuss the entire package here (see Rubin, 1971: 111-112, Johnson, 1970: 180-190, and Benjamin, 1972: 105-114); but it is of interest to note that their package, amongst others, clearly called for double nationalities – state and federal. It is also very significant to point out that the "Dual citizenship, as proposed by the Southern Cameroons delegation" (Konings, 1999: 297) graphically vitiates the claim of patriotism; and also points clearly to the fact that no federalism was in fact intended – the act of going to Foumban being only a means to achieving something else. "For, as Dicey said," according to Chitepo (1964: 20), "if a federation is to exist, there must be among the peoples of the territories or states a connection of loyalty – by history, language, race or the like – which in the eyes of the inhabitants bears an impression of common nationality. No one doubts that there is today an American nationalism – a sense that all citizens of the United States belong to a single nation." Even in Canada which has been blessed with more geography than with history, the Fathers of Confederation, English- and French-speaking alike, said plainly and clearly and repeatedly (before the confederation deal was finalized) that they were founding 'a new nation', 'a new political nationality', 'a powerful nation, to take its place among the nations of the world,' '*une seule et même puisance*,' 'a single great power' (Hogg, 1996: 101-102; and Tremblay, 1993: 28).

Indeed, what West Cameroonians appear to have wanted (out of Foumban) was "a loose form of federalism" (Konings and Nyamnjoh, 1997: 209), that is, a confederation proper or Swiss-style,[103] and not the confusing Canadian and recent Swiss usage of that terminology. Both these countries, the experts (see Stevenson, 1989: 4-7) say, use the term 'confederation' for what is actually a federal union in the modern American sense. The Canadian union of provinces, like that of the United States (according to Hogg, 1996: 101), established a central government that was in no way the delegate of the provinces. It was independent of the provinces and coordinate with them and if there is any extent of their not being coordinate, it is the provinces that are subordinate to the central government – the opposite of confederation. That being so, the next question concerns the reason why Canada even chose, and has continued using, the term 'Confederation'.[104]

During the discussions of union in British North America before 1867 (see Simon and Papillion, 2008: 96-98), one is told, the terms union, federation and confederation were not used in any consistent or precise sense; and the latter has now become an accepted term for the Canadian union of provinces. There is no point, one constitutional expert (Hogg, 1996: 101) has concluded, in cavilling about this use of the word because for Canada, usage has made it correct. The invisible hand behind this usage, Stevenson (1989: 6) has explained, is that a word normally associated with the absence of a strong central government was deliberately misused by those who in fact intended to create a "centralized 'Macdonaldian' constitution" in an effort to confuse those who might find such a project alarming.[105] There is further evidence regarding the 'confusing usage' in the nature of an attestation from a former Canadian High Commissioner to Australia (a

---

[103] That is, what Tremblay (1993: 63) describes as "*les confédérations suisses de 1803 et de 1815 (la federation date de 1848).*" See also Wheare (1963: 56).

[104] For further discussion of the Canadian 'Constitution in Historical-Cultural Context', see Simon and Papillion (2008: 93-97).

[105] For more light on the concept of "centralized 'Macdonaldian' constitution", see Nancy J. Christie, "Evolution, Idealism and the Quest for Unity: Historians and the Federal Question" in Hodgins *et al*, (eds.), *Federalism in Canada and Australia: Historical Perspectives, 1920-1988* (Peterborough, Ontario: Frost Centre for Canadian Heritage and Development Studies, 1989), 353 at 353: citing for the quote in the quotation, W.I. Morton, "Confederation, 1870-1896: The End of the Macdonaldian Constitution and the Return to Duality" in Bruce W. Hodgins and Robert Page, eds., *Canadian History Since Confederation* (Georgetown, 1972), 189-208.

country which also kind of employed the same 'confusing strategy' in 1901). The High Commissioner who has had the opportunity to observe the Australian Federation closely, after several years of involvement in the workings of Canadian federalism from both provincial and federal vintage points "can attest to the evolution and dynamics at work in both countries."[106] To the High Commissioner (*ibid*),

> All that [including the use of 'Confederation' as in Canada] is apparent is not real, however. As a case in point I refer to the recent and growing view that the Canadian provinces, although intended to be less comprehensive in their status than the federating original states of Australia, have somehow waxed while the states have waned. It is argued that in the course of the past forty years, the point of convergence was reached and indeed passed, so that today the Canadian provinces are 'more equal' in their federation than the Australian states in theirs. So the thesis goes. Needless to say this will spur even more analysis on the part of those motivated to prove or disprove such assertions. There may well be no final analysis, because of the very evolution of modern federalism, there is no static target.

Could it have as well been the same strategy with the West Cameroonian employment of "confederation" at the Foumban Conference? If that is so, who would have been alarmed by "federation": West Cameroonians or East Cameroonians? If "federation" had to alarm anyone at all, should one then even have a highly centralized unitary form anywhere in one's mind? On the other hand, it is very probable (as seen in Chapter 1) that the same "Canadian Macdonaldian strategy" was involved with the East Cameroon all-male delegation's use of 'federation' whereas a highly centralized unitary state was actually the case: in order not to alarm (both the East Cameroon 'stormy' opposition and) the 25 all-male members of the West Cameroon delegation. As Konings and Nyamnjoh (1997: 210) have theorized, "Ahidjo looked upon federalism as an unavoidable stage in the establishment of a strong unitary state, and employed various tactics to achieve this objective." These various tactics would evidently include, and call for a keen study of, the role of

[106] The Rt. Hon. Edward R. Schreyer, "Foreword" in Hodgins *et al*, (eds.), *Federalism in Canada and Australia: Historical Perspectives, 1920-1988*, Frost Centre for Canadian Heritage and Development Studies (1989) 7-9, at 7.

translation.

Translating In the Martian-Venusian Dialogue

Like the fearless Senegalese Judge Mbaye, *Je n'accuse personne. Je constate un fait.*[107] These are matters of public importance and I am entitled to analyze the facts as I can see them; a right which does not in any way prevent anyone else from getting into the discussion and proving me wrong. That is the real essence of academic discussions, especially on matters of public policy and public administration. The West Cameroon delegation also seems to have been effectively duelling in the interpreter/translator's darkness. I would say so because, were it otherwise, it would become inexplicable that people seeking a confederation proper would return from Foumban with a highly centralized unitary state, just having the word 'federal' affixed to it. Federalism proper would, of course, be the obvious compromise between those truly seeking a confederation proper and those really seeking the centralized unitary state. It is thus clear that *the real forces* at work in Cameroon (prior to, at, and after Foumban) were simply not the kinds that would usually impel the reaching out for what some federalism experts have described as a middle-way between the two polar perils of imperium and anarchy. The middle-way between Mars and Venus, for instance, could be Earth. Failing both to settle on earth has therefore meant completely transforming Martians to Venusians.

Absent confusion and manipulation in regard of the key role of the Foumban interpreter/translator, it is extremely hard for experts on federalism to comprehend the actual formation of the FRC, especially as the two sides do appear to have been on the different planets of Mars and of Venus. Some Canadian experts on the issue have been enormously intrigued. For example, David Bercuson, a history professor at the University of Calgary (Alberta), would appear to have looked at the various proposals for union put forward by the two sides in Foumban when he concluded that "It sounds as if one party [of the Foumban Conference] is on Mars and the other is on Venus. If they *were* [not], at least these results would be logical. What we have instead are two different groups looking at exactly the same

[107] See Elimane Fall, "Les scrupules d'un juge incommode" *Jeune Afrique* N° 1680 (18-24 mars, 1993), 28.

circumstances and data, and coming up with totally different conclusions."[108]

It would thus appear that a federation proper could not have approached what West Cameroonians might have been ready to settle for. Even their pre-Foumban chronic disagreements in both the Mamfe and Bamenda conferences could fortify this stance.[109] All this discord among West Cameroonians was capped by what Johnson (1970: 183, & also at 188) sees as "the severity of the disparity in their conception of the federation, and their contradictions in the West Cameroon position reflecting continued failure to understand the basis of that disparity." What then could actually have landed them on the other party's planet, absent the translator's handiwork? This question finds particular significance in the fact that Foncha's plebiscite campaign had been full of promises of constitutional and human rights guarantees, punctuated by much talk of how they (in West Cameroon) were going to teach their French-speaking "brothers" of East Cameroon the essentials of good and responsible governance (as to more on which system of governance, see Hogg, 1996: chapter 9; and Dawson, 1970: 5-39). Why did they then cross completely to the other side rather than the reverse or the mid-way stance? Comprehension of the question would require finding out (1) the historic ties involved, and (2) the translator's key role and the invisible hand behind that role – his mission.

Historic Ties?

Some experts have used historic ties in explaining what happened in Foumban. This, like the *Kamerun Idea*, is not credible at all especially because of the time period (One-Hour-Thirty-Five-Minute) that Johnson (1970: 184) gives as the duration of the official Foumban Conference when both delegations – 25 members in the western or Anglophone and 12 members in the eastern or Francophone – were actually in meeting. This 'haste' is also talked about by Konings and Nyamnjoh (1997: 209 n.8). One has then to ponder about what exactly these *historic ties* were that should have been

---

[108] Cited in Charles Macli, "Dueling in the Dark" *The Globe and Mail Report on Business* (April 1991) 29, at 35. See also Enonchong (1967: 84-85 & 24-26).

[109] See the 51-page *Record of the Mamfe Conference on the Plebiscite Question and Register, August 10th and 11th, 1959* (Buea, November 1959); and the 129-page *Record of the All-Party Conference on the Constitutional Future of the Southern Cameroons, Held at the Community Hall, Bamenda, from 26th to 28th June 1961* (Buea: 1961).

moving the Foumban One-Hour-Thirty-Five-Minute Enterprise at such great speed: when, between themselves, West Cameroonians (or the Martians) could not agree in the pre-Foumban much lengthier debates in both West Cameroonian cities of Mamfe and Bamenda. This disagreement of theirs could not even be resolved in the *five days* in Foumban during which Johnson (1970: 188) and Anyangwe (1987: 128) say they "repeated Bamenda" before the official 'one hour thirty-five minutes' meeting with the other side. Would there be more historic ties between them and East Cameroonians than between themselves? The SDF, of course, answers yes here with its four-state federation as seen above.

To some critics, the West Cameroonians' unfortunate 'failure' to agree among themselves and present a united front in Foumban (as they are still doing to date) would appear to be the effective beginning of the taproot of the human rights problems (especially for the English-speaking) in Cameroon today. British Southern Cameroons thereafter effectively 'moved' from a sub-colony in Mars (1916-1961) to a sub-colony in Venus (1961-1972) and finally to outright *Venusation* or assimilation in Venus from 1972 forward? This dire and unfortunate transformation, according to the critics, is the inevitable price that English-speaking Cameroonians have been and are still paying for British *naiveté*; a *naiveté* that Franck (1968a: 15) says manifested itself in Britain's refusal to let British Cameroonsians have their own state as well as its reluctance "to abandon the principle of Westminster parliamentary democracy as the model for Africa." But other critics like de Smith (1964: 281) have flatly denied that the blame could be put solely on Britain because "English statesmen and their advisers, when they addressed themselves to the problems of Ruritania, could hardly be blamed if they began with the presumption that what had worked admirably in Britain was likely to work better for Ruritania than what had worked rather badly in Arcadia and Utopia."

Yet, the critics of British colonial attitude in the Cameroons and Africa generally are still adamant and have proceeded to elucidate that their charge particularly finds something of a parallel in East Africa where, as Franck (1968a: 3) again charges, "a great federation" would have been formed between four nations "with historic, functional, political and personal ties so strong that their failure to seize the moment seems, at first glance, almost a flouting of destiny." Whether or not Britain played a major role in the failure of the East African federation could be debatable. But the important thing is that this glaring East African case would very unmistakably exclude any question of hiding behind historic ties in Foumban, a city where the flouting of the destiny of a "people" (for personal favours) seems to have been the overriding (if not the only) concern of its principal actors as can also be clearly seen in the breakdown that did not break down because of the key-holding bridge-man role of the translator.

Key-Holding Role and Mission of the Translator

It is not farfetched then to ponder, for example, if the impracticality and unreasonableness involved in their conceptions of the new state could have been making their reaching of consensus by the two sides impossible. Could this not be what was actually responsible for the apparent breakdown in the Talks at Foumban? Could the said breakdown not have also been due to the English-speaking people not understanding the East Cameroonian proposed federal text (*Loi N° 61-24 du 1er septembre 1961 portant révision constitutionnelle et tendant à adapter la constitution actuelle aux nécissité du Cameroun réunifié*[110]) which, being only in French, the "Anglophone" bilingual translator/interpreter alone comprehended? The West Cameroonians' chronic discord in Mamfe and Bamenda where they were dealing completely in their own language could fortify and direct the answer here. Moreover, Lantum (1991: 11) clearly points out that this bilingual "intellectual [Dr. Fonlon] was the political luminary of his time … a teacher of his people" who was "fully aware that [the] popular rural headmasters and other elite from the countryside [that he was dealing with] did not automatically become competent and knowledgeable statesmen in matters of government of a modern state." Would their disagreement not have easily played into the hands of the scheming translator?

Knowing the propensity of "Anglophones" in Cameroon to devour each other rather than jointly confront a common adversary,[111] the following question from the 'lost Cameroonian youths' becomes inevitable. Could it not be quite possible that the refusal by Prime Minister Foncha (as leader of the English-speaking camp) to accept the 1961 French Foumban

---

[110] "That's it. This full title tells the whole story. *Res ipsa loquitur.*" Anyangwe (1987: 128 n.6).

[111] See Canute N.N. Tangwa "Our Patrick Akoh Mbawe: Casualty of Dare-Devilling" *Cameroon Post* N° 0021 (20-26 August 1996), 8; and Konings and Nyamnjoh (1997: 212-213).

Constitution – without actually understanding both it and the exact position of the other parties or party – might have been what was actually leading to the breakdown in Foumban when Dr. Fonlon (then a conspicuous member of Foncha's government) saw his 'chance' and volunteered to serve as interpreter (with only the devil knowing what interpreters can do to two fools of each other's language) so that he could then, in Lantum's (1991: 20) words, be easily "spotted by the then [automatic] Head of State [of the federation], Alhadji Amadou Ahidjo, summoned to Yaounde to serve as Chief of Missions soon after the Reunification on 1st October 1961"? I have put 'automatic' in square brackets here because that this is exactly what the "Federal" Constitution (then properly understood by only the interpreter from West Cameroon) in article 51 made Ahidjo to be "until the end of his present term of office."

One can only largely speculate about the Foumban Federation generally because of the manner its principal participants have either not talked about what actually happened or, if they say anything at all, have very much twisted and/or compounded the facts. As a West Cameroon lawyer now in exile in Britain (Gorji-Dinka, 1996) has put it, "I ran foul first with Foncha, then with Jua, and Muna [these are successive West Cameroon prime ministers] because they didn't seem to stand by the truth. Each time a thing is clearly defined, and you want to follow it, for convenience they changed it. They told so many lies to the point of believing their own lie. The most problematic people are politicians who think they are entitled to tell lies." The exiled barrister cannot be far from the point because in Cameroon even as one speaks Fohtung (1995) says "there are quite a handful of victims of this mental and optical illusion… [who] create their illusion and hallucinations and, for repeating them with religious conviction, mixed with doses of fear and calculation, start believing, seeing and even feeling their mirage."

Whatever the case, my position on the translator/interpreter's role is not speculative, being principally based on the sane interpretation of material that has been furnished by Lantum (1991: 20) who is a "specialist [who] enjoyed such close association with Dr FONLON and for so long that he could lay claim to be able to state with fair accuracy a lot of Dr FONLON's political activities." There is no doubt then, according to Stark (1976: 441), that "The West Cameroon elites who arranged 'federation' were badly advised, had little experience or education, and were confused by the ... [translator]." Stark is obviously right but people could be astonished to hear this talk of 'little experience or education' especially as the leader of that delegation is being addressed as Dr. Foncha. How some of these titles (including Dr. Biya) have come about will only go to mystify the mystery that is Cameroon. Impossibility is truly not Cameroonian?

No justice, I think, would be done to the Foumban federalism enterprise in Cameroon without a clear call for an end to the seemingly ceaseless emasculation of the translator's impeccable anti-federalism role in the Foumban Enterprise. Translators in any society are, in a lot of ways, like teachers and lawyers who often abuse their unique 'key to knowledge': "You teachers of the law… are really in for trouble! You carry the key to the door of knowledge…. But you never get in, and you keep others from getting in."[112] The 'key to knowledge' of translators/interpreters enormously surpasses that of lawyers because it is translation that "opens the window, to let in the light, that breaks the shell, that we may eat the kernel, that puts aside the curtain, that we may look into the most holy place, that removes the cover of the well, that we may come by the water."[113] The shoddy doings of Mosé Yeyap are a living concrete case of what translators' power of abuse can amount to. I do not need to set out here the details of the unfortunate events created by this Foumban man (Mosé Yeyap) and their lasting effects on the Bamum traditional court (see Geary, 1983: 15). One may not even need to peruse all of that Bamum history to comprehend translators/interpreters who are largely known to "impose themselves upon their world."[114]

The Foumban translator, without looking ahead to see the violent storm on the horizon, obviously imposed himself upon his world by 'volunteering' (out of the blue?) to help make real what was perceptibly crumbling. Benjamin Franklin's popular thesis on the giving up of essential liberty for the purchase of a little temporary safety would apply here with full force; being strongly validated by the poor human rights situation in Cameroon that soon devastated Fonlon himself; as aptly captured by Kubuo's incisive declaration:

---

[112] Luke 11: 52. See also Williams (1987: 401-403 – the Meta-Story).

[113] See "The Translators to the Reader", King James Version 1611, as cited in *The Contemporary English Version* (of the Bible), Canadian Bible Society (1995) at vii.

[114] Roderick A. Macdonald, "Legal Bilingualism" 42 *McGill Law Journal* (1997), 119 at 141.

> That is strange. But it all stems from the [Foumban FRC] law of the jungle, which [later] shocked and completely devastated the late Bernard Fonlon [himself], who was wont to ask with wonder and dread: 'Whither Africa? What do we not see, as far as we survey the present political African scene?: mad ambition, run-away greed, insatiable lust for power, callous indifference to public misery, the almost general absence of a sense of public service, treachery, betrayals, stabbing in-the-back, assassinations, massacres: Lord, what have we not seen! Indeed we have seen much that we are now inclined to take it all with a shrug of the shoulders, as rather in the nature of things.'[115]

The role of the translator could thus, in large measure, explicate how the confederation proposals from West Cameroon were transformed overnight in Foumban into President Ahidjo's unitary centralized state with 'federal' just attached to it. And all of these things are the handiwork of intellectuals in politics with 'towering IQs' and special missions! The next important issue becomes that of knowing what the missions reserved for the spotted translator/interpreter consisted of. Some have wondered if it entails "going out for CPDM campaigns? Does it entail transferring public revenue from Cameroon to private accounts in the Swiss Banks?"[116] Having given that hint or the answer itself to the type of missions, Lantum (1991: 21, emphasis added) refutes the suggestion that any of these suggested missions had anything to do with those of the Foumban bilingual intellectual who, "Besides nature and nurture,…had a unique vision", having as

> His early ambition, which never left him even till death,… to live the life of priesthood, but somewhere along the way he was thwarted and seemingly assigned a *political mission* by what he [himself] called the inscrutable ways of the Almighty. And as it was the Almighty's assignment, the Lord Almighty – also apparently – provided the essential requirements for the success of that mission.

---

115 John Kubuo, "Is the Mentality of Some Politicians Akin to that of Honourable Baboons?" *The Post* (24 October 1997), 4, citing from page 8 of Bernard N. Fonlon, *As I See It* (Buea, 1997).

116 Lord W. Degaulle, "Retrench Ministers to Fight Economic Crisis" *The Herald* N° 356 (13-15 September 1996), 4.

And, at last, what is that successful mission? Lantum (1991: 22, emphasis added) clearly states what the spotted translator's "mission" consisted of (perhaps without realizing it himself): "From []his vintage point of the <<inside man>> he [Dr. Fonlon] stood the chance of *understanding the East Cameroon Government and the political master plan* for harmonizing [i.e. assimilating] the Federated States after Reunification." Lantum has now also debunked his very own thesis that gives the impression that Dr. Fonlon was first known to the East Cameroon leadership *only* in Foumban because of his 'brilliant show-up' there. Quite apart from being a conspicuous member of the Foncha government in Southern Cameroons, Dr. Fonlon's pre-Foumban close *connaissance* with the French Cameroun leadership (Ahidjo in particular) might not be hard to establish when one considers Suifon's indication that Dr. Fonlon "had been well groomed in the School of *Présence Africaine* in France."[117] Again, it is hard to see how Dr. Fonlon could have translated that country's secretive constitution (long before Foumban), as Suifon (*ibid*) also indicates, without in the least knowing Ahidjo with whom the 'mission deal' must have been made in order to have the Foumban manipulations get smoothly through.

Whatever these "intellectuals in politics" really are, this writer may not quite know; but this one thing is certain. Someone who has deliberately taken up confusing and manipulating others as his profession would often (if not always) end up himself gravely confused. This thesis could largely explain why Lantum (1991: 20) did even bury his angel twenty-five days before the angel was dead (if angels do die at all):

> Dr. FONLON was always a member of the ruling party from the time he returned to Cameroon in 1961 till he *died on 26th August 1986*.... Dr. FONLON was elected into the Central Committee and he remained a Member till his death *on 26th August 1986*. At his burial which took place in Kumbo town on *1st August 1986*, the personal representative of the Head of State and Leader of the Delegation of the Central Committee of the CPDM stated....[emphasis added; different spellings of Fonlon are as in original]

---

117 Takwa Suifon, "Eleven Years after Bernard Fonlon: A Postscript" *The Herald* (26-28 September 1997) 6.

Translation might have had nothing to do in Kumbo town but can it (translation) provide a good explication for the Foumban Enterprise? The manipulated act of "federation" alone introduced a diabolical "missionary" factor and significantly opened the way to the full and unencumbered use of the hitherto slightly 'hedged' 1959 *pleins pouvoirs*. As already noted in Chapter 1, the Foumban Enterprise brought about very drastic political changes in East Cameroon. The existence of *pleins pouvoirs* in that state was not good for human rights respect but Foumban aggravated the situation. Amadou Ahidjo was able to easily get his 'modification' of East Cameroon's Constitution (transforming himself from prime minister to president) by using the upcoming Foumban meeting with the 'Anglos' as excuse. (Could this be the origin of the Anglo-war-cry thesis in Cameroon?[118]) The door was thus thrown ajar to *pleins pouvoirs* by the complete destruction of the power-splitting parliamentary government in place before then. The 'modification', purportedly aimed at incorporating West Cameroon that was returning like the Prodigal Son, swept away the last vestiges of any checks to the absolute governance of the newly fashioned automatic President of the 'Federal' *République du Cameroun*. Thereafter there was no longer a place for the parliamentarians and the Courts.

There is no denying that the first (East) Cameroon's 1960 Constitution (whose 'slight modification' became the 1961 Foumban Federal Constitution) still accorded autocratic powers to the premier and had itself only been enacted – despite that the south-central and coastal regions voted overwhelmingly against it – on the basis of support from Ahidjo's *The Grand North* (see Bjornson, 1991: 111). But, put alongside what was rubber-stamped in Foumban, that 1960 constitution is preferred for some of its few human rights guarantees that have been discussed further (alongside the dramatic and traumatic alteration) by Johnson (1970: 184-194) and Enonchong (1967: 80-82). Foumban swept those away; with both parties obviously benefiting from their secretive dealings. This exercise in the interpretation of plain facts includes wondering if the parties to the secret pre- and post-Foumban dealings (not without the translator) did not sufficiently reap their fruits of the secrecy, as shown in the concluding remarks of Chapter 1. What else, absent the benefits of the secrecy, can in fact be the Foumban Invisible Hand

---

[118] For more on this thesis, see Fossungu (2013:23-25).

that was that strong as to occasion apparently blatant and irrational behaviour on the part of the western (or BSC) delegation?

It is very difficult, absent confusion and manipulation, to believe that the people largely responsible for the foregoing drastic changes are the same West Cameroonians who did not only know exactly where they were leading their people to but also went to Foumban with double nationalities in their proposals for union. Could all the results of Foumban be the fulfilment of the political dream of 1954? In that year, Lantum (1991: 21) states,

> Bernard FONLON had dreamt a political dream: that he was designed to be a leader of his people. He took it seriously and wrote for himself a code of conduct which would guide his every move in the political area. He wrote: "Looking at these, I saw that, to make a good leader, it is absolutely necessary that i) I should know where I am leading the people to, ii) I should know how best to lead them there; should wage [a] perennial war in my life, against all the attractions, enticements and seductions of money, ease, pleasure, worldliness, against the thirst for power and glory; must come to no terms whatever with vice, must live in the world with a spirit that is totally dead to the world".

That spirit seems indeed to have been totally dead to the West Cameroonians' world in Cameroon. It is thus not clear what one is to believe in. Should we consider that the entire Foumban Enterprise was geared toward the dreamland for Dr. Fonlon's people or toward his own narrow dream? That is, was the sole goal in Foumban Dr. Fonlon's political dream and mission that would seem to have been designed to give the 1959 *pleins pouvoirs* their wide open doors OR his people's political advancement through this 'fascinating Federalism'? Are the intellectuals in politics confused or actually confusing? Whatever the case may be, the basic fact remains that the Foumban actors were all-male and are all responsible for turning federalism into secession.

Chapter 3

The Politics Of Federalism, Self-Determination, And Secession: Is The Cameroon Administration Above International Human Rights Law Too?

> In many ways, pronouncements about national unity and national identity [in Cameroon particularly and Africa generally] served [only] as instruments that allowed a small majority of the population to maintain its own wealth, power, and status by offering the rest of the people symbolic gratification for their real needs and by distracting their attention from the true causes of their misery. The system perpetuated itself largely because the privileged class expanded to incorporate a relatively large number of educated individuals, who then had a vested interest in preserving the existing social order. [Bjornson, 1991: 110]

Is federalism a vehicle for self-determination or one for secession? As indicated in the Introduction, this question, and many more, can be best answered mostly with an adequate understanding of the politics of secession in Cameroon; this politics finding its roots in the concept of federalism through which the English-speaking minority thinks it can feel protected in the larger state. Backed by some of the self-seeking "intellectuals", African leaders have been brandishing ethnicity as being responsible for their country's poor human rights record. To achieve their objective of confusion and oppression, they tend to sometimes pin federalism (and/or self-determination) to the chest while at the same time presenting it as a totally foreign concept to Africa; also making federalism the synonym of secession and/or a threat to national unity and development. This critical study on confusioncracy and human rights will attempt washing up these nasty and confusioncratic self-determination theses by elaborately examining the African oppressors' three related theses, namely, (1) whether federalism is foreign to Africa, (2) whether it is the same thing as secession, that is, whether self-determination is compatible with the centralized unitary state, and (3) what international human rights law and practice would offer those who are oppressed by the supreme majority like Southern Cameroonsians.

Is Federalism Foreign To Africa?

I argue in this book (as elsewhere) for a system of governance that synchronizes with the African peoples' realities (rather than just a useless copycat). Expert studies like those of de Smith (1964: 280-83) have shown that there is a close relationship between federalism and the special protection of human rights, both of which are typical manifestations of constitutionalism. Federalism is thus proffered as the appropriate channel through which respect for human rights is instituted and promoted in radically diverse societies like most African states are. The political principles that animate federal systems unavoidably emphasize the primacy of bargaining and negotiated coordination among several power centres; they stress the virtues of dispersed power centres as a means for safeguarding individual and local liberties.[119] The idea of not having powers concentrated in one person's hands has long been a vexatious issue in modern African politics generally but Francophone Africa in particular. Some experts like Fombad (2005) have already elaborately discussed the twin principles of the separation of powers and constitutionalism in Africa; a study that, although with axis on Botswana (like this book turns around Cameroon), is very important for also treating the issues in regard of both Anglophone and Francophone Africa.

All that can be added here is that in the absence of constitutionalism any talk of federalism could become just one in confusion since federalism clearly cannot function without liberal or constitutional democracy. The regime of personal and absolute power in Cameroon would think otherwise. Consequently, in this 'Miniature Africa', federalism has been deceptively 'embraced' and then immediately accused and denied; being presented as another name for secession; with the high-handed response thereafter being in the nature of 'the minority can never dictate to us, the supreme majority'. Deception thus abounds in every conceivable sphere in this country; this trickery having awkwardly displaced and replaced brotherhood, sincerity and patriotism; and also transformed truth-telling from the noble nation-building deed that it is to an offence; all of these taking roots from the secretive dealings in public matters in Foumban (Cameroon's Philadelphia, it is said).

---

119 *The New Encyclopaedia Britannica* Volume 4, 15th ed. (Chicago: Encyclopaedia Britannica Inc, 2002) at 712.

The human rights situation in Cameroon is worsening by the minute; yet, the international community seems to be unaware of the reality there.

It is most probably because the ruling elites have planted a lot of confusion around the three interwoven concepts of federalism, self-determination, and secession; wrapping the confusioncracy with the all-too-familiar national unity cloak. It is not hard however to straightforwardly determine their relationship to one another. Simply put, (devolutionary) federalism provides the means for self-determining *within* the state while secession furnishes the way for doing so *without* the oppressing state. That is to say that an unnecessary denial of self-determination within the state (federalism/decentralization) often necessarily opens the road to self-determination without the state (secession). That is as elementary as the connection is, although the dishonest tendency in Africa has been to confuse, complicate and compound everything so as to easily dictate and oppress under the cover of national unity.

It was in view of strongly rooted diversity (cultural, ethnic, linguistic, and religious, for example) in some polities like Cameroon that federalism has had to be engrafted unto democracy as a means of uniting diverse communities, without destroying their individual unique characteristics, into a single *internationally* recognized state. The whole idea would be to avoid the obvious drive to 'uniformize' or assimilate that is bound to follow in a unitary form. All this has been especially ushered in by the realization, according to Goell, first, that the so-called 'nation-state' is now outmoded; and, second, that recent expert studies have found the underlying assumption of previous studies of nationalism and modernization (based on the one-nation-per-state as the only way) to be a misconception or an incorrect reading of political reality.[120] The misconstruction of political reality in Africa is out in the open in the hot pursuit for the 'perfect nation' by those in power; it is also more elaborately uncovered in their theories on federalism, secession, and self-determination.

Africa's policy-makers, according to Ekob'a Njembu, are well known for their disdainful and anti-African comportment ("*mutisme et dédain pour l'Afrique*"). Before reaching this conclusion, Ekob'a Njembu would first have documented several burning continental crisis areas and issues where,

---

[120] Yosef Israel Goell, *Bi-Nationalism and Bi-Lingualism in Three Modernized States: A Comparative Study of Canada, Belgium, and White South Africa* (Ph.D. Diss., Columbia University: University Microfilms International, Ann Arbor, Michigan, 1978) at 341 & 1.

normally, then African Chairman (President Paul Biya of Cameroon) should have been in his Chair with pencil and paper taking stock, and attempting solutions, etc.. But, paradoxically, in all the instances, the African President is instead on some beautiful beaches in Europe lavishly enjoying himself rather than in the blood-spilling hotspots in Africa (*"le président de l'OUA est plus que jamais absent de la scène africaine*").[121] And most of the blood-spilling would have been occasioned by the oppressed people's demand for democracy and federalism. To these un-African African administrators, federalism is not African because this continent is composed of multiethnic states whose national unity federalism works against. To Biya (1986: 18 & 31), therefore, the demands of the English-speaking minority for a federal devolution are frivolous and unacceptable because federalism is not only a strange thing to Africa but also "an instrument of political destabilization used against multi-ethnic [African] States" like Cameroon which, "more than any in Africa, is a land of socio-historical multiplicity and diversity, the melting pot of various divergent and opposing forces, and of an infinite number of sectarian or even hostile communities which are living in a kind of permanent vigil of arms [and] where ethno-geographical particularisms are strongly evident." Quite Amazing, isn't it?

The specialists are however very loudly asking these African "intellectuals in politics" on what they rest their premise. To the critics, to begin with, Cameroon cannot even claim to be alone in facing these hurdles. As Johnson (1970: vii) has clearly pointed out, "Every African society is now confronted with a severe problem of cultural and political integration. Cameroon is not alone." Eleazu (1977: 7) has also indicated how ethnicity is part of the problem in Nigeria, but then Nigeria is not the only country that has many ethnic groups; with Magstadt (1991: 309-310) discussing India's own intriguing diversity that has not turned that country overnight into a dictatorship. Like Nigeria, India is a federation. Douzinas and Warrington (1987: 33) do not only question the base of their theory but also clearly show how "the 'unconscious' text [is] undermining the 'conscious' pretensions." In

121 Ekob'a Njembu, "9 mois après le 32e sommet de l'OUA: L'Afrique en sang, Biya à la plage" *Le Messager* (3 mars 1997), 9. See also Boniface Forbin, "OAU: The Challenge of Yaounde" *The Herald* (8-9 July 1996), 4; Awung Jem, "OAU Chairman: Is Biya Up to the Task?" *The Herald* (16-17 September 1996), 4; and John Mukum Mbaku and Joseph Takougang, (eds.), *The Leadership Challenge in Africa: Cameroon Under Paul Biya* (Trenton, N.J.: Africa World Press, 2004).

other terms, these experts have questioned, do all those attributes of Cameroon (and by extension, Africa) not provide palpable justification for a federal devolution to begin with? Is it not strange that people in power in Africa instead view federalism only as secession (separatism)? Could it be that they actually do not know the distinction between the two concepts?

Some critics hold that it is not the question of their not being aware of the differences. For instance, Fossungu (2013:73-80) has shown that in Cameroon the politics about/on federalism has simply been the politics of killing two birds (the hardworking Bamileke and the English-speaking minority) with one potent stone, the federalism net. This un-African inverted and mischievous view of federalism all paradoxically began with someone who was bent on uniting diverse Africa while preaching the emergency of strong unitary centralized states on the continent. I am here talking about Kwame Nkrumah of Ghana. While Nkrumah's goal of African unity was and is still unquestionably laudable, his complete exclusion of the federal devolution as a possible if not the exclusive, form is highly questionable. Benjamin (1972: 203 n.14) cites Kwame Nkrumah as stating in his *Africa Must Unite* (1963) that

In order to improve effectively and quickly the serious damage done to Africa as a result of imperialism and colonialism, the emergent African States need strong, unitary States capable of exercising a central authority for the mobilization of the national effort and the co-ordination of reconstruction and progress. For this reason, I consider that even the idea of regional federations in Africa is fraught with many dangers. There is the danger of the development of regional loyalties, fighting against each other. In effect, regional federations are a form of balkanization on a grand scale. These may give rise to the dangerous interplay not only of a power politics... but can also create conditions which will enable the imperialists and neo-colonialists to fish in such troubled waters.

I can begin to see why the Ghana-Guinea-Mali union could not go beyond the rhetorical stage, let alone act as the nucleus of African unity. Nkrumah's Ghana must obviously have been bent on 'unitary-centralizing' (assimilating) the two French-speaking members of the union. Why would Sékou Touré, for example, who (unlike Ahidjo, Houphouet, Senghor, Bongo, etc) had boldly told the French General-President to go to hell with his fake 'independence-association' concept then have to accept such "assimilationist nonsense" from Nkrumah? Moreover, does the case of 'strong unitary centralized' Cameroon prove or disprove Nkrumah's thesis on 'their capability of exercising a central authority for the mobilization of the national effort and the co-ordination of reconstruction and progress'? I am sure both Bjornson (1991: 108) and Johnson (1970: viii), if no one else, would cleanly say DISPROVE.

The Indonesian case might be understood in the sense that the Dutch had ruled the territories as a single unit until then (although that argument is apparently not valid now[122]). Indonesia stiffly rejected federalism by branding it as Dutch attempts to limit its sovereignty. As Morton Grodzins has clearly indicated in Chitepo (1964: 20), the Dutch imposed a federal system in Indonesia after World War II clearly as a means of perpetuating Dutch control in those islands. This federalism was smashed as a consequence of independence movements. But how, for example, can Nkrumah's vision of a unitary centralized Africa that had been colonized by different European powers be explained? It is not hard to do that by adding to the Sékou Touré example just given. To most African leaders, only the unencumbered consolidation of their already acquired positions (rather than the welfare of the general public) is most often the point of departure for any discussion; otherwise, federalism cannot be regarded in the strange way they look at it. Cameroon's leaders also claim that federalism is not African. Federalism, they have thus concluded, must be shunned because it simply does not promote national unity in Africa. But many experts do not seem to buy their idea. I will next demonstrate that federalism (like democracy, a precondition for federalism) cannot be a new concept to Africa in general and Cameroon in particular with (1) a brief survey of the democratic African pre-colonial system and then (2) narrow down to Cameroon with the Bangwa federalist tradition.

The Democratic Nature Of Africa's Pre-Colonial System

In a vivid and fascinating account of the African political system, Geary (1983: 4 & 8) has noted the existence of "acephalous and federate political formations" in Cameroon (e.g., in the Mentchum Valley, Fungom, and We

---

[122] Some analyses do nevertheless consider federalism as the only solution to Indonesia. See Gwynne Dyer, "Federalism Only Hope for Indonesia" *Montreal Gazette* (15 June 1999), B3. The events and atrocities in East Timor since the 1999 sovereignty referendum there seem to be proving the correctness of the critics of the Indonesian rejectionists.

chiefdoms) even before the arrival of Europeans.[123] Geary (1983: 1) has also described how German Captain Ramsay, on visiting Foumban, "the capital city of Bamum," was struck by the impressive trench and wall fortifications, the royal compound, and the opulence of the court. In the former Gold Coast (current Ghana), the Akan political system, according to Appiagyei-Atua (1999: 8), is one of the most prominent among the various strands of political systems which have been identified in Africa. Potholm has also identified this Akan political system under the umbrella of Pyramidal or Federated Monarchy.[124] As it appears then, it is rather the idea of highly centralized political organizations that is somewhat foreign to Cameroon or Africa.

One cannot over stress on the human rights protecting features of the political institutions in Africa before the arrival of Europeans. In this continent's pre-colonial system(s), for instance, the Chief could not rule or take certain crucial decisions without the approval or consent of the other recognized traditional dignitaries who, moreover, were in a very comfortable position to easily dethrone an unbecoming chief without any bloodshed. This chief and the council of elders were even better governors and legislators than the mess Africa is littered with today, modern rulers whose 'modern' style of legislating leads only to mosaic confusion – see Fossungu, 2013: 227-230 & 210-212). Anyangwe (1987: 9) has shown how traditional African rulers made laws that were straightforward prohibitions and/or injunctions, for better conduct of communal affairs or to abolish old usage that the community had outgrown. In Southern Africa also Marc Epprecht recounts how Chieftainess Mantsebo was much liked by her people because her style of rule was pivoted on the principle that "A chief is a chief by the people", "a person who listens well and judges according [to] the will and advice of her

[123] For further discussion of some of these kingdoms, see Merran McCulloch, "The Tikar of the British and French Cameroons" in Daryll Forde, ed., *Ethnographical Survey of Africa – Western Africa Part X : Peoples of the Central Cameroons* (London: Hazell, Watson and Viney, Ltd., [no year]), 1-52. For 'federal' entities in Africa generally, see Davidson (1991: especially chapter 2) ('Ancient Glories'); and Peter Lloyd, "The Political Structure of African Kingdoms" in *Political Systems and the Distribution of Power*, American Sociology Association Monograph N° 2 (New York: Praeger, 1956).

[124] Christian Potholm, *The Theory and Practice of African Politics* (Englewood Cliff: Prentice-Hall, 1979) at 19-21. See also Kwame Arhin, *Traditional Rule in Ghana: Past and Present* (Accra: Sedco Publishing, 1985); and G.B.N. Ayittey, *Indigenous African Institutions* (Transnational Publications Inc., 1991).

people."[125]

The traditional legislative style, as already noted, obviously contrasts vividly with the mosaic confusion of modern African administrators. Davidson (1991: 145) has explained that the straightforwardness of the rules of traditional rulers was necessary because

> these societies depended for their survival on such rules being thoroughly understood and strictly applied. Nothing was punished as severely as their abuse [by whomsoever]: it was precisely for abuse of rules of magical and supernatural belief and behaviour that persons presumed to be witches were tortured.

The Night Society in Bangwa, for instance, was what Brain (1972: 6) describes as the feared arm of the law, the secret weapon of the chief who carried out fearful punishment on witches, adulterers, and murderers.[126] Even this necessary torture did not go without checks on those who exercised the powers because Johnson (1970: 53) says various "counterbalances" to abuse of powers by the ruler were in place. Some of such abuses came especially from chiefs who used the powers, e.g., of the Night Society in Bangwa, to wreck vengeance against their personal rivals (Brain, 1972: 6-7).

But the important thing is that there were effective means of curbing such abuses in place. Geary (1983: 4 & 8) lengthily recounts how the Chief (known variously in Cameroon as *Fon*, *Fo*, *Mfo, Sultan,* etc.) stands at the apex, with spiritual and political authority and other ritual prerogatives "that

---

[125] Marc Epprecht, "Gender and History in Southern Africa: A Lesotho 'Metanarrative'" 30:2 *Canadian Journal of African Studies* (1996), 183 at 203. For more on the human rights-respecting African political institutions in place before the arrival of, and destruction by, colonialism, see, e.g., Davidson (1991:.145-155); Nelson *et al.* (1974: 1-12); Anyangwe (1987, chapter 1); and Nelson Mandela, *Long Walk to Freedom* (Boston: Little Brown and Company, 1994) at 287-288. See also Lakshamann Marasinghe, "Traditional Conceptions of Human Rights in Africa" in Claude E. Welch, Jr. and Ronald I. Melts, eds., *Human Rights and Development in Africa* (Albany: State University of New York Press, 1984), 32; and Thimothy Fernyhough, "Human Rights in Pre-Colonial Africa" in Ronald Cohen, ed., *Human Rights and Governance in Africa* (University Press of Florida, 1993), 42.

[126] See also Anthony Chungong, "Tombel: Man, 56, Lynched for Alleged Witchcraft" *Cameroon Tribune* N° 6574-N° 2853 (8 avril-April 8, 1998), 15; Chia Adamu, "Kibaranko Juju Forcefully Collects Debts in Nso" *The Post* N° 0067 (8 May 1998), 6; and John Mbiti, *African Religions and Philosophy* (London: Heinemann, 1988).

are necessary for the well-being of all." This, Davidson (1991: 155) explains, is because of the same type of kingship, with its firm belief that the health and welfare of the king were inseparably and spiritually linked with the health and welfare of the whole society. There were the same notions of religious identification with ancestors, of beneficial magic and harmful witchcraft, of methods of making war or keeping the peace. The chief is assisted by "Influential secret societies of men" (such as *kwifo*, *mabu*, *nko, ngondo* in Cameroon). These arrangements, as Geary (1983: 4 & 8) says, thus provided a counterbalance to the possible misuse of power by the chief, fortified by the council of advisors as a third element beside the chief and the secret societies. Appiagyei-Atua (1999: 93-97) has provided an elaborate 'Historical Analysis of African Traditional Concept of 'Civil Society'; with his article in 2000 also being an excellent further reading on the subject of the conceptualization of African notions of human rights.[127]

Some experts have then concluded that the traditional African political system was/is more democratic than what is in the West today. As Gobata (1996) indicates,

> many of the traditional African kingships (fonships), circumscribed as they were by sundry taboos, ritual restrictions and sanctions, were arguably more democratic than some contemporary western democracies. I could write a whole book defending this thesis but that is not necessary for our purpose here and now

If anything, Davidson (1991: 145) also writes, "the comparison between Africa and Europe is likely to be in Africa's favour. Throughout the medieval period most African forms of government were undoubtedly more representative than their European contemporaries. Most African wars were less costly in life and property. And most African ruling groups were less predatory."

That is the highly developed and human rights-respecting African political system. This survey of the system is essential in understanding the confusion in Africa that is today passing under the name of rule of law, of institutionalized guarantee of individual liberty, of development, etc. It is

---

[127] See Kwadwo Appiagyei-Atua, "Contribution of Akan Philosophy to the Conceptualisation of African Notions of Human Rights" 33:2 *Comparative and International Law of Southern Africa* (2000), 165-92.

obvious that the traditional African system stands in the way of despotic and absolute governance. And this system is still very strongly entrenched especially in Savannazone whose capital is Bamenda – a city well known to be at the centre and forefront of the quest for responsible governance in Cameroon. That could explain why the Biya regime is bent on eliminating any vestiges of it. According to Biya (1986: 51), therefore, the villages "will be given special attention and transformed into real decentralized territorial communities with extensive prerogatives to choose their leaders democratically... [which] will mean a parallel reduction of the traditional power, often hereditary." Why is decentralization so important only for the villages, but not for Cameroon as a whole?

Responding to the question, Nantang Jua, for example, has tersely noted to Ndi Chia (1995b) that the New Deal Craze in Cameroon (of actively seeking the complete destruction of traditional authority which is still prominent in North-West Cameroon especially) is "understandable for it is often said that if the gods want to kill you, they first make you crazy." The journalist, Ndi Chia (1996b), to whom he was talking pretended not to understand the doctor and asked him to explain what he meant. Jua then responded: "You simply have to read *Communal Liberalism* that is the bible of political theology in this country which harps on the need to democratize traditional authority. If this proposal... [was to be] implemented, it would mean that henceforth, Chiefs would be elected and I would guess that the modalities regulating this particular election would also be fixed by a Presidential decree!"[128] Still in the context of this controversy, Carolyn Logan and others have provided interesting analyses and further reading regarding the long-standing debate about the proper role for Africa's traditional rulers vis-à-vis modern state power.[129]

---

[128] See also D. Fopoussi, "Les élections ont-elles tué les chefferies traditionnelles à l'Ouest?" *Dikalo* N° 196, 25 janvier-1 fevrier 1996), 11; David Tendong, "Lebialem Chiefs in Disarray as South West Chiefs Plan Assembly in Menji" *The Herald*, N° 597 (20-21 April 1998), 1 & 3; and "Fons Should Belong to Any Party in Power – Fon Angwafor" *The Herald* N° 315 (30 May-2 June 1996), 6 (an interview).

[129] See Carolyn Logan, "Selected Chiefs, Elected Councillors and Hybrid Democrats: Popular Perspectives on the Co-existence of Democracy and Traditional Authority" 47 *The Journal of Modern African Study* (2009), 101; Piet Konings, "Chieftaincy, Labour Control and Capitalist Development in Cameroon" 37-38 *Journal of Legal Pluralism* (1996), 329-46; Michael Awah, "Mankon Traditional Authority and Modernisation," *The Herald*, N° 585 (18-19 March 1998), 4; and S.K.B. Asante, "Nation-Building and Human Rights in Emergent African Nations" 2 *Cornell International Law Journal* (1969), 72.

The persistence and fortification of the French colonial policy of appointing chiefs (including *chefs d'état*) in Cameroon would also apparently account for the blossoming tension between the villages and cities in this country. This tension is rooted in their different perception of what the ruler's relationship with the ruled should be. Most of the villages or traditional authorities in Cameroon find it hard to comprehend what they now have as government. The villagers do not seem to see why the traditional African political system has to be completely ignored even now that Cameroonians are claiming independence and a system of governance of their own. To buttress their incomprehension, these village critics of city intellectuals in politics do easily point to the experiences of South East Asian nations where constitutions, according to de Jorge, have had to be rewritten to reflect cultural realities as well as demands of the international community. All the said nations have enjoyed records of steady economic growth and development in the last decades, providing enough evidence that there is no strict blueprint for democracy – there being only some identifiable universal values on which each democracy is based.[130]

Africans must learn to remain African even while evolving with the rest of the world because that is the only way they can become anything authentic and worth respecting from others on this earth. Copycat institutions that do not reflect African realities are not helpful because these institutions would render Africans just as more rootless and ineffective than 'political science without history' is. Most Africans often hide behind the fact of having been colonized. That is part of the problem but not the entire problem. Almost all of Asia was also colonized like Africa but the Asians are globally far ahead of Africans principally because when Asians said 'independence' they meant it and got it; which also largely explains why what has "evolve[d] in East Asia is a democracy that is quite unlike a liberal democracy but which produces the good life and wholesome society, economic and social progress and a political and social system that is consonant with the values and traditions of their society."[131]

---

[130] Hans de Jorge, "Democracy and Economic Development in the Asia-Pacific Regions: The Role of Parliamentary Institutions" 14:9-10 *Human Rights Law Journal* (1993), 301 at 304, 301-302 & 306.

[131] *Id.* at 302. See also "Democracy and Good Governance: Challenges and Solutions Reflecting National Circumstances" (Being a report to the heads of governments of Commonwealth African states adopted after a roundtable conference on Democracy and

Against this background, many researchers have advocated for awareness of the African traditional system that works against concentration of powers and its abusive use.[132] But the avowed policy of African administrations has been to destroy such an eventuality. They have consequently turned the stronghold of the traditional values (the villages) into the very definition of ignorance, superstition and witchcraft (Biya, 1986: 11). This definition of the villages that these African leaders want 'decentralize' is understandable, first, because it is from there that Cameroon's 'stupid and ridiculous advanced democracy' (as some critics describe it) has been clearly deciphered by the "village Old Man" (cited in Fossungu (2013: 12). That 'Old-Manish' deciphering wisdom is certainly not the kind of civic education that the dictators want. Second, as Davidson (1991: 149) has pointed out, there still does "remain today beneath their [villages'] veil of bush and thorn, a powerful indicator of the depth of culture that can lie behind the apparent simplicity of…African village life." African villages thus remain the haven for the much more democratic traditional African political system that has now been largely destroyed by colonialism's teaching of *demoncrazy* in Cameroon especially.

In short, the attempt by the African leadership to present both democracy and federalism as not being native to Africa is very suspect. Federalism is a politico-constitutional rights-protecting mechanism that obviously works against the rise of the potentates that most of the said leaders always want to be. The federal governing method has always been the product of reason that aims at uniting divergent interests without throwing away realities of those concerned in the enterprise – an undertaking which must itself be based on popular will. In Majeed's (2008: 5) wise words, the federal system is a device of shared governance, and the constitutions of federal polities usually envisage a "creative balance" between the need for an effective federal centre and the need for effectively empowered constituent federal units. There is also a need to balance the factors promoting a federal-institutional model of self-rule with those promoting shared rule. The notion of power-distribution and power-sharing arrangements must be addressed by

---

Good Governance in Africa in Gaborone, Botswana, on 23-25 February 1997), as found in *The Herald* N° 427(3-4 March 1997), 6.

[132] See David Fossong, "Bansoa: Chief Advocates Cultural Awareness" *Cameroon Tribune* (8 avril-April 1998), 7; and Peter Ateh-Afac Fossungu, "Intellectuals in Politics: Essential Education from the Village?" *The Herald* N° 604 (6-7 May 1998), 10.

both the national and regional constituents of a federation. As Donald Rothchild (cited in Benjamin, 1972: 203 n.13) has then stated in apparent amazement,

> Constitutionalism and legalism at the modern state level, broadly accepted as means of reconciling interests in the west, are frequently looked upon by African [leaders] with widespread indifference and even fear, as imported systems dangerous to their countries' unity and therefore to their modernization.

Nowhere on the African continent could this 'up-side-down' and 'rolling-back' tendency be more marked than in the 'Africa in Miniature' called Cameroon. And this is a country that is conspicuously said to be infested with "intellectuals in politics" with 'extraordinary intelligence quotients' (Lantum, 1991: 21); with Biya (1986: 11) adding that "Of course, we can boast to the world of having a literacy level which puts us among the developed countries in the Third World." Will people with such super-intelligence and literacy level truly see federalism as foreign to Africa when the Bangwa exemplary case is right there in Cameroon?

The Bangwa As Federalists

The Bangwa are in Debundschazone and their federalist tradition would also mainly explain their numerous palaces. The question has been asked as to whether the Cameroonian administration's love of palaces is a contamination from the Bangwa? If so, then why are they infected by only the palaces and not also by the federalism that is behind those many palaces? And why are the palaces restricted to only the two branches (executive and legislative) to the detriment of the judicial branch that is supposed to stand between the other branches of government in particular and human rights violations? The heads (or members) of the other two 'branches' in Cameroon are lodged in palaces but no 'palace-justice' is done to the judicial 'power'. Concretely, the legislature's home is known as the Glass Palace (*Palais des Verres*) in Yaoundé. This palace is supposed to be Cameroon's Capitol Hill (as one can say just to give Americans in particular a clear idea of it) or Parliament Hill (to Canadians). This is in contradistinction with the 'Unity Palace' or Presidency.

Cameroonian politicians/administrators love palaces so much that even the dependent courts (headed by its un-supreme Supreme Court) are known as justice's palaces (*palais de justice*) despite that their head, in the person of the President of the Supreme Court, according to Nyo'Wakai (1991: 18), lives "in a tumble-over house while boys who had just graduated from ENAM [National School of Administration and Magistracy] and appointed Ministers were living in palaces." One can thus easily find executive palaces (including even ministerial palaces); legislative palaces, including congress palaces or *palais des congrès* (although these legislative officials do not live in them, as is actually the case with the executive members); but not a single judicial palace. Is there therefore a 'judicial power' (or any other power other than the 'executive') in Cameroon? So what rule of law (and which law by the way) would be possible without an independent adjudicator? Is Cameroon not just an unconstitutional kingdom hiding under 'republic'?

In answer, some experts have suggested a return to the traditional African system. They think the apparently much more democratic African traditional system (with its many palaces too) can show the way not only to proper representation per se (as already noted above) but to democratic federalism as well. The Bangwa (who are of Bamileke stock) are now quite a different people from the Bamileke solely because of the division of German Kamerun between the English and French in 1916. As specialists like Brain (1972: 9) have elucidated, one of the reasons for the difference "was that British rule in Bangwa [very unlike that in Bamileke] was very indirect indeed."

With the Bamileke in French Cameroon (specifically in Bamboutouszone), the atmosphere was quite different. The French, of course, continued the German policy of recruiting plantation labour in the grassfield with or without the co-operation of the chiefs. Many of their chiefs, Brain (1972: 10) concludes, were thus forced to abdicate and French appointees were put in their place. This French appointive trend would not end only with the traditional chiefs; extending as well to the country's past and current leadership or 'chief of state' (*Chef d'État*), after also having chased the upécistes into exile and/or underground; it being only normal to Davidson (1991: 151) that such appointed "kings became more powerful and despotic by a shift in authority from ascription to appointment. They raised soldiers and governors from men who were their own personal servants or appointees, rather than from men who owed their rise to nobility of birth." One would expect that the situation would have been corrected at 'independence' but, thanks to the lack of vision (resulting, of course, from their illegitimacy) on the part of the country's imposed unpatriotic and dishonest politicians, this regressive colonial development continues to be advanced and fortified in "independent" Cameroon.

Hence, not wishing to create an 'autonomous' power base for chieftaincy in the federal republic, according to Konings (1999: 301), Ahidjo only reluctantly agreed to the Southern Cameroons delegation's demand for the preservation of the bicameral character of its state legislature, in recognition of the important role Anglophone chieftaincy had played in the coming about of reunification , but the PFR bluntly refused to create a House of Chiefs in East Cameroon, where none had existed before reunification. As a result, a potentially dangerous disequilibrium was created between the two federated states, which could in the long run have frustrated the chiefs in East Cameroon. No wonder that Ahidjo was quick to abolish the West Cameroon House of Chiefs after the promulgation of the unitary state in 1972. The negative development on the traditional African system in French Cameroon is thus being pervasively extended these days to the British side generally and in particular to Bangwa with its highlands "where the mist, pools and rivers were reminiscent of Scotland" (Brain, 1972: 10).

Experts have narrated how Cadman, the first British District Officer to this Bangwa area, wrote a long and admiring report on the Bangwa way of life, advising that the chiefs be left alone to run the country as they had in the past.[133] This story accounts for the fact that today the Bangwa, according to Brain (1972: 10), still think kindly of their English rulers, particularly as independence and 'reunification' with East Cameroun brought with them hardship and bloodshed. It is understandable that the Bangwa should feel that way. The Bangwa are federalist by their culture and political set-up; having nine fondoms or chiefdoms that constitute the clan or ethnic group. These chiefdoms are known today under the following names (which are actually mostly titles of their paramount chiefs or fons): Fonjumetaw, Fontem, Foreke Cha Cha, Fossungu, Fotabong, Fotabong II, Foto,

[133] Brain (1972: 9). To the priest and district officer the Bangwa were a romantic people lost in the mountains, ruled by autocratic and eccentric chiefs with a splendid material culture, working their women hard and living in huge polygamous compounds. *Ibid.* See also Scholastica Achankeng Asahchop, "Multiple Roles of Women in Rural Areas. Case Study: Nwangong Village in Lebialem Division" (Project Submitted in Partial Fulfilment of the Requirements for the Award of a B.Sc. in Sociology and Anthropology, University of Buea, Cameroon, 1998).

Fozimombin, and Fozimondi. Each of them has its paramount chief or fon (to distinguish from the numerous other chiefs and subchiefs in the fondom) and they do function very independently of each other. There is thus no single central sovereign as such for the entire clan: it being that clan affairs must necessarily involve the participation of all nine fons and their entourage. That is precisely why it is reported that the British district officer who visited Bangwa no more than once a year had to make the long trek from Mamfe to Tali, a nasty climb to Fontem and then innumerable journeys from chiefdom to chiefdom, to sub chiefdom and to lonely ward.[134] These innumerable journeys should have been unnecessary if Bangwa had a *centralized* system as Cameroon and most African states are today; making very easy for the French to have all of Cameroon in their hand by just having the occupant of the Etoudi Palace in hand. That is just my interpretation of Biya's well known boastful saying that "When Yaoundé breathes the whole of Cameroon lives."

The Bangwa set-up meets the essentials of federalism despite the difficulties encountered in defining the concept (as seen in Chapter 1). Having studied those difficulties, Stevenson (1989: 8) has admonished that any definition of federalism that has to be meaningful should meet some three essential criteria. First, the definition should not be unduly restrictive; second, it should serve to distinguish a federal state from a unitary state (such as Cameroon) and from other looser forms of associations; and third, it should emphasize the political aspect of federalism. With these criteria in mind, like Tremblay (1993: 62) and Wheare (1963: 35), Stevenson (1989: 8) has then defined federalism as

> a political system in which most or all of the structural elements of the state (executive, legislative, bureaucratic, judiciary, army or police, and machinery of levying taxation) are duplicated at two levels, with both sets of structures exercising effective control over the same territory and population. Furthermore, neither set of structures (or level of government) should be able to abolish the other's jurisdiction over this territory or population. As a corollary of this, relations between the two

[134] Brain (1972: 3). A Bangwa claims no clan or lineage membership, and no corporate group takes responsibility for any of his or her actions. Kinship is an aid to the business of making a living: trading, inheriting, acquiring a title, farming, ruling and marrying. And as the business of living is complex in Bangwa so is the kinship system. *Id.*: 1.

levels of government will tend to be characterized by bargaining, since neither level can fully impose its will on the other.

The Bangwa traditional political set-up does meet these requirements. So where do people (in Africa) who are saying federalism is not African come from?

The nine Bangwa chiefdoms are little states, with their elaborate administrative structure and complex political hierarchy giving them particular personality. The overall effect, the experts (Brain, 1972: 3 & 5; Johnson, 1970: viii) have concluded, is that the political structure of these chiefdoms was thus highly fragmented: sub chiefs, notables and even compound heads competing with the paramount for political power over their subjects. Appiagyei-Atua (1999: 104-111) has also offered an elaborate analysis of the African Traditional 'Civil Society as Tool for Community Development'. Moreover, even within the same Bangwa chiefdom or what the experts call statelet, there is no single and exclusive centre of power. Brain (1972: 4) clearly indicates that a

> Bangwa chiefdom does not have one chief. There is the paramount, known in Fontem by the grassland term 'Fon', and lesser chiefs, the most distinguished of whom are descendants of formerly independent chiefs who were conquered or who submitted (sometimes under colonial pressure) to Fontem. The subchiefdom has the same groundplan and structure as the chiefdom. The subchief is a 'chief', with his own palace, sometimes his market. He has his own 'subchiefs' and his palace is the centre for another spider web of tracks leading off to the 'palaces' of his subordinate 'chiefs'.

Although not specifically termed 'federalism' by those concerned, the essentials of that concept are clearly in place here. That is, there is the effective diversification of power centres. What is federalism that does not involve this effective territorial and institutional competition for power over citizens? Is the aim of this not the protection of the "subjects" from the tyranny of a single centralized chief? Are the essentials of federalism not clearly in place in Africa as here exemplified by the Bangwa? What is federalism but a political arrangement that maintains fundamental political integrity of diverse communities under the same umbrella by requiring that basic policies be made and implemented through negotiation, so that all the members (i.e., federating states or provinces) can share in making and executing decisions?

Until reunification, the Bangwa had not been used to concentration of powers, personally or territorially. Territorially (for instance), as Brain (1972: 9, 7, & 3) explains, although a police station was established and for a short time a dispensary was based in the palace, Fontem (the capital of the largest Bangwa chiefdom) became an administrative centre only in the sixties, after independence. Primary schools had been set up by the Roman Catholic mission (as well as a government school). But until 1967, when a mission was established, he concludes, the local priest living in Mbo at Mbetta made only periodic visits to Bangwa where the change in the environment can be startling after a few miles walk. As Brain (1972: 3) further elucidates,

> The Bangwa are astride a changing environment, between the grassy plains and the lowlands of dense tree growths. It is a dark, wet land, precipitous in the extreme. They are Bamileke chiefs but they share a forest environment with their very different neighbours, the Banyang. Their staple is the cocoyam, not corn. The roofs of their huts, still conical like those of the Bamileke, are thatched with palm, not grass…. The Bangwa are in fact between two worlds. Each of the nine chiefdoms – with one exception – has a boundary with the savannah and one with the forest. This is of vital importance, since the track which winds down from the grassfield markets to the Bangwa royal palace and market and from there to the forest is the life-line of each little state, a trade route for oil, wine, salt, meat and fish and, formerly, slaves. The Bangwa live in the mountains to trade, their existence depends on supplying the needs of the forest and savannah peoples, acting as middlemen in a trade which continues to the east as far as Bamun and then in the west to Nigeria – Calabar and the Cross River regions.

In view of this concise historical, cultural and sociological survey, it is understandable that Franck (1968a: 5) has concluded that the failure of much in modern Africa today concerning human rights protection is not due to "a defect of the African personality, it is a defect of teaching [Western] democracy through a colonial system, a project [that is] as impossible as teaching a bed-ridden man the theory of riding a bicycle and expecting him actually to *do* it when he is let up." This bed-ridden man theory is even more devastating in regard of Africa's unpatriotic and un-African leaders' undemocratic equation of federalism to secession. Before I take you to that unnecessary equation, it is essential that we draw some constitutionalism lessons from both Germany and Canada in order to 'modernize' those derived from the Bangwa.

Constitutionalism Lessons from Germany and Canada

Germany is one other country (the other being Canada) that I would highly recommend to Cameroonians. Cameroonians ought to be interested in this European country not just because it was Cameroon's first colonial master (1884-1916), but mostly because there are several things to be learned from there in respect of human rights protection mechanisms. Germany is a classic case of people who have suffered from the same types of governmental abuses like Cameroonians are today, and yet have been able to successfully institute a democratic regime afterwards. It is one of the 'free for all' cases from which Africans generally can wisely draw.

The Germans restored democracy not by merely waiting on the ruling party to decide to legalize other paper parties but by first of all guaranteeing fundamental rights and freedoms to all persons; just like the Belgians also guaranteed 'Individual and Collective Rights' (Dumont *et al*, 2008: 37-38). As the experts (Kommers 1985: 198; Magstadt 1991: 110–15) have pointed out, Germany's Basic Law in its 19-article Chapter I now guarantees 'Basic Rights' among which the following can be outlined: protection of human dignity (article 1), freedom of assembly (article 8), freedom of expression (article 5), personal freedom (article 2), freedom of association (article 9), equality before the law (article 3), freedom of movement (article 11), freedom of religion (article 4), marriage and family and children born outside marriage (article 6), school education (article 6), and privacy of correspondence, posts and telecommunications (article 10). Some Cameroonian officials do consider the last guarantee (which is also notoriously gapping in Cameroon) as posing a particular problem because of its international nature.[135] But the question becomes that of why, for instance, purely internal mails are tampered with in Cameroon without the aggrieved party being able to seek and obtain redress?

---

[135] See "The Violation of Private Mail is an International Problem – Mvondo Abessolo, P & T Littoral Delegate [interviewed by Christopher Andu, Ezieh]" *The Herald* N° 633 (15-16 July 1998), 9.

The Germans further secured their democracy by setting up a system of party democracy within a well-defined political and social structure that ensures the defence of constitutionalism (article 20), together with a constitutional ban on parties which seek to impair or abolish the free democratic basic order (article 21). They also brought forth a strong chancellor responsible to parliament (article 63); reinforcing the system in article 67 by what is called the constructive vote of confidence that keeps a chancellor in place until a parliamentary majority can agree on his or her successor. There is also provision in article 39 for the holding of 'direct, free, equal, and secret elections' of members of the Bundestag (or Lower House of Parliament). Finally, and above all in importance to specially note, the Basic Law incorporated a new model of judicial authority, providing a high court of judicial review to protect the fundamental rights of persons (see Schneider, 2008: 133). The judicial situation is the same in Canada, as well exposed by Russell (1987), Simon and Papillion (2008), and Dawson (1970: 383–410). That is how meaningful and constitutional democracy can be made to flourish, with equally consequential organs and personalities. That is a precondition for the devolutionary federalism that Cameroon now requires. And I am recommending the combination of federalism with the parliamentary system.

1. The Federal-Parliamentary Mixture

The choice for a presidential system by the 65-member Anglophone Standing Committee, according to Konings (1999: 314), seems to have been made for two reasons: "In the specific Cameroonian context marked by great ethnic and regional diversities, a presidential system, according to the authors, was more likely to forestall administrative chaos and political instability than any other form of government." Confusioncracy, isn't it? Then why are they also proposing the parliamentary system for the states to be headed by a prime minster? The nation is presidential with a president who is both head of government and head of state; the two states (why two?) are parliamentary with a prime minister as head of government (and who is 'head of state' of the states? Still the P.M. or the federal president?); and the provinces are what, with a governor? You just cannot separate the different (vertical) levels with different governmental systems without both confusing powers; as well as compromising the ability of a person to "rise", say, from district head to president of the federation. It is either all one or the other, not the confusioncratic mixture of theirs.

The problem with these people, I think, is one of trying to eat their cake and have it. They find, for instance, that the North West and South West exhibit "great ethnic and regional diversities" but they just would not countenance the two regions developing separately within a ten-state union but try to twist the facts by lumping them up in a small-one-state against the rest of the eight-province-Mighty State. Let us get real here. If we recognize a Divide, the best way to deal with it is to let the Divide be and deal with it as such, rather than pretending over it because such pretence is what would actually result in "administrative chaos and political instability". If we still need two and eight provinces within the two culturally-based states, why not just have those provinces as the ten states with each competently managing itself while electing the required number of their representatives to the federal parliament? And we should not forget that the "great ethnic and regional diversities" are not limited only to the 'inter-state' or 'inter-provincial' level but would apply as well within the same state or province, for instance.

Parliamentary democracy is not the best form of government according to some experts (Berkeley, 1968: 17; Crossman, 1972) although being to yet others (Mirkine-Guetzévitch and Prélot 1950: xi) "the most perfect modern form of government that is without doubt also the one that has been largely adopted by other nations" (my translation). When combined with federalism and with other new elements grafted onto it, as it is done in Canada and Germany, I think the parliamentary system provides a better system of protecting both the rights of individual citizens and groups as well as those of state institutions, and in particular the judiciary and its independence. This protection results from what I would term the system's "rights-protecting combination", alluding to (1) its practice within the federal structure, (2) genuine multiparty politics, including strong third parties, (3) bicephalism, (4) bicameralism, and (5) parliamentary procedure.

The rights-protecting character of the parliamentary system results from its potential to fragment power and authority and diversify their centres. The parliamentary system is able to furnish this because of its *bicephal* executive (i.e., head of state and head of government are vested in two different people, with each having particular competence) and its *bicameral* legislature: which means, the existence of Upper and Lower Houses of Parliament.

These diverse independent organs, *inter alia*, further ensure judicial activism and independence: an inevitable consequence of the existence of several potential disputants, none of whom will afford to see the arbiter's impartiality jeopardized (Wheare 1963: 53; Mallory 1984: 381; Dawson 1970: 283–84; and Dickson 1985: 6–8). This applies equally to the executive heads in situations of effective bicephalism, with its effectiveness being heavily tied to real multipartism. With these features effectively in place, coupled with proper public enlightenment, we could be entering an era of active citizen participation and, therefore, human rights respect in Cameroon particularly and Africa in general. Only the first two 'combinations' will be further surveyed here, since the other three (examined in the next Chapter) necessarily follow when the first two are effectively in place.

There are several things to be learned in this respect from Canada and Germany. Like Germany, Canada also creatively combines federalism and the parliamentary system but goes a little bit further. The peculiar federal nature (bicultural/bijural and bilingual) of Canada has meant, for instance, according to Mallory (1984: 273, 62 n.46, 282 & 220) and Hogg (1996: 164–68), that the *real* Opposition in the country against any infringement to judicial and other organic independence is found in the provinces, rather than just the stormy one in the federal Parliament – where the usual two-party system in the United Kingdom, according to experts (Crossman 1972: 51; St. John-Stevas 1968: 7, 9, & 10; Hollis[136]) easily leads to a prime ministerial government. This mixture of the system with other features constitutes what I characterize as "the rights-respecting combination".

It will be seen that the combination of the parliamentary system of government with the federal structure could properly explain why the German system is regarded by some experts as being more federal than is that of the United States. Thus, any serious study on comparative government must largely highlight some of the significant differences between the deficiencies of the British parliamentary cabinet, on the one hand, and those of Canada and Germany on the other. The latter countries must have overcome or mitigated some of those problems solely on account of their federal character and the survival of third parties that are strong enough to infuse their politics with innovation, leading them to succeed

[136] C. Hollis, *Parliament and its Sovereignty* (London: Hollis and Carter, 1973) at 12-31.

where others falter. This feature is most notable and very unlike in both the United Kingdom and United States where third parties have generally withered and died. The 'Third Forces' would result from the combination of federalism and parliamentary democracy, and take several forms or shapes.

(a) The Political Parties Form of Third Forces

Federalism often gives the parliamentary system (that is said to have been existing in both British and French Cameroons until Foumban completely killed it in 1961) another peculiar feature – the "Third Forces", including strong third political parties. Canada and Germany best illustrate this point. By 'third parties' one is referring to the existence of more than one opposition parties in a country's governmental system. In Canada, for instance, the two main parties currently are the Conservative Party of Canada (in power) and the New Democratic Party (the official opposition). The 'third parties' currently are (1) the Liberal Party of Canada, (2) the Bloc Québécois, and (3) the Green Party. The unique 'third parties' phenomena in Canada (see Mallory 1984: 222, 223–24, & 273; Dawson 1970: 413–33) and Germany (see Kommers 1985: 217–25; Magstadt 1991: 115–17) should rather be lauded because of the beneficent effects of their strong and surviving third parties which the cited experts have more elaborately discussed as well as the reasons for their survival – principally the combination I am here discussing.

This feature is most notable and very unlike in both the United Kingdom and United States where 'third parties' have withered and died. Mallory (1984: 222), for example, regards the survival of "Third political parties" in Canada as "a sign that Canadian politics is not the same as politics in the United States [or Britain], and not a sign that our society is sicker." The formation in the early 1990s (by billionaire Ross Perot) of the Reform Party (a third party to the usual Democratic and Republican parties) in the United States could confirm this, and the reverse might even be the case. For instance, Kirkpatrick sees American impatience with complexities – a characteristic feature of Cameroon's current administration (see Fossungu, 2013:124-130) – as a potentially dangerous phenomenon that can explain the disintegration of the party structure and the failure of much domestic policy over the decades. This, she has predicted, could ultimately change the shape of American institutions.[137] Without the entrenched federal structure, it is even doubted that the American two-party system can be able to boast of any effective prevention of a "prime ministerial" system. The federal structure is of great importance to judicial and other organic independence; and so too is effective multipartism to the federal structure, a structure that combines with the parliamentary system to facilitate the growth and existence of 'third forces'.

(b) The Other Form of Third Forces

In addition to strong "third parties" in Canada there is even what some writers like Cairns have termed a "Third Force" that was provided initially by the Maritime Provinces and latterly by the non-founding language groups whose non-recognition in Canada's Constitution today is only justified on the need of not having to "balkanize" Canada.[138] Some observers would also give the impression that the federalism situation in Cameroon (1961-72) could have been different if President Ahidjo had gone ahead with the rumoured annexation of Spanish-speaking Equatorial Guinea since there would then have been a "third force". Such reasoning is flawed from inception. First, "third forces" can only germinate in a true federation (that combines with the parliamentary system like Canada and Germany can attest). Furthermore, I am not at all sure that there would have been any positive difference because the very idea of "annexation" naturally negatives any intention of creating a federation. Annexation is anathema to the basic principles of co-ordination and of co-operation that are of the very essence of federalism. As already noted above, the meaning of federalism today lies in the process of joint action, and not so much in the manner of legal status. It has to do not simply with what governments are, but much more with what these governments do. These requirements of intergovernmental cooperation can be fully realized in Cameroon without necessarily having to absorb Savannazone and Debundschazone into Bamboutouszone and Wourizone, as per the SDF federation project, if federalism and self-determination are

---

[137] See J.J. Kirkpatrick, *Dictatorships and Double Standards: Rationalism and Reason in Politics* (New York: Holiday House, 1983), as reviewed in 15:2 *New York University Journal of International Law and Politics* (1983), 743 at 744.

[138] Alan C. Cairns, "Constitutional Minoritarianism in Canada" in Ronald L. Watts and Douglas M. Brown, eds., *Canada: The State of the Federation 1990* (Kingston, Ontario: Institute of Intergovernmental Relations, 1990), 71–96 at 71.

actually the goals of the scheme. Their federation would seem to be worse than the current CPDM concentrated state.

Perhaps the said trilingual union (had it been formed in Cameroon in the 1970s) could only have aided in avoiding over concentration of powers in the midst of three (foreign) language groups or cultures? My answer here is simple and clear. This could have helped only if the real forces pushing for such a union (as already seen) existed. Without those real forces (but instead union by annexation like also happened with Southern Cameroons before and in Foumban), who can be sure that the French-speaking majority (or President Ahidjo, now Biya) would not have still put the two minorities (English- and Spanish-speaking) at each other's throats while oppressing them? If Anglophones could have been, and still continue to be, so easily 'used' in this fashion – the so-called North-West/South-West Divide) – how could the majority not have more easily done the same to those whose tongues already divided them?

The self-fighting West Cameroonians even had all the chances of *practically* creating a three-state federation by providing a veritable "Third Force" to the "lively controversy" that Johnson (1970: 190, 191–194 & 185–186) has shown to have already developed around the 1960 Constitution of French Cameroon (before Foumban enormously helped in killing it) between that region's Moslem North and Christian South. Did the Anglophones need Equatorial Guinea's Spanish-speaking to do just that? Paradoxically, the same English-speaking people (minority) who should have been more concerned with human rights guarantees and the most ardent defenders of the federation instead facilitated the crucifixion of rights-balancing mechanisms such as multipartism that must *always* marry with federalism. (Is the current SDF comportment any different?) And it must be remembered that these are the same people who went to the Foumban Conference with 'double nationalities' in their federation proposals. It is not exactly clear just how on earth double nationalities and the single national party can find themselves in the same federation suitcase. The two (and especially the second, single-party) are not compatible with federalism.

2. The Federal Structure and Effective Multipartism

Genuine democrats will understand that only in an effective multiparty system can parliament/legislature be the sole legislation-making organ(s). Authentic multiparty politics is very essential for the parliamentary system.

Genuine democrats cannot doubt that the existence of effective multiparty politics in the parliamentary system is graphical in the existence of rights such as freedom of expression. The merit and general usefulness of political parties need not be elaborated on here. But, while it is dangerous to idealize the party system (the apparently much more democratic African traditional system even had no such things as political parties), there is no doubt that its merits decidedly outweigh its drawbacks (Dawson, 1970: 415). This is because Dawson (*ibid*) explains that in

> all democracies they [parties] keep the public both informed and aroused by giving forceful expression to opinion and criticism on all subjects of general interest. They enable those who are concerned with these matters (whether they are actuated by selfish motives or otherwise) to organize for the more effectual propagation of their views and more ready implementation of these views through practical political expedients. These parties are the outstanding agents for bringing about co-operation and compromise between conflicting groups and interests of all kinds in the nation; for as a rule it is only by a merging of forces that these can hope to become powerful enough to secure office.

Not to limit to only federal states, the importance of effective multipartism in preventing personification of power and, therefore, also furthering "responsible government" is also seen in France. Despite the showing by specialists like Fombad (2003: 83 & 102-103) of the absence of an independent judiciary in France,[139] effective multipartism and effective bicephalism do give that country its democratic character. As Cameroon's case in Chapter 4 can prove bicephalism simply cannot be effective without effective multipartism. It is due to useful multipartism in the French system that its citizens enjoy certain basic freedoms known to other Western polities. There is government and opposition balancing each other in the political process. The influence of public opinion can therefore be noticed since politicians on both sides must constantly be thinking of the electorate or what some experts call the 'unseen presence'. The democratic strength of the French system is thus not hard to divine – multipartism. A multiparty

[139] Some experts like Radamaker do question this however: Dallis Radamaker, "The Courts in France" in J.L. Waltman and K.M. Holland, eds., *The Political Role of Law Courts in Modern Democracies* (New York: St. Martin's Press, 1989), 129 at 129.

system, properly speaking,

> is superior to the one-party state because it is a defence against tyranny or, leaving aside the harsher aspects of tyranny, against selfish or myopic rule. It is a device for securing justice as well as order, and its abandonment signals a need to assert order, if necessary, at the expense of justice. A benevolent ruler, whether an enlightened despot of the eighteenth century or a Nyerere or Kaunda of the twentieth, will try to preserve justice in other ways; but these are intrinsically frailer.[140]

The benevolent preservation of rights in a despotic regime can hardly amount to any protection and could be largely the explanation of the easy equation of federalism to secession in Cameroon

Is Federalism The Synonym Of Secession?

Another way to put this question could be to ask why none of the nine Bangwa fondoms ever seceded from the clan, non-centralized as they were/are. The shortest and clearest answer would be: because of their sense of freely belonging and of full participation in clan affairs. The United States of America would answer in the same way. The federalism-is-secession rhetoric in Cameroon derives from President Ahidjo's visceral disgust for the federal concept that preaches the splitting of powers. From the discussion above, it is of course not surprising for someone whose power has an illegitimate base to behave that way. A discussion of sincerity, patriotism, and brotherhood in this country in regard of federalism and democracy cannot be complete without Ahidjo. The confusion and manipulation around human rights and the federal system all began with President Amadou Ahidjo. His alternating Yes-No position on federalism has been variously described as mischievous, devious and unpatriotic.

The Yes-No Stance On Federalism

Ahidjo's view on federalism *before* the 1961 Union in Foumban, was that "only a federal system would be appropriate in light of the linguistic,

---

140 Peter Calvocoressi, *Independent Africa and the World* (New York: Longman, 1985) at 23.

administrative, economic, and cultural differences between the two regions" (Johnson, 1970: 183). The Southern Cameroonsian persistent discord that I have already described in Chapter 2 was proving to be fatal to Ahidjo especially with the confederation that was actually what they wanted, judging from their proposals for union that included double nationalities. Viewing all these adverse issues and earnestly wanting his *pleins-pouvoirs* 'federation' as swiftly as possible, Mr. Ahidjo – as leader of the East Cameroon delegation – went on at the opening of the Foumban Constitutional Conference to lengthily expound his stance:

> You know that, in our [secret] meetings with Mr. Foncha (leader of the Southern Cameroons delegation) before and after the referendum, we had chosen a federal structure for our future state. Why this formula? Because of the existing linguistic, administrative and economic disparities we cannot seriously and reasonably envisage a unitary centralised State; because, on the other hand, a very loose federal system would not permit the specific reconciliation and close link which we want.[141]

This position that settles on federalism as the middle-way between the unitary devolution and confederation proper is acceptable in most parts of the world (including East Cameroon *before* reunification). That is why Pierre-Elliott Trudeau, a well-known former Canadian prime minister would thus have come along to applaud them for this brilliant choice (see Fossungu, 2013: 64). But Prime Minister Trudeau was kind of wrong in reacting swiftly, assuming that he was in a country like Canada where politics is played at the level and style known to their 'less advanced' democracies; erroneously supposing that the (apparent) bridge-building was a durable and lasting one. When the Canadian prime minister got to Cameroon a few days later for the champagne feast, he could unfortunately not find the 'bridge' because the same federalism-bridge is simply to be shunned in Cameroon *after* Foumban (that had already crowned Ahidjo the automatic president of the federation

---

[141] Henri Cazalou, Note Relative à des difficultés d'application de la Constitution fédérale du Cameroun (Yaoundé: Directeur des Affaires judiciares et du Sceau, 1964) at 3, cited in Enonchong (1967: 93 n.20). Note must be taken here again of the fact that these people were already scheming long before Southern Cameroons voters had even chosen a side in the UN plebiscites, what Ahidjo is here referring to as 'the referendum'.

in article 51 of the Federal Constitution). From then on federalism would become only a hindrance to progress because it is secession.

Already crowned through it, federalism (according to the same President Ahidjo) becomes, to all intents and purposes, only "a snare, a false façade and a parade, an instrument without any real effectiveness for true evolution."[142] According to Konings and Nyamnjoh (1997: 210-211), the President's justification for the 'glorious revolution of 20 May 1972' was that federalism fostered regionalism and impeded economic development. A growing number of articulate Anglophones, however, were inclined to attribute the emergence of 'regionalism' and lack of progress not to federalism *per se*, but rather to the hegemonic tendencies of the francophone-dominated state. Of course, the proof of this thesis could be seen in the inhuman *Code Pénal Camerounais* that would be brought in by the POR to deal with anyone who tries to say otherwise to their twisted theories like "Telling the Truth Is an Offence". Yes, in the same year of his anti-federalism speech (1965) in Bafossam, President Ahidjo introduced the barbaric *Code Pénal Camerounais.* I am not going into the details of the "Doomsday" Code here, being concerned solely with the questions revolving around Cameroon's "fascinating federalism" that is claimed by the intellectuals in politics to have provided independence (as it often does to other federating entities).

Yet, Cameroon's 'Model African Penal Code' prohibits this same independence-providing instrument in no unclear terms. According to Konings and Nyamnjoh (1997: 224), "From the very start, the President has also tried to equate federalism with secession." Thus, the prohibition on federalism is well covered by the CPC by the terms of which federalism or any territorial diversification of power centres is simply equated with secession – and specifically ordaining in section 111 that "Whoever undertakes in whatever manner to infringe the territorial integrity of the Republic shall be punished with detention for life." This is the bedrock of the federalism-is-secession theory and to be able to grasp its full force and application, it will be crucial to dig into (1) the meaning of 'whoever' and 'whatever manner', and (2) whether the POR can also be detained for life in connection with this offence; that is, whether there is rule of law in Cameroon.

---

[142] Ahidjo's Speech to the *Union Camerounaise* Party Congress in Bafoussam in November 1965, as translated and cited by Rubin (1971: 193).

On The Meaning Of 'Whoever', And 'Whatever Manner'

CPC section 111 has "Secession" as its title. But I wonder if only secession can actually "infringe the territorial integrity of the Republic" "in whatever manner". Looking up for synonyms of 'infringe', I come up with breach, disobey, break, violate, contravene, and flout. For 'integrity', the following are synonyms: truthfulness, honour, truth, veracity, honesty, reliability, and uprightness. 'Territorial', on its part, brings forth two, namely, defensive, and protective; I therefore go to 'territory' which gives the following as synonyms: field, subject, area, terrain, province, region, land, and country. In Cameroon article 61 of the 1996 Constitution indicates that the ten provinces "shall become Regions," a provision that has been fortified and actualized lately by the president's decree of 12 November 2008, notwithstanding that nothing in their administrative status has changed.

As most of you from 'less democratic systems' are obviously wondering about the value or utility of the 2008 presidential decree,

> I will tell you what and why right away..... It is just a confusing way of saying that the constitution (which is still the POR's decree sort of, but requiring the rubberstamping of Ndi Chia's (1995) 'rented jesters and political contractors' who approve in a place in Yaounde called the National Assembly) stands in an inferior position to the president's decree that does not need the whitewash of the National Assembly and the yet-to-be-created Senate (Fossungu, 2013: 3-4).

This information will also aid you in comprehending the meaning of not only "whoever, and whatever manner" but also that of "rule of law and democratic society" in the next section. I do not quite think Adolf Hitler, if he came to Cameroon today, would accept that he had as much 'enabling' powers as the Ahidjo-Biya 'full and complete powers' (*pleins pouvoirs*). But how, in a way, did the Germans (from whom there is much to be learnt by Africans) come back to democracy and constitutionalism after "their own 'less complete' version of Paul Biya"?

In addition to what has already been outlined above, after the Nazi regime's atrocities, we are told by experts like Kommers (1985: 197-198) that Bonn's founders sought to ensure the democratic character of their new regime in several ways. Essentially, the principles of federalism and popular parliamentary democracy have been permanently frozen into the Basic Law –

the country's Constitution since 1945. Its eternity clause (Article 79) declares inadmissible any amendment of this Basic Law that will affect the principle of democracy or the division of the federation into states. As concerns the modification of boundaries, Kommers makes known that the Basic Law in article 29 prohibits the indiscriminate re-creation of states from the existing ones. Before reunification of the two German states, the federalism of the Federal Republic of Germany (West), although functionally based on earlier German models, embraced ten states (excluding Berlin) of relatively equal power. One must also note Wheare's (1963: 56) indication of the safeguard in Article IV, 3(1) of the United States Constitution that prohibits any new state from being formed or erected within the jurisdiction of any other state, nor any state formed by the junction of two or more states, without the consent of the legislatures of the states concerned as well as of the Congress.

All that is very unlike in Cameroon where a similar Enabling Law as Hitler's (*pleins pouvoirs* acquired by Ahidjo in 1959 from the French before "independence") has resulted in a constitution-inflation for confusioncracy in Cameroon; and which Fombad (2003: 104) thinks clearly demonstrates how "with no effective means to control the constitutionality of laws, regular changing and amending of the constitution has become a favourite pastime of Cameroonian politicians." These critics are undoubtedly correct about Cameroon where some other columnists have even seen the haphazard presidential decreeing and re-decreeing of provinces, divisions, subdivisions, etc. as being directly responsible for the numerous ethnic wars, especially in Savannazone – the well known heartland of the traditional African system in Cameroon. "What puzzles some of us is that the North West Province as of late has been characterized by tribal wars and disasters such as Oku/Noni, Bamunka/Bamali, Bambalang/Babessi, Bambili/Babanki, Bali Nyonga/Chomba, Bambui/Bafungui, and some areas in Donga and Manyung, Menchum and Momo divisions."[143]

Knowing very well now that a country (the republic) is composed of provinces, regions, or lands (to take just these), I am bound to think that the republic's "territorial integrity" cannot be "infringed" only by secession, as

---

[143] John Nsup, "Balikumbat/Bafanji Wars: Role of the Administration" *The Herald* N° 592 (3-5 April 1998), 10. See also Kum Set Ewi, "Death Toll Rises to 21 in Renewed Balikumbat-Bafanji War, Troops Reject Commandant's Order to Arrest Fon" *The Herald* N° 569 (9-10 February 1998), 1; and B.W. Wanlensum, "One Year of Military Occupation of Oku" *The Herald* N° 592 (3-5 April 1998), 10.

we know it; especially as the infringement can be "in whatever manner". It follows then that violating the territorial integrity of a province or region in the republic, is as well contravening the territorial integrity of the republic 'in whatever manner'. Now, if I am right (and I am sure I am), does 'whoever' in CPC section 111 include the President of the Republic (POR)? In other words, does the arbitrary creation and recreation of provinces and/or divisions by the POR not also infringe the territorial integrity of the Republic *in whatever manner*? Does that not warrant the detention of the POR for life? Can the President ever be detained in Cameroon for the ceaseless infringements of the republic's "territorial integrity"?

As very important cases in point, I would call attention to President Ahidjo's splitting of 'West Cameroon' in the 70s into the current two regions of Debundschazone and Savannazone (not to leave out his changing of 'Federal' Cameroon to 'United' Cameroon seen in Chapter 1). Interest is also drawn to President Biya's politically motivated administrative division of 22 August 1983 noted in Chapter 2; as well as the 1984 change from URC to République du Cameroun, also seen in Chapter 1. Of course, all these changes would simply not occur in a 'true federation'; or, at least, the changes cannot occur without the courts being involved like in *Reference re Secession of Quebec* (seen in Chapter 1). Once more, would CPC section 111 duly apply to the president's infringement?

I am sure it would not and cannot apply, perhaps, because the POR's case obviously does not "infringe the territorial integrity of the [President of the] Republic" since there is plainly no 'territorial diversification of power centres' involved in their territorial administrative reorganizations. In both instances of presidential recreation of provinces in Cameroon the whole idea has simply been that of divide and rule (the North-West/South-West Divide, for Ahidjo – now Biya;[144] and, for Biya, getting the upper hand over Ahidjo in his northern stronghold during their power squabble that culminated in

[144] Konings and Nyamnjoh (1997: 211) have theorized on the point, indicating that, to reduce the growing dangers of united Anglophone action, Ahidjo decided to divide the erstwhile federated state of West Cameroon into two Provinces, albeit well aware of the internal contradictions within the Anglophone community between the coastal forest people in the South West Province and the grassfield people in the North West Province. The former had acquired a head start over the latter by being exposed to early contacts with western trade, religion, and education. The intelligentsia that emerged in the coastal areas, notably among the Bakweri, had quickly risen to the forefront in the nationalist struggle and dominated the Anglophone political scene for a number of years.

the April 6, 1984 failed coup d'état), not decentralization of decision-making. A further critical discussion of decentralization in Cameroon, and especially under the 1996 Constitution has already been skilfully proffered by Mback (2007). The question then becomes that of where the democracy and the rule of law are, when some people are above the law; and when people who indicate same are simply guilty for the telling of the truth.

Rule Of Law And Democratic Society In Cameroon?

CPC section 111 can never apply to the POR simply because of the absence of the generally known democracy and its handmaid of rule of law. Rule of law is nonsensical without separation of powers and an independent judiciary. With independent courts, confusioncracy would be on its way to being stemmed in most African states since there would then be real political science in practice, with such judiciary constituting Russell's (1987) 'Third Branch of Government' and Wade's (1980) 'Constitutional Fundamentals' – making 'Rule of Law' proper, a general discussion of which is found in Fombad (2005); Tremblay (1993: chapter 3); and Dickson (1985). This type of constitutionalism is what gives meaning to a (true) democratic society. Is that what is really in place in Africa's Cameroon?

To the country's administrators, the answer to this important question is affirmative and Biya (1986: 37) explains:

> A democratic society is one in which, first and foremost, the law prevails. It is a society in which all relationships among members are clearly defined in such a way that everyone knows at any moment what he can hope for, what he may expect of others and what other members may legitimately expect of him. In this respect, how can one not be pleased with the many laws which govern all fields of human activity in Cameroon?

Quite apart from the fact that relations are far from being clearly defined as claimed (see later, and especially Chapter 4), in making the first sentence of their Democratic Society definition, the African authorities do seem to have in mind only what Tamanaha (1993: 196) castigates as John Austin's "long defunct formalist perspective of law." Austin (whose contemporary is Auguste Comte) claims: "A command, then, is a signification of desire" and that "Laws and other commands are said to proceed from *superiors*, and to bind and oblige inferiors."[145] Riemer (1983: 182) regards this type of rule of law as having been the guiding philosophy of Nazism.

The African authorities hotly refuse being put alongside the Nazis, with Biya (1986: 13) saying that they (unlike the Nazis) "are convinced that political science has to do with the day-to-day situation as experienced in a given country, and that a political theory is worthy of attention only if it stands the test of this situation." That is why they consider it essential that their Democratic Society be reinforced, confirmed and promoted by one of the "Thirty objectives for Cameroon" (Biya, 1986: 123-35), namely, Objective 5 by which Biya (1986: 126-127) says "The promotion of a democratic society presupposes the rule of law. This implies that all relations between members of the society are precisely codified so that everyone should clearly know his rights and obligations. In this connection, a Charter of Liberties will be proposed to the people." This is supposed to be the foundation of the new Communal Liberalism Society, which Biya (1986: 13-14) defines:

> The society of communal liberalism we want to build is one of openness, and one that fits into a modern world that tends towards *a more interdependent mankind*. This community of interests is the basis on which we henceforth have to build the *new political society*, a society whose economy will be *at the service of Man* and in which *social justice* will be the guiding rule in the distribution of the fruits of our development [emphasis as in original].

The general trend of this Communal Liberalism Society, according to Biya (1986: 13), "goes from this general view of the world to our specific vision of Cameroon. In fact, our new society should not be seen [by prospective importers of advanced democracy] as being cut off like a monad." Quite apart from it actually 'being cut off like a monad', there is certainly much to be said about Africa's Democratic Society. I will dwell on three here, namely, (1) that unknown laws are ruling because there is no independent judiciary, (2) the escapist role of the un-masterly masters of the word, and (3) the strategies of the regime for turning the watch-dogs into

145 J.W. Mohr, "From Saussure to Derrida: Margins of Law" 18 *Queen's Law Journal* (1993), 343 at 360 n.53.

watched dogs.

1. Rule of Law and Democracy without an Independent Judiciary?

The first thing to note is that *Unknown Laws Are Ruling Because There Is No Independent Judiciary* in Cameroon. The Judiciary can only successfully accomplish its task if it is 'completely' independent from government generally and the executive branch in particular. Because of these essential requirements, according to Wambali and Peter (1987: 131), judicial independence "has developed into one of the most sacred principles since the rise of the modern nation-state, [this principle evolving]… together with that [of the] rule of law and the supremacy of Parliament." Judicial independence is so vital to the successful accomplishment of its delicate and indispensable role in society that any judiciary lacking it cannot be a *state power* (or 'Judicial Power').

Because of the vitality of this independence, anything tending to subvert it should immediately provoke an outcry from what Archer and Reay (1966: 13) describe as a lively political community, vigorous and imaginative and which watches carefully for infringements against individuals. Thus, the general public, the legal profession, academia, and the press must support the court in resisting any subversion on its independence and impartiality. This they must do if they place any value on their own rights and freedoms because the courts alone will not withstand the pressures of the other branches. This requirement of independence is very important since Russell (1987: 20) says adjudication is a form of third-party conflict resolution and therefore the adjudicator-judge must be genuinely a third party and not an ally or active supporter of one of the disputing parties. Should it be otherwise, the whole process will become an open farce and difficult to sustain as a public institution.

Statesmen truly dedicated to the freedom of their fellow countrymen from unnecessary interference by other individuals and the overwhelming state apparatus attest to this fact.[146] For example, Denning (1955: 15)

---

[146] Even though the focus in this study is more on no unnecessary state interference, it shares the view that the state's primary task in respecting individuals is not fulfilled only through non-interference with individuals and the respect for negative rights of individuals. See A. Acorn, "Consensus and Difference in a Women's Agenda for Constitutional Reform" in David Schneiderman ed., *Conversations Among Friends << >> Entre Amies: Proceedings of an Interdisciplinary Conference on Women and Constitutional Reform* Edmonton: Centre for Constitutional Studies, 1992), 25 at 26; and S. Bandes, "The Negative

quotes Sir Winston Churchill in a House of Commons debate on 23 March 1954 concerning the salaries of judges, as stating that:

> The principle of the complete independence of the Judiciary from the Executive is the foundation of many things in our island life. It has been largely imitated in varying degree throughout the free world. It is perhaps one of the deepest gulfs between us and all forms of totalitarian rule. The only subordination which a judge knows in his judicial capacity is that which he owes to the existing body of legal doctrine enunciated in years past by his brethren on the bench, past and present, and upon the laws passed by Parliament which have received the Royal assent. He also – and this is one of his most important functions considered incomprehensible in some large parts of the world – has to do justice between the citizen and the State.

Judicial independence need not necessarily be viewed in the negative way (African administrations generally see it) in a society that is truly worthy of the description 'open' or 'democratic'. Thus, we also hear Queen Victoria saying the same thing like Prime Minister Churchill when she is cited as declaring that "The independence and learning of the judges supported by the integrity of other members of the profession of the law are the chief security for the rights of the Crown and the liberties of the people."[147] These words aptly apply to Canada, without modification; but to apply them to Cameroon, as well as the United States, one must substitute 'country' for 'Crown' as Stason himself points out.

Africa's position on the issue can be gleaned from the utterances of its own statesmen. Listen, first, to President Julius Nyerere of Tanzania who, in essence, wants courts to simply convict whoever the government accuses. Concerning courts that acquit persons accused by the government, the Tanzanian chief of state (cited in Wambali and Peter, 1987: 139-40) stated: "We have a problem on what to do with these people. However, we have not yet decided on the course of action… I ask the magistrates to forgive us if we

---

Constitution: A Critique" 88 *Michigan Law Review* (1990), 2271 at 2346-47 & 2273-74. Compare Justice Rehnquist in *DeShanney v. Winnebago Department of Social Services* (1989) 109 S. Ct. 998 at 1003-04.

[147] E.B. Stason, "Judicial Selection around the World" in G.R. Winters, ed., *Judicial Selection and Tenure* rev. ed. (Chicago: American Judicature Society, 1973), 45 at 45.

hesitate to take culprits to courts of law. At times racketeers have been taken to courts where they have either received light sentences or have been set free…." President Biya (1986: 49) of Cameroon grudgingly offers the following: "As a custodian of freedoms and of the security of citizens, Cameroon justice must become a real judicial power vis-à-vis the executive and legislative powers."

The appearance of 'justice' before judicial 'power' is well calculated; a calculation already exposed above in 'the palace story'; as it is seen all through this book. Biya cannot be seriously desirous of this institution actually being a custodian of freedoms etc. when, as head of state and of government, Biya still "guards" the independence of the judiciary in article 37 of the 1996 Constitution and expects Cameroonians to seriously "believe that something awful is going to happen to us if we follow the example of nearly every other country in the world" by instituting genuine judicial independence and freedoms and rights of the people.[148] This is, in fact, what Biya (1986: 13) has in mind when he implores Cameroonians who are after democracy and federalism not to "borrow[]... rules of conduct" from other countries, excepting his own slavish copying from France.

Another notable problem encountered with the doctrine of judicial independence is that most, if not all, Third World governments shrink from or panic at the mere mention of 'judicial independence'. This is usually because governments in said countries always see judicial independence as a threat to their rights (which is true to the extent that these governments always arrogate to themselves rights that are properly not theirs) in favour of the people's liberties and rights. Unlike the others who pin the problem on the lack of natural resources (see Fossungu, 2013:194-195), it seems that Antonio Cassese very well understood why most of the states called Third World are in fact Third World. "Third World countries", Cassese is cited in Fossungu (1998: 44) for having written,

> have two other factors in common: a concept of law which, while differing from one culture to the other, is always profoundly distinct from that predominating in the [developed] West and a tendency towards authoritarian structures in their respective domestic legal systems…

[148] Lord Hailsham, House of Lords Debates 1382 (November 29, 1978), quoted in Wade (1980: 76).

[with] highly centralized and basically autocratic systems of government which tend to rely on power structures where the law is easily disregarded whenever it suits the ruling group.

Cassese would have perfectly described the Cameroon system and regime, with its rule of unknown laws.

Advanced democracy is based on *the rule of a law that is yet to be known.* I am talking about Anyangwe's (1987: 263-64) "framed legislation", which is to say that "enactments often contain provisions to the effect that a particular aspect of the law will be dealt with in detail by a future enactment – often a presidential decree or a ministerial order. Also, it sometimes happens that laws are so hurriedly [and secretly] drafted that no sooner have they rolled out of the printing press than there are amendments." Almost every vital subject of the constitution of this country is written in this framed style; typical examples from the 1996 Constitution being "the composition of, the taking of cognizance by, and the procedure of the Supreme Court" (article 32(2), the referendum procedure (article 30), "Parliamentary immunity, disqualification of candidates or of sitting members and the allowances and privileges of members" of the National Assembly (article 18), elections to the legislative institution (article 17), and the nomination of presidential candidates, supervision of such elections and proclamation of the results (article 6(3)). Although more will be said later on this 'framed rule of law' in Cameroon, it is important to immediately note a clear case touching on the point of discussion here.

Talking of the decentralization it announces in its article 1, the 1996 Constitution states in article 56 that "(1) The State shall transfer to [the] Regions, under conditions [to be] laid down by law, jurisdiction in areas necessary for their economic, social, health, educational, cultural and sports development. (2) The [unknown] law shall define: - the sharing of powers between the State and Regions in the areas of competence so transferred, - The resources of the Regions.-The land and property of each Region."[149] I would not even want to waste my valuable time on this one-man decentralization because it is not worth the energy; but just tell me now

[149] For further discussion of 'The Ambiguities of the Constitutional Principle of Free Administration of Local Governments' in Cameroon, see Mback (2007: 64-66); and Peter Ateh-Afac Fossungu, "One Cameroon against Unknown Laws" *The Herald* N° 700 (15-16 December 1998), 10.

which is the real law or constitution here: this one announcing its subsequent arrival or the unknown one whose subsequent coming is being here announced? Can there therefore be any *known* legal or constitutional processes to be dubbed 'rule of law' in Cameroon?

In addition to the dependence of the courts on the president in article 37(3) of the 1996 Constitution, many experts like Mback (2007: 65) clearly do not think there are because, "On that basis, the 1974 law and the 1973 decree cannot be contested constitutionally and legally." Some critics have therefore come to the conclusion that Rule of Law (*Respecter les Institutions*) in Cameroon can properly only mean that the Cameroon people must accept the 'election' of the POR by his personal appointees like supreme court judges, mayors, district officers, governors, and ministers; that no one has to cough about anything the POR does, not even when the POR turns the country into his private property, etc.[150]

Moreover, Africa's rule of law is *still to be punctuated by a Charter of Liberties and an independent judiciary to uphold it.* Some experts have therefore placed the advanced democratic rule of law alongside what Couloumbis and Wolfe (1986: 8) call "This rhetoric [which] generally remains, however, outside the gates of practical application." For their charge, these specialists would first point to the numerous calls for "*La nécessité d'une réforme judiciare [au Cameroon]*" from both Laski (1950: 258-261) and Nyo'Wakai"[151] – necessary reform that Anyangwe (1987: xiv) thinks must be undertaken "to get rid of old and out-of-date colonial laws; to unify and modernise the law, profitably borrowing from other countries on certain matters and inventing improvements of our own so as to make the law responsive to our national character, culture and social milieu."

Yes, only this requisite reform, the critics have explained, can inter alia

---

150 *C'est-à-dire, "accepter l'<élection> du président de la République par les sous-prefets et la Cour suprême, accepter les manipulations et le mépris de la Constitution par le MINAT et ses patrons, accepter la domestication de l'Assemblée nationale par l'Exécutif, accepter l'entretien incontrolé d'un Conseil Economique et Social fantôm, accepter la nomination de fonctionnaires RDPC à la tête de municipalités élues, accepter le financement par le contribuable d'une CRTV de service... privé. Et, bien sûr, laiser à Biya le monopole de la recherche des <appuis divers> en France et en francophonie, au Commonwealth, au FMI, à la Banque mondiale et à... l'OUA."* Daniel Rim, "L'OUA en vacance" *Le Messager* (3 mars 1997), 2 (omissions as in original). See also "Forfaire politique à Yaoundé: la Cour suprême intronise le roi Paul Biya à Etoudi" *Le Quotidien* (24 octobre 1997), 1 at 2-3.

151 See Justice Nyo'Wakai, *Under the Broken Scale of Justice: The Law and My Times* (Bamenda, Cameroon: Langaa RPCIP, 2008); and Nyo'Wakai (1991).

ensure active citizen participation because it is their sane belief that a citizen, bold and fearless as he or she might be, could not exhibit those qualities without the assurance that the media, legal, and judicial institutions are credible enough to defend him or her. It is this process of active citizen participation that the experts have termed 'democracy', defined by Pearson and Rochester (1984: 593) as an open, pluralistic governmental system, allowing for the free expression and flow of ideas and for rival political groupings – a system which is clearly contrary to Africa's 'paper system', a confusioncracy that peacefully exists solely because of this continent's un-masterly 'Masters of the Word'. As such, the provision on secession and the infringement of the "territorial integrity of the state in whatever manner" cannot apply to the African PORs, as it would in America where no one is above the "Law [which] applies to all persons, public or private, high or low, even to the President."[152]

2. *The Un-Masterly Masters of the Word?*

The Un-masterly Masters of the Word have played an accentuated shameful role. Africans are wonderful people by nature but they have been transformed to something else (such as rascals or *voyous*) by bad governors and un-lawyerly lawyers. Eyoum'a Ntoh has posited that no one can doubt that Cameroon is a wonderful country inhabited by a wonderful people. Nevertheless, he has concluded, very serious doubts are cast on everything when real issues (among which are federalism, multiculturalism, and human rights defence) are carefully examined. On such an insightful examination, one simply finds that Cameroonians are only 13 [now almost 20] million proud rascals.[153] Demonstrations to the theses of these critics are not hard to come by in the area of human rights defence and the resulting fallouts on Cameroonians generally.

---

[152] F.D. Day, *Criminal Law and Society* (Springfield, Illinois: C.C. Thomas, 1964) at 11.

[153] "*Le Cameroun est un grand pays. Cela ne fait aucun doute. Un grand pays habité par un grand people. Cela non plus ne fait pas de doute. Là où le bât blesse, c'est quand on se rend, enfin, à l'évidence: le grand people du grand Cameroun est compose de 13 millions de…voyous! Oui, Mesdames et Messieurs les Camerounais: vous êtes, pardon, nous sommes tous des voyous! Et c'est ce qui explique que l'autre [c'est-à-dire, le président de la république] ait balancé, il y a 5 ans <<Me voice donc à Douala>> (sous-entendu, de manière très 'quartiésarde', <<vous pouvez me faire quoi>>, avant d'ajouter: <<Le Cameroun, c'est le Cameroun>>.*" Patrick-Thomas Eyoum'a Ntoh, "13 millions de voyous!" *Le Messager* (12 septembre 1996), 2.

It has been discovered that a money-chasing legal profession (as is the case in Cameroon) can hardly help in ameliorating things in this country since it cannot properly defend the rights of citizens and businesses, let alone those of other state institutions, notably the judiciary. That could be the main reason why most of the citizens have simply found it more advantageous to simply join the '*voyous* club' rather than stand up only not to be counted: since no one is there to defend their defending their rights. Maître Alice Nkom is even quoted as saying that some of the lawyers involved in the illegal sale of a Nigerian's property in Douala (capital of Wourizone) are looking for money through the wrong means: "They are running after money like blind men. I am afraid of their future in the profession. They have to go back to school...."[154] In another instance, one witness of the incident has described the acts of the "lawyer who at the same time claims to be a human rights defender" as "beastly" before asking whether it was the business of lawyers "to go nosing around for cases where they have not been invited."[155] Why are people in Africa not then to be frightened when, rather than go around nosing for situations of human rights violations, especially by the executive arm of government, lawyers only go around committing crimes themselves?

Another sickening case from the jurists in the academia would also be important. This has to do with Cameroon's infamous "judge-made" Law of the Preamble, as enunciated by its 'misnamed' Supreme Court in *l'Affaire Société des Grands Travaux de l'Est (SGTE) c. État du Cameroun*;[156] a decision that points obviously to the fact that independence is a sine qua non for judicial impartiality and activism. The Cameroon Supreme Court decided the case based on two arms. First, that retroactive legislation which violates the constitution is not unconstitutional and cannot therefore be struck down because the non-retrospection principle specifically violated is enunciated only in the preamble of the constitution. I would want to point out that this ratio grossly ignores the fact that 'the utmost interest of the state' (*l'intérêt supérieur de l'État*) which has been employed now and then to suppress the Cameroon people is also found embedded in that same preamble. Moreover, the principle of non-retrospection is also implanted in section 3 of the

---

[154] Hillary K. Fokum, "Can a Foreigner Get a Fair Trial in Cameroon? Lawyers Connive and Auction Nigerian's Property" *The Messenger* (20 May 1996), 8.

[155] Peterkins Manyong, "Bamenda High Court Judge Denounces Lawyer for Invasion of Residence" *The Herald* (13-15 June 1997), 1.

[156] (C.J.F. Arrêt N°4, 28 October 1970), (1962-1970) 1 *Recueil Mbouyoum.*

'Model African Penal Code' that also carries the vigorously enforced secession crime and 'truth-telling' offence that are being discussed.

The Supreme Court held further (second arm) that even assuming that the said legislation violated the constitution (as, indeed, it did), only the president – the violator (in the sense of being the sole legislator, as shown in Chapters 1 and 4) – could refer the matter to the Supreme Court as per article 10 of the same 1972 Constitution. This requirement raises the same problems that Wade (1980: 22) canvasses concerning the impracticability of having entrenched rights in the British system with its "dogma of Parliamentary sovereignty." Fombad (2003) has further discussed this issue of the POR being the one to refer for constitutionality checks in the context of the 1996 Constitution.

Commenting on the Supreme Court's decision, Pougoué and Kamto (1990: 8) have cited many French decisions that unequivocally affirm the constitutional value or importance of the preamble of that country's 1958 Constitution "from which our constitutional law heavily draws" (my translation). They then affirmed that the constitutional validity of the preamble of the 1958 French Constitution has been unequivocally established by the courts of that country but those of Cameroon continue to adopt a particularly unusual or shaky position on the issue. About an earlier decision of the Court, based not on the preamble but on an article of the Constitution but still justified in the same way, Pougoué and Kamto (1990: 8) declared that 'such a decision is wholly unjustifiable as the court was dealing with principles enshrined in the constitution itself' (my translation). It must be stressed here that the preamble is part and parcel of the constitution and even the most important portion of it.[157]

In respect of another (then) very recent retroactive law (the very July 1988 law on the regulation of the Supreme Court that is the topic of their commentary) Pougoué and Kamto (1990: 7) questioned whether the amendment was unconstitutional; but instead preferred to state that the answer remains open since Cameroon courts have not yet courageously settled the matter as is expected of them (*ibid*, 9 & 7). These public law professors rebuke the courts in Cameroon for grossly failing to definitively lay the issue to rest. It is submitted that this has not happened not only

---

[157] See Peter W. Rodino, "Living with the Preamble" 42 *Rutgers Law Review* (1990), 685.

because the court's hands are "chained to the back" as Nyo'Wakai (1991: 19) says. In addition and more importantly, it is because the university intelligentsia and legal analysts have for too long taken and continue to take an escapist stance on human rights issues. Rather than come out boldly (like Chief Justice Coke of Britain, Chief Justice Marshall of the US, and Chief Justice Laskin of Canada) and denounce illegality outright when it is spotted, most have always shifted responsibility completely to the courts or judges. And they do this without appreciating in the least that these judges are helpless in the absence of authoritative texts from the legal academia and political scientists (in particular) on which to pin their (judges') 'creative' departure from the 'traditional' or chained stance.

For a further example, on the 1972 Constitution as a whole, Pougoué and Kamto (1990: 8) agree that one can validly contest that it is not a constitution. But, again, instead of standing firm (like the Seven Bishops and their Jurors) and demonstrating to the judges just why and how that constitution can be struck down, they (as if hearing that the POR was around) immediately come in with: 'logically, however, the constitution should be upheld' (*ibid*). Their argument for this abrupt and surprising *re-prise de position*, they say, is that the Constitution should be upheld all the same because of fundamental liberties and human rights therein protected (*ibid*). But one cannot fail to ponder about the human rights and liberties they are talking about, especially as they themselves clearly state that these rights and liberties, 'in the 1972 constitution, were relegated to the preamble' (*ibid*). And, moreover, that is the preamble we are being told has no constitutional standing. Yet these professors are telling the helpless judges to still uphold that constitution because of that 'worthless' portion of it. Nothing would seem to describe it better than 'nonsensical escapism'. As Judge Learned Hand (cited in Ackermann, 1989: 71) put it in 1980, a "society so raven that the spirit of moderation is gone, no court can save; a society where the spirit flourishes, no court need save; and a society which evades its responsibilities by thrusting upon the courts the nurture of that spirit, that spirit in the end will perish." This is especially the case where society's watch dogs are transformed into watched dogs.

3. *From Watch-Dogs to Watched Dogs?*

The most intriguing thing is that the same escapist and crime-committing lawyers in Africa have been openly called upon by Biya (1986: 99-100) "to educate [all] Cameroonians about their most basic rights and freedoms, through a sustained initiation in the law and in the mechanisms of Cameroonian justice." Only such a militant exercise from educators, as Biya (1986: 73) indicates, would be able to transform Africans from mere anonymous elements in a shapeless and passive mass that they currently are "into citizens who are aware of their rights and obligations and who are determined to assure and assume them fully." It is only through this authentic civic education that the courts can become independent. This is a very significant call that has challenged teachers and the media in Africa to live up to their name because, like many experts,[158] Biya (1986: 127) thinks

> An authentic democracy requires the development of civic awareness in citizens and an increase in their level of education. This presupposes the possibility for all to have access to knowledge through school, the media and various means of informal education...[as well as] improving the school charter so that there should be no limit whatsoever to the people's right to learning.

That unlimited right to learning, of course, extends to their being taught their authentic history and the knowledge that their country can only be properly managed through a genuine federation. If history has anything valid to say regarding this state form, it will declare that there has never been any in Cameroon; which could elucidate why the mere mentioning of federalism and/or history has always been so scary to the country's administrators. It is due to this fright that the authorities are doing everything in their unrestrained powers to prevent the very 'Masters of the Word' they are inviting to do so, from actually teaching and defending Africans about/of their rights. In Cameroon, for example, these watchdogs have therefore been tactically transformed into watched dogs by the too many confusing laws that

---

158 Eko's (2003) article is a very good and interesting piece on the history and various strategies that the English-language press professionals in this country have employed in refusing to be transformed into watched dogs, rather than remain society's watch-dogs. For a detailed discussion of the role of the media (in the parliamentary system in particular and) in democratic societies in general, see Justice Anderson in *R. v. Frederick* (1978), 41 C.C.C. (2d) 532 at 537 (Ontario H.C.); J.P. Mackintosh, *The British Cabinet* 3rd ed. (1977) chapter 8 & 613-621; Loewenstein (1967 : 148-151); Banfield and Wilson (1963: chapter 21); Riemer (1983: 260-261 & 287-288); and François Ouellette *L'Accès des caméras de télévision aux audiences des tribunaux* (Montréal: Les Éditions Thémis, 1997).

have gotten even the masters of the word lost. The Cameroonian authorities would think otherwise, believing that Cameroonians ought to express immense gratitude for the confusion they call advanced democratic society because, as Biya (1986: 37-38) sees it, while the confusing "law is an instrument for managing the present, it is also a creative image for the future and, as such, can be improved." Therefore, the confusion that is being called law, according to Biya (1986: 38), "will be constantly evaluated and modelled so that it remains a practical tool consonant with the aspirations of the people and requirements of the moment. It is also for this reason that safeguards will be taken to guarantee not only the enforcement of the law but also its evolution and adaptation."

In addition to King Rex's strategy involved here (by way of the 'framed legislation'),[159] I need to clearly indicate that said 'constantly evaluating and modelling' have been very carefully fashioned so as to completely tie up the lawyers and also marginalize and keep out the university intelligentsia. For instance, university law teachers (not already in private practice in 1987) are excluded from practicing by Law N° 87-18 (Bill N° 322/PJL/AN). Like several others after it,[160] the 1987 Bar Law, according to Anyangwe (1989: vii), also

> effectively rendered nugatory the time honoured immunity which a barrister enjoys when conducting a case in court. The Bar Council put up a spirited fight. But the Bill was voted into law all the same. However, the President of the Republic, mindful, no doubt, of the malaise created within the Bar by the Bill, declined to promulgate it. The Law was tinkered with and in June 1987 sent back to Parliament for a second reading – the first time ever in Cameroon's legislative history that this has happened. It sailed through Parliament and was promulgated on the 15th of July 1987 as Law N° 87-18.

This whole tendency has been held by Anyangwe (1989: vii) to be a regressive provision and a gross "error" that only helps to remove law

[159] See M.D.A. Freeman, *Lloyd's Introduction to Jurisprudence* 6th ed. (London: Sweet and Maxwell, 1994) at 149-153 (discussing the legislative attempts of King Rex).

[160] See "President Biya Gives Fatherly Ear to Lawyers' Cry, Says New Bar Law will be Reviewed" *Cameroon Post* (31 July- 7 August 1990) 13-14, continued in *Cameroon Post* (8-15 August 1990) 7, 11, & 15.

teaching in the university "from practice and national realities." Thus, even as the legal profession and academy are unavoidably bound, the texture of that binding in Cameroon is precisely still captured by what Smith and Weisstub (cited in DeCoste, 1991: 968-69) some years ago castigated as "a theory without a profession and a profession without a theory." This is obviously the type of "binding" that couples with the internal friction within the legal and media professions, to give the Cameroonian 'advanced government' the free and advanced ride on human rights, the invisible hand of development.

This sad situation is further compounded by the virtual non-existence in Cameroon of law reporting and academic journals. All this, according to Anyangwe (1989: viii), can only have the inevitable "untoward effect of hampering a proper, harmonious, rational and progressive development of the law in this country." Add all the confusion up and then tell only a businessman who has nothing else to do with his capital to come and invest it in Cameroon where, in addition the civil service is so corrupt. It is not surprising since it has been shown that a sheepish academy, combining with a tame media and a divisive legal profession, can only conveniently furnish what Ndi Chia (1995a) describes as a very comfortable haven for gross public mistakes and unaccountability. This would visibly be unthinkable in a democracy; or at least, the one that is generally and properly known, and which is practised in diverse societies through federalism.

Furthermore, the experts would buttress their charge on the rhetoric in Cameroon's Objective 5 by easily citing a very convenient model 'Charter of Liberties' (*Model Human Rights Charter for Developing Countries 1989*[161]) that the Canadian Bar Association/Cameroon Bar Council specifically proposed to Cameroon in 1989 and which has so far been treated as if it never existed. The treatment given to this invaluable separation-of-powers proposal would simply render incomprehensible and confusing the desire and call of the authorities, as far back as 1986, for "The institution of a National Charter of Freedoms, a strong State effectively governed by the people's onward march" (Biya, 1986: 41-42). It is now more than twenty-five years later and no such Charter of Rights and Freedoms is in place in Cameroon; with only the 'strong State' being in place to effectively prevent 'the people's onward match toward democracy'. It must be noted that the proposed 1989 model

161 See *The Canadian Bar Association and the Cameroon Bar Council Committee Report: Model Human Rights Charter for Developing Countries 1989* (Ottawa: Canadian Bar Association, 1989).

Charter (from the Canadian Bar Association and the Cameroon Bar Council) does clearly provide for an independent judiciary as the ultimate arbiter and guarantor of rights in society. This judicial institution is necessary and indispensable for the Rule of Law proper. I do not think therefore that Africans should be expressing happiness for anything less than that 1989 model Charter. Cameroon's rule of law is thus the usual confusion all the way; with the selected and arbitrary application of the inhuman laws reigning unchecked and inaugurating and propping up the truth-telling offence. All this is principally because of the untenable theory of self-determination and multiculturalism within a highly centralized unitary state.

Self-Determination and International Human Rights Law

To the Ahidjo-Biya administrations, there is absolutely no need for federalism (the vehicle or channel for self-determination); since the Cameroon people are already having more than enough opportunities to exercise their right to self-determination in their 'modern Cameroon' (see Fossungu, 2013: 66 *et seq*). Having thus prevented them (or some of them) from participation, the gates of secession would seem to have been thrown ajar. Having worked tirelessly but in vain to have the institution of a real federal structure within which they can feel protected in Cameroon, Southern Cameroonsians cannot be rebuked by a knowledgeable international community if and when they use brute force to have their independent state; a thing that could happen solely because the regime in place is unnecessarily excluding the federal structure.

There is actually no need for complaining about federalism or effective decentralization in polities with representative governments. Such governments do significantly help in the avoidance of bloody secessionist wars as well as guaranteeing the independence of the judiciary and, therefore, human rights (see Pomerance, 1982: 3, 37-42 & 115 n384a; Tiruchelvam, 1987: viii & ix; and Couloumbis and Wolfe, 1986: 82). Federalism is also known to have provided great grounds for judicial independence and activism in Canada even before the arrival of the *Canadian Charter of Rights and Freedoms* in 1982. In Cameroon where power is viewed only in the 'me-and-me-and-me' terms, this generally accepted solution is regarded simply as a right to secession. Since they have chosen not to listen and emulate from Belgium and others, Southern Cameroonsians have to turn to international human rights law and practice to see what the situation looks like for them. I will thus first of all briefly survey the various secession debates before indicating, in the second place, what I think is the most plausible door open to Southern Cameroonsians, assuming, of course, that they are really serious about having their independent state.

The Secession Debates Reviewed

As I have indicated earlier, secession is a legitimate response to the denial of the right to self-determination within the state through federalism or decentralization. All the evidence indicates that the bulk of Cameroonians (including Southern Cameroonsians, of course) wish to build, and not to destroy, their country. The building of this country they can only effect if and only if adequate means for their full participation are in place. Having prevented them (or some of them) from this participation, the gates of secession would seem to have been thrown ajar. It is normal for a state or province or region of a federation (or any other type of state) to effect secession 'by unilateral act' for the purposes of legitimately exercising the right to self-determination. Although some critics of secession politics would find it outlandish, it is possible, and some like Hogg (1996: 127-129) would even say legal, to secede 'by unilateral act'. It is either sheer ignorance or the mere drive to confuse and concentrate powers that leads the people in power in Africa to regard federalism as secession, which they also equate to subversion.

It appears that the Cameroonian authorities do not even comprehend what self-determination means. Otherwise, the right to self-determination cannot be *necessarily* viewed as implying the right to secede from an established nation-state.[162] After a lengthy analysis, Buchheit has even posited that the history of United Nations practice does lend support to the thesis that self-determination "is primarily a vehicle for decolonisation, not an authorization of secession."[163] This theory would certainly not find favour with some current thoughts that would seem to equate it with what

---

162 See J.H. Chineball & T. Thomson, "Sovereignty and Self Determination: The Rights of Native Americans under International Law" 27 *Buffalo Law Review* (1978), 669 at 709. See also Murray Greensmith Forsyth, ed., *Federalism and Nationalism* (Leicester: Leicester University Press, 1989).

163 L.C. Buchheit, *Secession – The Legitimacy of Self-Determination* (New Haven: Yale University Press, 1978) at 87.

Appiagyei-Atua (1999: xvi) denounces as the untenable thesis that "Freedom was conceived of only as freedom from colonialism, but not individual freedom for citizens against the government." It is comforting still that Buchheit uses 'primarily' and thus not firmly closing the door on secession.

But the anti-secessionists are not about to capitulate because Wippman (as cited in Charette, 1996: 194 n.11) also thinks that, "As the Badinter Commission recently held, self-determination, whatever its precise content, does not – under international law – encompass a right of secession." Some critics like Scott (1991: 16) have consequently argued that, "So far as Québec is concerned, the population of Québec, through its elected representatives or its voters, opted for Canada in 1867 and again in 1980. I would argue that the issue of self-determination, if it existed, is closed; the people and province of Québec remaining free, like all others, to seek constitutional change within the Federation by constitutional processes." This powerful argument notwithstanding, Quebec sovereignty referendum still took place again in 1995 and the issue is not yet over in Quebec; perhaps because this is one of the available constitutional processes in Canada?

Awasom (2000: 92) has told us in Chapter 2 above that Anglophones unilaterally opted to achieve independence by joining the Cameroon Republic and that reunification was not imposed by Francophones. It could then also be posited that Southern Cameroonsians as far back as 1961 expressed their right to self-determination by voting to join their "brothers" in *La République du Cameroun*, and that this closed their right to any further self-determination; leaving them to seek constitutional change within the 'Federation' by constitutional processes. This argument is very powerful. However, it appears to find no home in Cameroon (quite apart from the findings above of there being no true federation in Foumban) for a couple of other reasons. First, only one side (Southern Cameroons) seems to be willing to do things constitutionally. It is well known that it takes two to tangle. Secondly, there are no known constitutional processes in Cameroon as I have demonstrated above under rule of law and democratic society; which leaves the people concerned with no other choice but secession or revolution.

As faulty and manipulative as the 1961 'federation' was, as unconvincing as the Southern Cameroonsian arguments for not acting determinedly in 1961 and in 1972 are, Southern Cameroonsians cannot be considered to have made a once-and-for-all decision in 1961 that would now oblige them to remain in the Republic of Cameroun at all costs. What is of capital importance in this debate is the will or determination of the people concerned. People (including this writer) who may clearly not be in favour of secession must equally be conscious of the fact that if and when a "people" is really determined to secede, there is nothing that naked force can do to prevent it from happening. In refusing to reform and recreate a country that reflects imperative changes, it is surely the Biya regime that will be judged by posterity for the ensuing secession when and if it happens.

It has even been countered further by SCFAQ (Question 18) that the very fact that Southern Cameroonsians freely exercised this right in 1961 necessarily entails that "we could also freely opt to get out of the union. In 1972 Southern Cameroonians overwhelmingly rejected the unitary state. The fact that their wishes were never respected does not negate this expression of autonomy." Some critics would find it hard to countenance this Southern Cameroonsian thesis that they inherently have the right to opt out just as they freely decided to get in. Scott (1991: 16) of McGill University, for example, has opined that

> It is difficult to discern any consensus at all as to the conditions of an internationally-recognized right of self-determination: who enjoys it; when and how it may be exercised; and what territory it applies to. It cannot plausibly [he would then conclude,] be a right to assert repeated fresh claims, each of which would bring the state to an end at any time [because] It seems preposterous to assert that Canada can be brought to an end at the demand of one of its provinces.

This is quite true for a true federation as amply seen in Chapter 1. This is the elementary lesson; and which is quite normal and logical but does this logic apply to the case of Cameroon? In other words, what is the position of provinces or regions in a state that is not a 'true federation'? It looks like he was responding directly to this question when Jay A. Sigler (cited in Charette, 1996: 194 n.10) posited that "Minority rights do not include the right to revolution and secession except upon the same basis as do individual rights. Only the direct and substantial threat to life, limb, and the integrity of family life would ordinarily justify group resistance to constituted authority." Does this argument apply to and exclude the rights of Southern Cameroonsians? What is the most apposite avenue for them?

The Most Appropriate Path for Southern Cameroonsians

The foregoing standpoints have, however, not prevented or stopped secession of oppressed peoples and it can never do so because, first, Wade (1980: 3) defines revolution as "a logical safety-valve against governments which ignore the popular will." The right to revolution is a right that Pomerance (1982: 7) says was viewed by US President Woodrow Wilson as "sacred" and not be interfered with in any way.[164] Pearson and Rochester (1984: 118) have thus used militant leader Ayatollah Khomeini's case as clean evidence that even unlimited US military supplies to Iran could not stop a determined commitment to change. Konings and Nyamnjoh's (1997: 228-29) discussion of the failed attempts to intimidate the SCNC leaders from meeting the people in the townships also points to same message.

Second, the international documents and covenants dealing with the self-determination issue do expressly confer the right on "all peoples", including Quebecers who Bissonnette (1963: 20) sees as clearly meeting the definition of a "people": *Une société commune formant un tout moral et attachée à un territoire déterminé.* Although the Biya regime, through the SDF projected four-state federation, is out to take this away from them, Southern Cameroonsians do also fulfil this 'people' requirement (see Fossungu, 2013: 80-84), and Anyangwe further cements it:

> I suppose you know that the British Southern Cameroons was also a UN trust territory. It was a separate unit of self determination within the trust territory of British Cameroons administered by the United Kingdom of Great Britain. I take it further that you also know that as a distinct and separate colonial territory, the British Southern Cameroons was not part of the territories comprised within French Cameroun either before or on the date of its achievement of independence on 1 January 1960. The territories of the two countries, the British Southern Cameroons and Cameroun Republic are separate and distinct and have always been and will always be so.[165]

---

[164] See also Tracy E. Higgins, "Foreword" 63 *Fordham Law Review* (1994), 1 at 3, n.14.

[165] Carlson Anyangwe's Interview with *La Nouvelle Expression*, November 12, 2008, found @ www.southerncameroonsig.org/2008/11/professor-carlson-anyangwe (last visited in March 2011). According to Anyefru also, "The territory for which the Anglophone leaders claim nationhood is relatively well defined; it does not cut across existing state borders, and

The right to self-determination can be invoked even by those who are oppressed (like Southern Cameroonsians) and wish to secede from an already independent state.[166] I think this is where Southern Cameroonsians could be advised to principally pin or anchor their case rather than placing it on some confusing go-for-before-for-back and not-so-solid arguments. Their arguments so far are stuffed with a lot of the 'yes-no' rhetoric that is characteristic of Cameroon. For instance, they would begin by arguing in the Independence Proclamation (1999) that they are entitled to unilaterally declare their independence because, as the 1961 Foumban union "was between Sovereign competent La Republique du Cameroun and minor incompetent Southern Cameroons, discussions there were not held on a footing of equality, and their result known as Cameroon reunification was null and void AB INITIO." But the very next thing you hear after this thesis is an endless string of proofs "that pending the termination of the trusteeship agreement, the Southern Cameroons under United Kingdom administration became De Facto Independent…." Are they too confused with the oppression or is it just the normal confusing way of doing every business in Cameroon?

Southern Cameroonsians should abandon all these unconvincing talk and arguments and just focus on the undisputable and consistent strategy being proposed here. For this better and firmer stance, they can look to the highly respected Supreme Court of Canada. This court is highly venerated because "In several key recent decisions, direct Canadian influence is evident in Israel's approach to a variety of separate issues, including gender equality, the application of constitutional remedies, and even in the area of procedure." [167] At the portals of this Canadian apex court, Southern Cameroonsians will

---

it is occupied by a majority of Anglophones." E. Anyefru, "The Refusal to Belong: Limits on the Discourse on Anglophone Nationalism in Cameroon" at http://www.thefreelibrary.com/The+refusal+to+belong%3A+limits+of+the+discourse+on+Anglophone...-a0279891521 [accessed on 11 February 2013].

[166] See D.B. Knight, "Self-Determination for Indigenous Peoples: The Context for Change" in R.J. Johnston, D.B. Knight, & E. Kofman, eds., *Nationalism, Self-Determination and Political Geography* (New York: Croom Helm, 1988), 117 at 120; and Y. Dinstein, "Opening Remarks" 21:3 *New York University Journal of International Law & Politics* (1989), 451 at 455.

[167] Hillel C. Neuer, "Canadian Content: Why Israeli Judges Read Canadian Cases" 19 *Canadian Lawyer* Issue 3 (May 1995), 14. See also Adam M. Dodek, "From Vancouver to Jerusalem: A Year at the Supreme Court of Israel" 54 *The Advocate* Part 6 (November 1996), 905. Ethiopians are doing the same, as reported by Paul Pelletier, "Letter from Ethiopia" 54 *The Advocate* Part 6 (November 1996), 911.

find that, regarding the legitimacy of Quebec's threatened unilateral declaration of independence, this Supreme Court in a decision in August 1998 (*Reference re Secession of Quebec* [1998] 2 S.C.R. 217) – about one year before the Southern Cameroons futile Independence Proclamation – *unanimously* held that international law did not apply in Quebec's case simply because Quebecers were not a suppressed or colonized people. International law has therefore to unfailingly apply to the case of oppressed and/or colonized people, as is plainly the case with Southern Cameroons.

The Southern Cameroonsian case through this pathway is thus formidable because Anyangwe's 2008 book (*Imperialistic Politics in Cameroun: Resistance and the Inception of the Restoration of the Statehood of Southern Cameroons*), according to the publisher, focuses on the unresolved Southern Cameroons colonial predicament, giving insightful accounts of how the Cameroun Republic hijacked the Southern Cameroons and is *holding its citizens under colonial bondage.* The insights include details of the stratagems resorted to by La République du Cameroon to exact submission to its annexation of the Southern Cameroons and to conceal this crime from outside censure.[168] It is thus clear that Southern Cameroonsians are oppressed or suppressed. International law has to therefore apply, making the right to self-determination for them one that cannot be held back by any amount of arms or legal jargons because, in addition, the apt conclusion from all the investigation into this inalienable right is that "If self-determination has a future as a legal rule beyond decolonisation, it will not be as a general rule in favour of representative democracy, still less a widespread right to secession. It may appear, though, *as a justification for action against governments of States which wholly disregard the basic interests of their people.*"[169]

It cannot be overemphasized that the basic interests of Southern Cameroonsians, as a people, have been widely, if not entirely, neglected by and in the Republic of Cameroon. In the words of SCFAQ (Question 13),

> The Southern Cameroons provides close to 70% of the Gross Domestic Product (GDP) of Cameroon but gets less than 3% in return in

168 http://www.langaa-rpcig.net/Imperialistic-Politics-in-Cameroun.html [last visited in March 2011] (emphasis added).

169 C. Warbrick, "Book Review of *Self-Determination in Law and Practice* by M. Pomerance" 32 *International and Comparative Law Quarterly* (1983), 542 at 542 (emphasis added).

infrastructural and other developmental investment. Industrial and commercial development is practically non-existent in the Southern Cameroons. All enterprises of importance to Southern Cameroons like POWERCAM, Cameroon Bank and the Produce Marketing Board (to name just a few) have either been run to bankruptcy or liquidated by Cameroonians of La Republique du Cameroun origin. Commerce has been diverted from formerly vibrant sea and river ports like Victoria, Tiko and Mamfe to ports in La Republique du Cameroun, leaving these former commercial centers to wallow in ruin. The development of communication infrastructure in the Southern Cameroons is practically zero. There are no roads linking major towns like Kumba, Mamfe and Bamenda. A Southern Cameroons province like North West has only 25 km of tarred roads to link its main city to a town in La Republique du Cameroun. Even the Southern Cameroons division of Ndian that produces the oil has been completely isolated and neglected. Ndian is not accessible by any good all-year round motorable roads despite its agricultural and oil wealth that is siphoned by sea for the development of La Republique du Cameroun. There are practically no functional airports in the Southern Cameroons despite the fact that prior to 1972, the Southern Cameroons had the Cameroon Air Transport Administration with functional airports in Bali/Bamenda, Mamfe and Tiko. No energy resources have been developed in the Southern Cameroons despite the hydro-electric energy potential of waterfalls like Menchum. The tele-communication service in all towns of the Southern Cameroons is most unreliable, and whenever service is available it has to be rooted [sic] through a town in La Republique du Cameroun. Even mass media services like radio Bamenda and Buea have to be boosted from towns in La Republique du Cameroun. The Southern Cameroons has no television station to serve her citizens. All of this is not just neglect, it is abandonment.

It can thus be easily visualized that all what the Cameroonian authorities are saying in regard of the doctrines of self-determination, of federalism and of secession are only their usual confusioncracy tales meant to frighten ignorant (because miseducated) Cameroonians away from democracy and thus perpetuate the dictatorship. The sole purpose of brandishing 'national unity' is to confuse and therefore oppress without being branded in the West as "oppressor" and they would seem to easily do so because of the funny theories of the myriad of (English-speaking) sycophants being called *intellectuals in politics* that they have comfortably surrounded themselves with.

There are several other swaying factors that also buttress the entitlement of not only Southern Cameroonsians but Cameroonians generally (I am now talking more of the preferred ten-state federal solution to human rights protection for all in Africa) to the right to self-determination, which is not only a universal right but is also clearly embodied in, and guaranteed by, the African Charter on Human and People's Rights. Cameroonians are clearly entitled to this right as is evident from the very elaborate analysis of the right to self-determination in the context of this African Charter by El Obaid (1996: 248-295), a McGill University professor of human rights law. As some recent studies clearly indicate, Eritrea and Ethiopia are the only member states of the defunct OAU that have, as of May 1998, not ratified this African Charter.[170] Cameroon, having ratified this instrument to which it adheres,[171] the African Charter has become part and parcel of Cameroon law. In interpreting article 1 of Cameroon's 1961 Federal Constitution which talks of "attachment to the Universal Declaration of Human Rights etc.," Enonchong has ably argued that the entire picture of the Constitution cannot be properly assessed without taking into consideration every provision both of the Universal Declaration of Human Rights and the United Nations Charter because each of these instruments has become an integral part of the Cameroon basic law.[172] Similarly, it has been strenuously theorized, for the people of the oil-producing communities in the Nigerian Delta, that the right to a clean environment, currently regarded as 'soft' law at the international level, can only be fully realized in public law, against the backdrop of sustainable development because this right was aptly made in 1981 by the African Charter on Human and People's Rights to which Nigeria is not only a party, but has incorporated into her corpus juris by the African Charter

[170] See Chili Anselm Odinkalu and Camilla Christensen, "The African Commission on Human Rights: The Development of its Non-State Communication Procedures" 20:2 *Human Rights Quarterly* (May 1998), 235 at 235 n.4.

[171] See *Décret N° 87/1910 du 29 décembre 1987 ratifiant la Charte Africaine des droits de l'homme et des peuples.*

[172] Enonchong (1967: 88). See also Franz Viljoen, "Application of the African Charter on Human and Peoples' Rights by Domestic Courts in Africa" 43 *Journal of African Law* (1999), 1-17.

(Ratification and Enforcement) Act, 1983.[173]

What is even more important is the fact that Cameroon's attachment to international human rights law is not sanctioned only by the preamble that most of Francophone Africa is still labouring to recognize as part and parcel of the enforceable constitution (see Pougoué and Kamto, 1990 ; and Verhelst, 1971). In Cameroon now, by article 45 of the 1996 Constitution, "Duly approved or ratified treaties and international agreements shall, following their publication, *override national laws*" including even the 1996 Constitution itself. The proviso in this article 45 "that the other party [or parties] implements [or implement] the said treaty or agreement" has no effect of stopping this overriding of Cameroon's inhumane laws and constitutions by the ratified treaties and agreements (especially where there is inconsistency between them).

Other nations of the international community, parties to these important conventions, have already implemented them. It is now left to them (through their common forum, the United Nations or OAU, now African Union) to see to it that Cameroon actually adheres to its international commitments and immediately stop the massive killing of innocent people whose only crime is their determination to exercise their legitimate rights. Double standards have to be put aside because the Libyan murdered president is not the only one 'murdering innocent citizens'. And some of those countries that spearheaded the attack on Khadafy (France, to be specific and in calling a spade a spade) are also the ones overseeing the 'Rwanda-style' genocide that is coolly taking place in Cameroon. The international community had better wake up now. Or must Southern Cameroonsians/Cameroonians have to actually begin fighting fire with fire before the UN *et al* can realize just how serious the human rights situation in this West-Central African country has escalated?

Southern Cameroonsians would however seem to think that the force of argument, rather than the argument of force, has to be the favoured rule. The willingness of Southern Cameroonsians to do everything in their power to

---

[173] Patrick D. Okonmah, "Right to a Clean Environment: The Case for the People of the Oil-Producing Communities in the Nigerian Delta" 41:1 *Journal of African Law* (1997), 43 at 43. See also Tom G. Svensson, "Right to Self-Determination: A Basic Human Right Concerning Cultural Survival. The Case for the Sani and the Scandinavian State" in Abdullahi An-Na'im, ed., *Human Rights in Cross-Cultural Perspectives: A Quest for Consensus* (Philadelphia: University of Pennsylvania Press, 1992), 363-384.

negotiate and peacefully resolve their current conflict with La République du Cameroun is couched in their slogan: "The force of argument, not the argument of force". Do their overall arguments really have any force (the way they are put)? Is that not also a capitulation from the use of force on their part? "This however does not imply", SCFAQ (question 11) has pointed out, "that the Southern Cameroons will not defend herself if attacked. It only guarantees that the Southern Cameroons shall never be the aggressor in this brotherly squabble." Is this not a bundle of nonsense that clearly tells the oppressor to go ahead and continue oppressing because of the 'guarantee' of inaction on the part of the oppressed? Just how many times, and for how long, must the attack be before the defence starts? Does this standpoint show the resolve and fighting spirit that some experts (cited in Fossungu, 2013: 44) say diplomats want to see before placing their careers on the line for a cause? Is the employment of the 'the force of argument' with someone who only knows the 'argument of force' a sensible and practical approach in this matter?

Concluding Observation

While some critics would be lauding Southern Cameroonsians/Cameroonians for attempting to arrive at a solution without (un)necessary bloodshed, others (the majority) will take this same fact as evidence that they are not as determined to have their independence just like other oppressed 'peoples' that have done so before them. The history of independence dictates that, if it has to be independence, it is snatched or paid for with the hard currency of one's blood; it is not 'granted' or negotiated. The crux of the matter is so overwhelmingly on Cameroonians' side to the extent that some human rights activists like Newman (1968: xii) are now simply stupefied by their failure to seize the moment, first wondering silently ('This is, no doubt, *The Distemper of Our Times*') before turning angrily on Cameroonians with "Has our good luck, taken for granted for so long, run out? Can't we just forget about the politicians and get on with our lives? Oh God!" If a Canadian is saying this, then their case is surely one that would put anyone off.

Americans who are said to believe so much in the written Word and the "[hot] pursuit of happiness"[174] must take this Canadian's words to be, above all, an intimation to Bjornson's (1991: 162) "blind[]... Cameroonians who assured themselves of wealth and status by collaborating in the European exploitation of Africa" that (as Le Vine puts it) there is simply no happiness and freedom for a people who negotiate independence rather than buy it with the currency of their own blood.[175] This strong independence message, according to Mirkine-Guetzévitch and Prélot (1950: viii), was also forcefully delivered to *La France libre* in 1944: "*la liberté appartient à ceux qui ont le courage de la conquérir et de la défendre après qu'ils l'ont conquise.*" Not comprehending this independence message could be the singular explication why Africa's 'Paradise on Earth' has not yet arrived in the Hinge of Africa.

To summarize those experts' counsel to Southern Cameroonsians particularly and Cameroonians generally, there comes a time when forceful argument has to simply give way to the force argument. It does not make any sense for Southern Cameroonsians to go on forever babying the authorities of La République du Cameroun in an endless attempt to build a country in which they simply don't exist or matter. Southern Cameroonsians, in exercising their right to self-determination by actually seceding, would be violating no laws/constitutions of Cameroon because all its constitutions, including the latest one in 1996, have affirmed the country's unwavering attachment to the various international conventions and treaties that guarantee them this right. Since 1996 onward, "We, the People of Cameroon," these (unnecessarily?) myth-consuming proud Africans would tell anyone who is interested in listening, "Declare that the human person, without distinction as to race, religion, sex or belief, possesses inalienable and sacred rights; Affirm our attachment to the fundamental freedoms enshrined in the Universal Declaration of Human Rights, the Charter of the United Nations and The African Charter on Human and People's Rights, and all duly ratified international conventions relating thereto, in particular, to the following principles:...." This is the ranting of the 1996 Constitution's

---

[174] A.C. Cairns, "A Tribute to Donald V. Smiley" in R.L. Watts and D.M. Brown, eds., *Canada: The State of the Federation 1990* (Kingston, Ontario: Institute of Intergovernmental Relations, 1990) at viii. This Idea of the Preamble of the American Constitution seems to have gone so much into the lawyers' head that it is now a negative on the happiness of the masses. See Reno (1994: 8); and Williams (1987: 401 & generally).

[175] Victor T. Le Vine, "Political-Cultural Schizophrenia in Francophone Africa" in I.J. Mowoe and Richard Bjornson, eds., *Africa and the West: The Legacies of Empires* (New York: Greenwood Press, 1986), 159-173 at 169.

preamble; and the list goes on and on and on, enumerating all the human rights that exist so far in international human rights law lexicon. So where are the patriotism and sincerity on the part of these African leaders who are more than ready to unnecessarily spill the blood of their own citizens at the behest of a foreign power?

Chapter 4

Africa, Bicephalism, And Bicameralism: The Impossible Is Really Not Possible In Cameroon?

> Democracy is an attitude of mind towards the political process. It embodies certain values that are realizable through certain processes and institutions. Admittedly, when and where such processes and institutions are moribund, it becomes difficult to realize those values that have come to be associated with democracy. The death of institutions, the abolition of processes in and of themselves do not abolish democracy, it is the will of the people, that indefinable attitude of mind, that in the end will sustain democracy [Eleazu, 1977: 5-6].

Overview of Separation of Powers (Bicephalism And Bicameralism)

What is the precise meaning of bicephalism and of bicameralism in this African country called Cameroon? Bicameralism and bicephalism in Cameroon, like any other constitutional or political question hinging on separation of powers, are loaded with much confusion and manipulation – confusioncracy. Bicameralism and bicephalism are first and foremost forms of the principle of separation of powers, a doctrine about which experts like Fombad (2005) have advanced important democracy lessons such the one that opens this book. Parliament is not only supposed to represent people who, by virtue of distance and other contingencies, cannot themselves attend; but also the law-making or legislative organ, as distinguished from the executive and judicial organs.[176] The representation role and the membership incompatibilities of parliament in Cameroon are the sole concern of the second part of this Chapter. Through the discussion of these main concerns, it is shown that parliament as generally understood does not

[176] For further discussion on the development of parliament and the splitting of these roles, see G.P. Bodet, ed., *Early English Parliaments: High Courts, Royal Councils, or Representative Assemblies?* (Boston: D.C. Heath and Company, 1968); Laski (1950: 93-138); and Loewenstein (1967: 27-34).

exist in Cameroon. Therefore, the legislation-making role cannot be attributed to it but to the President of the Republic (POR) who is the only organ or person performing all the functions normally assigned separately to the three traditional branches.

Both bicephalism and bicameralism are devices for furthering separation of powers. Bicephalism which is mostly, if not exclusively, tied to the parliamentary system of government, refers to a double-headed executive; that is, where two distinct personalities, each with particular competences, are respectively head of state and head of government. Bicameralism, on its own side, describes a situation where the parliament (or legislature) of a country or community consists of two chambers: an upper one known in most countries as the Senate and a lower one that is popularly called House of Commons or of Representatives. In Cameroon, according to article 14(1) of the 1996 Constitution, "Legislative power shall [henceforth] be exercised by the Parliament which shall comprise 2 (two) Houses: (a) The National Assembly; [and] (b) The Senate." There is therefore (1) a lower House called the National Assembly which, in this country as article 67(3) says, "shall exercise full [doubtful] legislative power and enjoy all [unknown] parliamentary prerogatives until [(2)] the Senate is set up."

The added words in square parenthesis are justified generally on the basis of the discussion in Chapter 3 above and specifically on article 14(6), namely, that "The conditions for the election of members of the National Assembly and the Senate, as well as the immunities, ineligibilities, incompatibilities, allowances and privileges of the members of parliament shall be determined by [a yet-to-be-enacted] law." It is the politics of the upper chamber (with its incomprehensible 'yet-to-be-determined' but 'already determined' elections modalities (examined below in the fourth Part) that is the principal focus of bicameralism since I would have already said something about the existing lower chamber in regard of the other important concepts of parliamentary representation (in the second Part) and bicephalism (in the third Part), all three instruments being the recent innovations in the confusion of powers in Cameroon.

From the already noted resemblances of the Cameroon set-up (in the Introduction of this book) to the well known governmental systems of the world, and the apparent multiplicity of separation of powers heads, the logical conclusion (of the 'quick jumpers') will be that democracy and separation of powers are overflowing in Cameroon. Using representation and parliamentary membership and other incompatibilities, it is argued that Cameroon is not any of the three governmental systems that it is attempting to pass for, not only because of the staggering absence of any separation of powers but also because even the French neo-presidential regime the Cameroon regime is known to slavishly copy from, has not been copied intact but has instead been very disastrously deformed in Cameroon – thus taking it very far away indeed from the parliamentary and congressional systems, both of which differ only in the (flexible versus rigid) manner of separating state powers. Cameroon's parliament then would seem to exist for no other reason than that of rubber-stamping and decorating executive acts. There is no political pluralism despite the semblance of many heads, organs, etc. in this country. Of course, there can still be effective pluralism without the traditional separation of the branches (executive, legislative and judicial) – traditional branches that some Indian experts on electoral studies like Shiv Lal (1976: 11) even stiffly question. As seen in Chapter 3 above, the apparently much more democratic and power-splitting African traditional system even had no such things as 'executive, legislative and judicial' branches; yet, the African king or chief could not just rule absolutely without effective reference to the effective input of the other recognized institutions and personalities.

Loewenstein (1967: ix) is of the stance that "to understand the essence of parliamentary government, it is imperative to grasp its historical origins, which date back to the High Middle ages in England." This system is founded upon flexible separation of powers (as opposed to the American congressional system of rigid separation) which allows for checks and balances while still making room for collaboration between the executive and legislative branches. These two systems of government that exist in North America have been elaborately distinguished by many experts, as cited and discussed by Fossungu (2010: 284-85). Essentially, it should be noted that the principle of separation of powers dominates in both systems. It is only a matter of how (not whether) power should be separated, that separates them. While one of them talks of flexible, the other preaches rigid, separation of powers. One can then visualize that, in especially the parliamentary system, what makes separation of powers really meaningful are, first, the traditional independent judicial branch and, second, effective pluralistic politics. In further putting Cameroon's camouflage of separation of powers and constitutionalism out there for all to see, the second part will examine the dialectics of representation in the context of the prime minister garbage over which selfish Anglophone bellyticians are fighting themselves; part three looks at bicephalism in the context of parliamentary and other incompatibilities; while part four handles the senate politics and elections.

The Prime Ministry, The Politics Of The Inside, And The Dialectics Of Parliamentary Representation And Legislation-Making

The best way to comprehend Anglophone contribution to propping up the dictatorship in Cameroon will be through reviewing the prime minister post in the context of parliamentary incompatibilities (in the next Part) together with this cataloguing here of the current mode of in-fighting over that post. As for the 'national' level, from Simon Achidi Achu (NW) the prime minister post went to Peter Mafany Musonge (SW), then to Ephraim Inoni (SW), and now to the country's long time ambassador to Canada, Philemon Yang (NW). At the centre of the issues here would be the NW/SW Divide which is bound to puzzle any right-thinking person because nothing important actually divides the people inhabiting these two Cameroonian (English-speaking) provinces or regions. It is only the confusion and manipulation of incompetent and selfish politicians that would put a wedge between them, as initiated by the *Endeley-Foncha 'Vote-Winning Pendulum'* noted in Chapter 2.

As the director of a professional teacher-training school (*École Normale Supérieure*) in Savannazone has lamented, "It puzzles my imagination that a problem between the Student Union president and some members of his executive should automatically involve the whole province of origin of the petitioner."[177] It must be stressed that the concerned students are not just "anybodies" or *les hommes de la rue* but teachers-in-training who are supposed to be teaching children the next day; also justifying the numerous critical theses from the numerous education critics discussed in Fossungu (2013: 175-189 especially). The ENS director did not fail to blame "the South West students of his institution for allowing themselves to be used by politicians 'to create tension, confusion and turmoil'."[178] The regrettable attitude of the

---

[177] See "ENS Bambili Crisis: Director Says SW Students Were Manipulated" *The Herald* N° 471 (11-15 June 1997), 1.

[178] *Id.*: 3. See also "PCC Accuses Politicians of Divisive Tendencies" *The Post* (8 May 1998), 3. PCC is Presbyterian Church in Cameroon.

English-speaking minority has meant that (1) people cannot be properly represented by those they vote for, because it largely prevents (2) the Quebec factor in Cameroon politics.

Cameroon's Regionalization and the Dialectics of Representation and Legislation-Making

The lamentable attitude of the English-speaking bellyticians is so pervasive and widespread that even the formation of political parties in Cameroon has not been spared of it; consequently preventing the rise of an effective opposition in the country.[179] The other name for the tendency is *c'est notre tour de bouffer* politics and/or 'politics of the inside'. This *notre tour* (for short) politics can be clearly seen in the demeanour of Southern Cameroonsian North-West parliamentarians of the ruling CPDM in 1996. In that year they attempted to block the passage of their ruling CPDM government bills solely in protest against President Biya's action of having, as they put it, transferred 'their prime minister post' from Simon Achidi Achu to a South-Westerner, Peter Mafany Musonge (also an Anglophone).[180] Why wouldn't they consider the post as "theirs" when, because of the secretive dealings in public affairs, the one-man appointive system was installed in Foumban, easily making all West Cameroon "prime ministers" until then of North-West origin (Foncha, Jua, Muna, Achu)?

On the other hand, one would also find the same attitude in the new prime minister's tribesmen (such as Njoh Litumbe) who had formed their own political parties (notably the Liberal Democratic Alliance – LDA – perhaps simply because the SDF was, and is still, headed by a North-Westerner) that "opposed" the ruling CPDM government. They would now not only abandon their own parties and join the *unchanged* CPDM party but would also go as far as categorically declaring that "good people are hardly found and when we find one like Musonge, we should all support him," concluding that "it would be a cardinal mistake for Cameroonians if they fail to support Musonge by voting against CPDM candidates."[181] So how is

---

[179] For elaborate critical discussion of the multipartism concept and law in Cameroon, see Fossungu (2013: chapter 3).

[180] See Chris Mbunwe, "North West Reaction to Achidi's Sacking" *Cameroon Post* (20-26 August 1996), 9.

[181] 'Litumbe Joins CPDM" *The Herald* (16-17 April 1997), 3. See also Konings and Nyamnjoh (1997: 227-28).

federalism (the SDF's version or whichever) that requires effective multipartism going to function in Cameroon or Africa with these kinds of bellyticians? Do you begin to clearly see what is lurking behind the 65-member Anglophone Standing Committee's confusioncratic federal draft that has all 'ethnic-eyes' only on the 'national cake'?

This *notre tour* politics is almost like the *pure party voting* (that is in contrast with *issue voting*) and has been defined as a vote for the candidate of the party with whom one identifies even if that vote is not in accord with one's issue inclination.[182] Pure party voting has subjugated parliament to the executive in two-party parliamentary countries like Britain, leading to what critics like St. John-Stevas (1968: 7, 9, 7 10) and Crossman (1972) have condemned as a Prime Ministerial Government. The difference though is that *notre tour* (unlike pure party voting) has no party with any program or issue it stands for, the only and sole concern being that of the belly and, hence, the other arm of 'politics of the inside': "We have reached a point in our political history," Waindim (1995) writes, "where the brain does the digestion, and does not prevent the inside from calling for more....why shouldn't our streets manifest a mode of life where hopes are gone? Any Hope?"

There is certainly no hope, in so far as this country's English-speaking people in particular continue to fight among themselves over the prime minister and other similar garbage rather than fight for their collective cultural and other human rights by, for instance, seeing to it that multipartism is real and effective. That is surely what will render the parliamentary (as any other) system unworkable in Cameroon, not the parliamentary system itself. When political parties exist for no other reason than bellytics, what is the guarantee that even the presidential system that people are acclaiming as the best system to prevent instability, would work and not become also nonsensical? It is mostly within the framework of the parliamentary government that parties like the Bloc Québécois (BQ) can exist and competently represent people who vote for them. Talking about the BQ smoothly carries us into a critical focus on the representation role of the National Assembly which essentially also exposes the 'separation-of-powers mind game' involved in the 1996 constitutional arrangements in Cameroon. Unlike the senators who will doubtfully represent their regions in article

---

[182] Norman H. Nie, Sydney Verba, and John R. Petrocik, *The Changing American Voter* (Harvard University Press, Cambridge, Mass., 1976) at 307.

20(1), each national assembler represents the entire nation in article 15(2). It is indeed paradoxical that each assembler represents the entire nation; but maybe that is precisely why they are called 'national assemblers' or 'rented jesters' and 'money-earners'. Representing the entire nation is not even actually what they individually appear to do in the 'Glass Palace' in Yaoundé.

As noted before, the Cameroon (Federal) Republic is itself so confusing and has confused so many people that it is simply difficult to clearly make a distinction between the intellectuals that are behind this confusion from those who are mere victims of the disorder. As I have also said before, many experts do seem to have easily become victim to the mystification in Cameroon because of their failure to pay the essential amount of consideration to non-constitutional aspects that have been found to be paramount, if not exclusive, in this mini-continent. All of these issues become more evident as this discussion proceeds, trying always to discover the meaning of parliament in the framework of separation of powers in Francophone Africa particularly. As long as there is no effective separation of powers – including effective multiparty politics – in place, a country's constitution is not proper by the mere fact that a spate of confusing and arbitrary laws has been enacted supposedly to give effect to its constitutional preamble's vague proclamation of liberty of association and paper multipartism. The constitution is not proper simply because there is a *chef d'état* and a *premier ministre* – having *chef du gouvernement* attached to it; because the real or important question from the experts (see Verhelst, 1971; Fombad, 2003; and others[183]) is: *Quelles sont vraiment les guaranties constitutionnelles relatives à l'individu face à la justice dans ce pays*? That is, are constitutional promises and values respected and fulfilled, with effective sanctions and remedies for breaking the rules?

Judicial and constitutional rhetoric would provide the most appropriate means to answering these questions. But it is obvious that judicial rhetoric in particular can hardly exist in the absence of real separation of powers and

---

183 See Anicet Abanda Atangana, "A la recherché d'un cadre juridique approprie pour une meilleure protection des droits des administrés au Cameroun" 105:818 *Penants: revue de droit des pays d'Afrique* (1995) 133-55; André Morel, "Le droit d'obtenir réparation en cas de violation des droits constitutionnels" 18 *Revue Juridique Thémis* (1984), 253; Marcelin Nguele Abanda, "De l'empéchement du président de la République au Cameroun"7:2 *African Journal of International and Comparative Law* (1995) 380-399; and Issa Abiabag, "Reflexions sur la deconcentration de l'executive camerounais après les révisions constitutionnelles des 9 juin 1975 et 29 juin 1979" 17-18 *Revue camerounasise de droit* (1979), 34-48.

judicial independence; and these are clearly absent in Cameroon, a so-called 'bilingual' country where one-sentence judgments from one-man unijural and unilingual courts are the rule (see Anyangwe, 1987; Ndi Chia, 1995a; and Bringer, 1981: 8-9). The many heads and organs, I will show in detail, are only mirages meant to deceive the bed-ridden man that he can actually ride a bicycle when he is let up. The bed-ridden man theory is the story today especially in Cameroon whose parliament has since 1959 simply become what a critic defines as "the motley crowd of political contractors and rented jesters... [who] approve in Yaounde in a place called the national assembly."[184] These critics are not at all exaggerating anything because a lot of other constitutional provisions and legal texts easily prop up their definition of this organ. Examples are *Loi N° 91/019 du 16 décembre 1991 abrégeant le mandat de l'Assemblée Nationale*; and especially Part IV (articles 25-36) of the 1996 Constitution, dealing with 'Relations Between the Executive and the Legislative Powers'. While some of these articles will be discussed later on, it is important to note that an appropriate understanding of these "relations between" the two "powers" cannot be divorced from the sessions of the latter, an issue that is necessary to discussed right away.

Sessions and Legislation-Making Role of the National Assembly

The "very sophisticated" constitutional separation of powers in Cameroon (as the Biya administration describes it) cannot be clearly understood without a deciphering of the provisions on the sessions of the National Assembly, the only chamber of the country's parliament that is actually in existence. The sessions of the National Assembly not only illustrate the legislation-making role of the "POR-parliament" but also clearly show how Cameroon has come to be what critics call government by decree. In Chapter 1 above I have discussed article 23 of the Federal Constitution that made the legislation-making role to belong *equally* to both the President of the Federal Republic (PFR) and the Federal National Assembly (FNA). The PFR seems not have been happy about this unequal equality which meant he was not as total as *pleins pouvoirs* permit or mean.

---

184 Ndi Chia (1995a). See also Bonny Kfua, "Legislators or Money Earners?" *The Herald* N° 474 (20-22 June 1997), 4; and Boniface Forbin, "National Assembly: A Case for Reduced Pay" *The Herald* N° 474 (20-22 June 1997), 4.

As Fossungu (2013: 94-95) has demonstrated in connection with the constitution and the educational domain, replacing the federal, the 1972 (Unitary) Constitution, therefore, in "allocating" legislation-making domains, listed the legislature's domains in article 20 and matters reserved for executive decrees in article 22. Its article 21 (being successor to Federal articles 23, 47, and 24) then says "the National Assembly may empower the President of the Republic [POR] to legislate by way of ordinance for a limited period and for given purposes" on the article-20 matters usually when the National Assembly is not in session. That 'limited period' and 'for given purposes' authorization, Fossungu concludes, has since become the usual method of law-making in Cameroon because National Assembly sessions were shortly thereafter made more infrequent by the POR through one of such article-21 *laws*.

Fossungu (1998: 7-13) has amply also shown that the effects of change in the frequency of the sessions of an organ (especially one that is normally meant to be supreme) are usually very debilitating on its overall duties, powers, stature and influence in the entire set-up. His theory in connection with the ICAO Assembly would also elucidate why, like those of 1984 and 1991, the current 1996 Constitution is itself an apt example of such article-21 laws: although the confusing claim in Cameroon is that such presidential legislation is called *ordonnance* – with *loi* being reserved for the enactment proper of the National Assembly in its article-20 domain (the equivalent of 1996 article 26(2)). It is simply not perceivable that proper governance can exist in such a system, one that is marked by the blinding lack of self-control and the persistent absence of institutional checks and balances, as a brief focus on both the ordinary and extraordinary sessions of the National Assembly would also show.

At the commencement of each legislative year, the National Assembly is to meet as of right in ordinary session under the conditions to be laid down by law (article 16(1)); holding each year three ordinary sessions, each lasting not more than thirty days; and electing its president and bureau members at the opening of its first ordinary session (article 16(2) (a)). During one of its sessions, it adopts the state budget; failing adoption of which "the President of the Republic shall be empowered [by himself, of course] to extend the previous budget by one twelfth until a new one is passed" (article 16(2) (b)). Why does this organ need to adopt the budget when the POR can still have his budget whether or not it is adopted? Voting of the national budget is normally one of the most effective means for parliament to exercise control over the executive branch. Therefore, the question of who does the empowerment of the president, and with what conditions, for the budget extension would become a very important one for the doctrine of separation of powers. From the discussion of the Federal Constitution in Chapter 1, it is, of course, no one else but the POR himself who empowers himself in Cameroon. The twisting is also seen in extraordinary sessions.

The National Assembly also meets in extraordinary session for not more than fifteen days on a specific agenda and does so at the request of the POR or of one-third of its members; with the session winding up as soon as the agenda for which it was convened has been exhausted (article 16(3)). Following Fossungu's (1998: 40-46) detailed critical discussion of the case of the ICAO Assembly as the 'Most Unsupreme of Supreme Organs in the United Nations System', the tenor of this entire Cameroonian provision does not make any sense of the concept of 'extraordinary session', being very indicative of the National Assembly being under the unbridled control of the POR. The story of frequency and duration of sessions would further cement it.

Regarding the important issue of the frequency of the sessions of Cameroon's National Assembly, we are told by article 14(3) that

> Both Houses [of Parliament] shall meet on the same dates: (a) in ordinary session during the months of June, November and March each year, when convened by the Bureau of the National Assembly and the Senate, after consultation with the President of the Republic; [and] (b) in extraordinary session, at the request of the President of the Republic or of one-third of the members of both Houses.

Quite apart from the vexed issue of curtailing the regularity of its sessions, Cameroon's modality of convening a 'supreme' organ (especially with the presidential consultation part) has also been frowned upon by Fossungu (1998: 37-40) for being unduly dependent upon the POR's discretion that there would seem to be nothing anyone else can do about it. And that would not be all that makes the Cameroon situation appalling.

Another practical and legalistic issue with the provision that needs to be pointed out is that, were Cameroon actually a 'democratic society' with a 'rule of law' that is not confusion, the National Assembly would not have been "meeting" since 1996 until the senate has been duly created and functional because the former cannot be meeting on any dates other than "the same dates" with and/or without the non-existent senate. That is exactly what an independent court of law would tell those 'representatives of the POR' at the Glass Palace, if citizens or even just one of them would bring up this matter. But that is not all that is wrong about this provision (article 14(3)) which was even violated just a few weeks after coming into force;[185] this violation being intimately tied to the historical and constitutional curtailment of the frequency of the sessions of this 'legislative' organ.

But the architect of the document seems to have heard about the criticism I have just levelled on the provision when the same 1996 Constitution violated sessions provision (article 14(3)) would then turn around with a 'however' that "the two Houses shall be convened simultaneously only if the business of the day concerns both of them." One of such instances of simultaneous convention concerns their being addressed by the POR (head of state and of government):

> The two Houses of Parliament shall meet in *congress* at the request of the President of the Republic in order to: be addressed by or receive a message from the President of the Republic; receive the oath of members of the Constitutional Council; [and] take a decision on a draft or proposed constitutional amendment. When Parliament meets in *congress*, the Bureau of the National Assembly shall preside over the proceedings [emphasis added].

There is certainly much to be said about these two houses meeting in *congress* in Cameroon. For instance, what would many Americans be thinking right now? Who owns the legislation-making role in Cameroon? What help would the courts get from the academia in order to, perhaps, rewrite the constitution themselves or ensure that it be correctly done by the parliament (as properly understood)? Such aid can clearly not be forthcoming from a legal academy and profession that cannot take firm and clear positions on

---

[185] For further discussion of this particular violation and the *advanced* reasons behind the 'illegal' move, see Pius Njawé, "Pour l'avenir" *Le Messager* N° 590 (3 mars 1997), 1; Boniface Forbin, "Biya Holds the Assembly to Ransom" *The Herald* N° 384 (18-19 November 1996), 4; and Randy Joe Sa'ah Azeng, "Government in Hide-and-Seek Game With Parliament" *The Herald* N° 383 (15-17 November 1996), 2.

important human rights and other constitutionalism issues. That duly explains why Fossungu (2013: 95) has posited that the same 1972 Constitution's articles 20-22 separation of powers mind-game strategy applies to date; hence, securing the disaster to the 1996 Constitution's local government. The confusioncratic modus operandi would thus have stayed on, but with more improved tactics this time in the 1996 Constitution's "relations" articles 26-28 – 'the more efficient running of a dictatorship', according to some critics.

It thus remains to be seen whether the unique-party National Assembly which has since the early 90s become "multi-party", will also actually become bicameral and move out of the hitherto unicameral single-party "cocoon" by emulating the British counterpart of earlier centuries. Until that emulation can be and has been done, critics like Eyinga (1996: 7) might be right in hotly objecting to any suggestion that it is not the POR but actually Parliament (as known elsewhere) that is enacting all the bad or oppressive laws that are suffocating the Cameroonian people.[186] Others have explained that all this happens primarily because the National Assembly is packed full with people who do not have the least idea of the law so as to enact laws suitable to the Cameroonian society. This organ has therefore simply been an object for decorating by rubber-stamping the POR's texts. Fohtung (1995) has then theorized that when the Cameroon People's demands for the usual and common type of democracy that is to be engrafted on federalism, seem to be overwhelming the neo-colonial regime,

> he [the POR] decides to revise the Satanic verses of the 1972 constitution through parliament....[and] furtively slipped the poisoned portion (constitution draft) to Parliament in one of the most risky gambles of his political life. In the last paragraph of his speech on the occasion he washed his hands off the matter and asked parliamentarians to take their responsibility. Yes, he had told them that they had the freedom to decide on what to do with the poison: dump it in the latrine or keep it and become partners in crime. Quite a gamble!

---

186 "*Non! Je ne crois pas que ces termes [allogènes et autochtones* in article 57(3)*] auraient figuré dans la Constitution si une Assemblée constituante avait élaboré ce texte [parce que] Un Camerounais doit pouvoir être chez lui partout dans son pays. Le régime actuel qui parle d'unité nationale n'en fait qu'un thème de discours.*"

The gamble being talked about is nowhere very poignantly brought out than in the portion of the "poison" that purportedly creates the upper chamber of the rubber-stamping parliament that is not even representative of anyone other than the POR.

Who Do National Assemblers Represent *Proprement Dire*?

The question of who is actually being represented by the assemblers of the Glass Palace also brings in doubts as to whether this National Assembly alone can be trusted to bring salvation to the bulk of Cameroonians who are desperately looking up to it.[187] Some critics even think it is unreasonable for the intellectuals generally, and those in the National Assembly in particular, to fold their hands and do nothing when the masses are suffering under the weight of discriminatory and unjust laws and other forms of injustices in Cameroon. According to the SDF Chairman, John Fru Ndi, for example, "We cannot be sitting [contented] in the National Assembly when those who elected us are behind the bars [merely for doing so]."[188]

It seems that most of Cameroon's parliamentarians cannot even raise issues of concern to their electorate: proving perhaps that they are not in 'The Glass Palace' because of these voters' decision. This is glaringly the case with the English-speaking parliamentarians who, on even attempting to do so, according to Ofege (1995), are always branded "regional, parochial, [and] partisan, as if they do not have a natural, legitimate right to fight for their interest." This fact alone must immediately also call into question Biya's (1986: 128) bragging on "major decentralization" that the 1996 Constitution is said to have instituted in article 1(2); through the creation of 'Regional and Local Authorities' in articles 55-62. Otherwise, it is inexplicable that

---

[187] As *L'Effort Camerounais* editorializes, "*il serait plus incensé, il nous semble, de taire de la misère de nos populations si désabusées, et dont l'imppressionnant silence pourrait un jour devenir une redoutable réponse à des injustices et frustrations longtemps accumulées. Notre auguste Assemblée de philosophes, de technocrates, d'hommes d'affaires, de pères et mères de familles, deviendra peut-être enfin une école où l'on s'attachera à dire la vérité, à enseigner et à pratiquer la justice, à construire l'unité nationale, à rechercher la paix et le bien commun.*" L'Effort Editorial, "Majorité honnête, opposition digne" *L'Effort Camerounais* N° 73 (1070) (28 juin-11 juillet 1997), 1. See also Nicolas Amayena, "Les députés SDF à l'école des pratiques parlementaires" *Cameroon Tribune* N° 6574- N° 2853 (8 avril-April 8, 1998), 5.

[188] Peter Ngea Beng, "SDF in Parliament! Fru Ndi Says Party's 43 Deputies Will Cause Earthquake: Schedules First Confrontation with Oben Ashu" *The Herald* N° 473 (18-19 June 1997), 1 at 3.

'Anglophone' parliamentarians (if they are actually the people's representatives) should not be able, for instance, to freely engage in the discussion of the "Anglophone Problem" (their demands for protection through federalism) in the country's own parliament without being branded regional, parochial, and partisan.

Could it be because, by article 15(2), each national assembler must represent the entire nation? Granted that this is the reason, it does not still make any sense for a host of reasons, the most important of which is that each of them is not normally elected by the entire nation but by the individual districts they run in. Again, even accepting that 'entire nation' argument, does the Anglophone community form part of that entirety or not? The 'Problem' is thus one that, among other things, hinges on the preservation of group identity and culture against assimilation and has led to Fossungu's (2013: xi-xii) strenuous argument that Cameroon national culture cannot be a national culture without embodying the distinct culture of the English-speaking minority, the cautious inclusion of which necessitates effective federalism or decentralization; and that anything else is nothing but deliberate confusion of assimilation for multiculturalism, a confusion that is heavily tied to the country's camouflaged independence. If the Anglophone community does form part of the whole, as it obviously does, why then can the entire assembly not engage in the discussion of the problems? The answer clearly points to the fact that the 'Glace Palacers' are not there representing anyone but their stomachs.

The national assemblers would not even be representing anyone (except perhaps the POR) if they cannot be regional. There is no sense in the major decentralization that is said to be epitomized by the 'Regional…Authorities' when being regional is "subversive"; and neither is there any acceptable meaning to the much-talked-of sense of participation of the people. The Bloc Québécois (BQ), for instance, is in the Parliament in Ottawa for no other reason than the interest of the Province of Quebec and even ultimately to take that province out of Canada. But no Canadian government is calling that parochialism etc. simply because the country is democratic. Moreover, it is not the government in Ottawa that 'legalized' the BQ but they are in Parliament Hill because they could organize themselves and win the required number of seats to become a national party, notwithstanding that all their seats are concentrated only in Quebec. Could Cameroonians generally learn anything here from my recommending the parliamentary (rather than the presidential) system for Cameroon? Furthermore, whatever the BQ (whose provincial version is the PQ, Parti Québécois) brings about will be the wishes of the people who voted the BQ/PQ and the outing of Quebec from Canada (if it does happen at all), it appears from the ongoing debates,[189] will be effected within a proper constitutional set up and known rules and conventions: all these under the umpiring role of the independent judiciary, as already seen in *Reference re Secession of Quebec* in Chapters 1 and 3. All this is very indicative of the fact that Parliament in Canada is the representative of the people.

On the contrary, Cameroon's parliament is not representative of the people but of the POR, with the parliamentarians themselves openly saying so. Understandably enough, being told how Cameroon's parliament was going to do this and that, Nantang Jua could not but retort:

> What Parliament would this be? Do you remember that in one broadcast of Cameroon Calling, one Member of Parliament [John Nformi Tatah from Njinikom in the North West Province], and an honourable one indeed, defined the role of the MP as the representative of the Head of State in his constituency! This being the case, I doubt that these same Parliamentarians would now begin to take the interests of the people into consideration.[190]

The Prime Minister Post and the Quebec Analogy

Democracy cannot implant itself in Cameroon until its democrats lose their ignorance. Paul Biya seems to know (and he must be duly given credit for this knowledge) that he is dealing with Laski's (1950: 323) ignorant democrats. Otherwise there would not be the NW-SW wrangling over the PM post with no real attributes to it. This far it is important to historically

---

[189] See Pierre-Elliott Trudeau, *Le Fédéralisme et la Société canadienne-française* (Montréal: Éditions HMHC, 1967) ; and Allan Hutchinson, Suzanne Lalonde, and Patrick Monahan: "The Significance and Implications of the Supreme Court's Decision in *Re: Secession of Quebec*/La portée et l'impact de la décision de la Cour suprême dans l'affaire du *Renvoi sur la Sécession du Québec*" in Joint Seminar/Séminaire Conjoint by Osgoode Hall Law School of York University and Faculté de Droit de l'Université de Montréal held at Université de Montréal on Monday December 7, 1998.

[190] Ndi Chia (1995b); and Nantang Jua, "Small Is Not Always Beautiful: A Case Study of the Njinikom Area Development Association" 11:3 *Nordic Journal of African Studies* (2002), 336-358 at 341.

situate the prime minister post that is at the centre of the so-called NW/SW Divide before seeing what to make of the Quebec analogy.

1. History of the PM Post in Cameroon

Like Britain and Canada, Germany also has a parliamentary form of government having a divided executive. The German president, provided for in the Basic Law (Chapter V: articles 54-61), is a figurehead who is indirectly elected and endowed with ceremonial powers exclusively. The chancellor is the true chief executive; a person receives this office in the same way that the British Prime Minister does – by being leader of the majority party in the lower house (the *Bundestag*).[191] If no party enjoys an absolute majority, as has often been the case in Germany, the leader of the majority party in the ruling coalition becomes the chancellor (Magstadt, 1991: 111; Kommers, 1985: 239). The question to be posed is: What is the value of having a prime minister in the set up of Francophone Africa (with Cameroon as case study), when s/he would not be clothed with the attributes of that office?

It is as if he was responding directly to the question when Blondel (1985: 167 & 166) tersely noted (as if having Cameroon specifically in mind) that in African and Asian states, "especially where the legitimacy of the regime is somewhat in question," the French "dual arrangements have become popular." But this popularity, he concludes at page 166, only has a place in Francophone Africa after having ensured that "the prime minister has a position which is… unlike that of the French prime minister." Etinge (1991: 6) would be more helpful to the strangers to advanced democracy by avoiding generalizations about the Third World, and specifically telling them that Biya's re-introduction of the suppressed prime minister post in the early 90s is "only a desperate effort of an uninspiring government pretending to the people that it is open to dialogue [because] The new deal government of President BIYA has failed very colossally to admit and acknowledge the importance of public opinion. The chaos, the holocaust that visited this nation only climax to ineffective leadership saddled with a corrupt

[191] For discussion of 'le premier ministre britanique', see Laski (1950: 145-156) and James Simon, *British Cabinet Government* (London; New York: Routledge, 1992). An interesting discussion of the post in federal polities is Patrick Weller's "Federalism and the Office of Prime Minister" in Hodgins *et al*, eds., *Federalism in Canada and Australia: Historical Perspectives, 1920-1988* (Peterborough, Ontario: Frost Centre for Canadian Heritage and Development Studies, 1989), 147-57.

administration which has elements of bent minds" (capitals as in original). The corrupt nature of the Cameroon administration is so limitless that even widely known and long established governmental principles must also be corrupted or bent.

The story of the prime minster post in Francophone Africa has therefore always been that of 'piston' or shield used by illegitimate governments to fence off any democratic wind of change. Using the so-called Foumban Constitutional Conference as pretext, Amadou Ahidjo then transformed himself overnight from that puppet post into the automatic PFR of Cameroon. The post was puppet because Tixier (1974: 16) clearly indicates that all "executive power was still held by the [French] High Commissioner who was directly responsible to the French Government." According to the accounts of Ahidjo's wife, Amadou Ahidjo was desirous of still ruling in retirement/resignation through "the docile Biya," so he had to hastily amend his constitution to make his prime minister (Biya) his constitutional successor before retiring.[192] Therefore, on 6 November 1982 Biya, who since 1975 was prime minister, became president "*en vertu de la Constitution (amendement du 29 juin 1979).*"[193] Biya then quickly abolished the prime minster post which had, in the meantime, been taken up from him by Ahidjo's fellow clansman (Bouba Bello Maigari – until then thought by many to be the natural heir to Ahidjo).

Why did Biya reintroduce the post in the early 90s? Was it not simply to fence off "precipitated multipartism" that was championed by Anglophones, by way of the SDF? Biya reintroduced the post in 1990 when the Demon of *le multipartisme précipité* began staging its return.[194] The whole idea was to use the highly respected Northern Moslem politician, Sadou Hayatou, to play the people's pluralism wishes off. When stopping 'paper' multipartism did not quite work, the home to those parties, the National Assembly (until then "The Anglophone Presidency"), could then not be trusted in the hands of

---

192 See "Confidences: Germaine Ahidjo à coeur ouvert à Honoré De Sumo" *La Nouvelle Expression* N° 319 (28 juin 1996), 1 & 12.

193 *See* 'Histoire du Cameroun', <www.camnet.cm/celcom/histoire/histoire>, visited in March 2011.

194 For details of which, see Barry B. Fohtung, "Parliamentary History in Cameroon 4: The Return of Pluralism I" *The Herald* (23-24 April 1997), 6; Boh (1991); and M.M. Mensah-Gbadago, "9 Years of Political Transition: From Ahidjo to Biya and the Hayatou Connection – How Far Have We Moved?" *Le Messager* **Special Political Issue** (6 June 1991) 1.

the 'Anglos'. Is that not precisely why this S.T. Muna's long time 'Anglophone Presidency' (National Assembly) had to be substituted with the prime ministry? Before it became the new 'Anglophone Presidency', the prime minster was the constitutional successor of or to the president. Why is the prime minister no longer the president's successor, now that it is an Anglophone? Is it because Anglophones are considered by the Biya regime to be "the enemies in the house"[195]? Rather than be demanding answers to questions like these, these 'Anglo-fools' would only be fighting themselves over the prime minister garbage. The existence of a prime minister in Cameroon changes nothing because the PM has no attributes and powers of his own.[196] This really makes the Quebec analogy predicated on that post very vexatious.

2. The Quebec Analogy: Making Sense?

All the NW/SW Divide trash in Cameroon would give a lot of force to Stark's (1976: 441) thesis that "An analogy which suggests that West Cameroon is the 'Quebec of Cameroon' has limited valued." Such an unhelpful analogy has been made by the author of "A Quiet Revolution", who would solely be harping on the so-called Anglophone *infiltration* into the reins of power in Cameroon with the appointment of one of them as the president's P.M.[197] It would appear, from the very brief discussion of the prime ministry here, to be abusing Quebec's splendid Quiet Revolution[198]

---

[195] J.S. Dinga, "What Cameroon for the Future?" *The Herald* (30 June -1 July 1997), 4; and Konings (1997: 307, quoting Foncha's reasons for his resignation from the CPDM vice-president post).

[196] "Is Musonge [the P.M.] the right person to carry out this fight [against corruption]? I don't personally think so... [because ministers] know that the P.M. cannot sack any of them and this is very true." Ayuk Henry Oben, "Fight Against Corruption: Biya and Musonge Should Apologise" *The Herald* N° 585 (18-19 March 1998), 10. See also Cameroon Post Editorial, "If Musonge Were Head of Gov't" *Cameroon Post* N° 0028 (8-14 October 1996), 2; Mavice Ambeno, "Prime Minister Musonge's Appointment: Praising the Unproductive Servant" *The Herald* N° 386 (22-24 November 1996), 4; Herald Editorial, "Musonge Now to Take Charge?" *The Herald* N° 559 (16-18 January 1998), 4; and Bate Besong, "From Achidi Achu to Peter Mafany Musonge: Will It Be Another Hen-Pecked Premiership[?]" *Cameroon Post* N° 0028 (8-14 October 1996), 9.

[197] See "A Quiet Revolution" *West Africa* (27 April 1992), 709.

[198] For more on the Quebec revolution, *see* Yvan Lalonde and Claude Corbo, *Le rouge et le blue. Une anthologie de la pensée politique au Québec de la Conquête à la Révolution tranquille* (Les Presses de l'Université de Montréal, Montréal, 1999); William Johnson, *A Canadian*

to describe the Cameroonian farce as such. Quebec within Canada clearly cannot be reasonably made analogous to 'Anglophone Cameroon' within Cameroon or vice versa. No one who has attended the lectures of Driedger in the field of 'The Quest for Ethnic Rights'[199] could even buy for free the Cameroonian Anglophone "revolution" predicated on the P.M. post because it is only reminiscent of Michel Crozier's *La Société bloquée*. That is, as Roy Pierce (cited in Fossungu, 2010: 282) puts it, a society whose vitality and capacity for change were very seriously obstructed by outmoded political institutions and excessive conservatism masquerading as progressive egalitarianism. This masquerade is in the form of the so-called separation of powers (typified by multipartism and bicephalism) that is being claimed to be overflowing in Cameroon, especially with the given impression that there are two executive heads, one being called the prime minister – over whose designation 'Anglo-fools' fight themselves while the ship of assimilation dangerously but smoothly drifts on.

It is simply not clear what the English-speaking bellyticians in question do find particularly wrong in the POR appointing any other person or a goat to the post: especially when the power of appointment (about which said 'Anglo-fools' find nothing wrong) is solely the appointer's discretion. The power to appoint the prime minister is solely the POR's discretion; and I do maintain this position in spite of this confusioncratic claim that is found on the internet: *"Avril 1991: Création du poste de Premier Ministre, Chef du Gouvernement (issu de la majorité parlementaire), conformement à la loi portant révision constitutionnelle du 23 avril 1991"*[200] The reality is simply that the POR of Cameroon appoints whomsoever he wants to appoint to this garbage with no conditions attached; whether or not the appointed person or animal is a parliamentarian (a point reinforced later on).

It is very doubtful, moreover, that the foregoing actions from both Anglophone sides would have been witnessed had Mr. Simon Achidi Achu been replaced by a Francophone. There would just have been what Boh

---

Myth: Quebec, Between Canada and the Illusion of Utopia (Montreal: R. Davies, 1994) at 19-34; and Jeremy Webber, *Reimaging Canada: Language, Culture, Community, and the Canadian Constitution* (McGill-Queen's University Press, Kingston & Montreal, 1994) at 92-120.

[199] See Leo Driedger, *The Ethnic Factor: Identity in Diversity* (Toronto: McGraw-Hill, 1989), chapter12.

[200] See 'Histoire du Cameroun', www.camnet.cm/celcom/histoire/histoire.htm, visited on 13 June 2011 (underlining added).

(1991) calls 'the usual sonorous clapping' from all angles. Yet, a lot of people in this country will very easily 'cry you a river' about the Anglophones' status and Francophone oppression of them. Who is actually oppressing whom in this illustrative NW/SW scenario that could be the real invisible hand of the SDF federation project? Who will really be oppressing Anglophones in the new SDF federation? A lot of critics of the Anglophone self-destructive attitude do think they have done enough investigation that has enabled them to have the answer. "Investigation," according to one of them, "has led me to the conclusion that most people are unaware of the real issues at stake and if they are, they have decided to bury them underneath the carpet. So then why [have all] the hoopla? Why can something be wrong in one situation and right in another? Do rules and regulations [have to] apply to people depending on their province of origin?"[201] Do rules and regulations also have to apply to people depending on the ethnic group of their predecessors? Indeed, as Mewett has also lamented, "to be told that a situation is admissible for one purpose but not for another….[is] something I very much doubt they can understand."[202] Is it really a case of comprehending but burying the issues underneath the carpet (confusion and manipulation) or that of pure ignorance of the real issues at stake? It seems to be more of the former as could be seen in the employment of 'four-state federation' by and through the Anglophone-led SDF to attain smooth and perfect complete sublimation (as seen in Chapter 2); or employing bicephalism to attain and camouflage more terrible concentration of powers.

Bicephalism and Parliamentary Membership and Other Incompatibilities

Parliament normally represents people who, due to the impracticability of all being present, send elected members to it. The people's representatives are to be known in Cameroon as 'national assemblers' in contradistinction to

---

201 Orock Ashu, "The University of Yaounde II and the NW SW Divide" *Cameroon Post* (11-18 December 1995), 2. See also Johnson Abachuku, "The Great Lesson that Anglophones Have Not Learnt" *The Herald* N° 300 (8-10 April 1996), 4; Michael A. Yanou, "The University of Buea Crisis: The Unspoken Truth and the Way Forward" *The Post* (February 2013); and Ernest L. Molua, "University of Buea: Unveilling the Real Truth and Grand-Plan for its Destabilization (Part I)" *The Entrepreneur Newspaper* (March 3, 2013).

202 Alan W. Mewett, "Editorial: Statements Admissible in Narrative" 38 *The Criminal Law Quarterly* (1996) 385-86 at 386.

the president's specially selected senators. Both groups constitute Cameroon's congress or parliament which critics say is neither a representative nor legislative organ and exists for no other reason than that of rubber-stamping executive acts. There is no political pluralism despite the semblance of many heads, organs, etc. in the country. What then is the use of the different heads, appellations, and organs? This question is even very apt as far as concerns the membership of Cameroon's parliament. The Cameroon National Assembly comprises 180 members (a number that may be modified by [the president's] law), elected by direct and secret universal suffrage for a five-year term of office (1996 Constitution, article 15(1)). But 'membership' as used in this book is not limited just to the one hundred and eighty national assemblers plus the 100 yet-to-come senators. It also applies to all persons and organs that effectively participate in the activities of the National Assembly (Parliament).

This somewhat 'wide' meaning given to membership here is important especially in regard of the host of the known[203] confusing incompatibilities of functions discussed below, as well as concerning the issue of who actually legislates in this country. Although the issues of this section cannot be easily dissociated, the dialectics of representation and legislation-making have already been surveyed above and I will here study mostly the membership incompatibilities. There appears to be a lot of 'membership' irregularities regarding Cameroon's parliament. The interesting thing, to begin with, is that Chapter II of Part III of the 1996 Constitution that is captioned 'The Senate' devotes one of its provisions talking lengthily about the National Assembly's agenda that "shall be drawn up by the Chairmen's conference" (article 23(1)), a Chairmen's conference which "shall be composed of Presidents of Parliamentary Groups, Chairmen of Committees and members of the Bureau of the Senate" (article 23(2)). It is not exactly clear why Chapter II is titled 'The Senate'. Illusion, illusion, illusion, and illusion are marked all over the scheme.

The illusory resemblances of the Cameroon set-up to some western

[203] A lot of them are not only confusing but also not yet known. For example, "The conditions for the election of member of the National Assembly and of the Senate, as well as the immunities, ineligibilities, *incompatibilities*, allowances and privileges of the members of Parliament shall be determined by [the president's] law." 1996 constitution, article 14(6) (emphasis added). But did not article 15(1) say national assemblers are elected 'by direct and secret universal suffrage'? What are these other conditions that must stay out of the constitution?

governmental systems have led the author of a certain "revised and updated Doctoral Dissertation presented to Georgetown University, Washington, D.C." (Enonchong, 1967: xi) to the thesis that "The Cameroon constitutional system is to all intents and purposes a hybrid between the French and American systems, insofar as the concept of the separation of powers is concerned" (Enonchong, 1967: 94-95). What is found in Cameroon is clearly not what occurs in France, not to mention the USA. France is already a hybrid between the USA and, say, Britain. With Cameroon now being a hybrid between another hybrid and the USA, it becomes almost impossible to correctly locate it. Of course, 'impossible' is clearly not possible in this country. Furthermore, I would not think it is even correct to talk of a child as the 'hybrid' of two parents of opposite sex whereas that child is just a clone (and a very nasty one moreover) of one of them. For instance, some experts like Ondoa (1996: 11) have been trying to know whether, by merely and blindly transplanting French institutions (as is largely the case with the1996 Constitution), Cameroon has at last been dotted with a stable and viable constitution. Has Cameroon by doing so "*enfin trouvé une constitution stable*?" Or is Cameroon really the hybrid of the two systems (French and US) as claimed?

For the "parliamentary" focus here, I will especially prefer to use the 1991 Constitution (especially its article 26 (*nouveau*)) all through because it fascinatingly captures what is scattered in various subsections of many other articles of the 1996 Constitution (especially its articles 33 and 34). It is my belief that this preferred employment can greatly facilitate comprehension of the Cameroonian Confusion-and-Oppression called advanced democracy. Genuine democrats will understand that only in an effective multiparty system can parliament/legislature be the sole legislation-making organ. Authentic multiparty politics is very essential for the parliamentary system; I talk only of this system here since there is this too much talk of a *chef-du-gouvernement* prime minister (which implies a non-executive head of state such as king/queen, governor-general, emperor, etc.) having access to parliament and participating in its debates. Is s/he a member of parliament? How about the incompatibilities of functions? To better respond, it is essential to see what other prime ministers or chancellors (having a president) are like. Germany and Britain have already been noted.

Bicephalism and its accompanying instruments (motion and vote) are only meaningful in an effective multiparty setting; a setting that has been nicely precluded in Africa's Cameroon, as already elaborately shown by Fossungu (2013: 130-140), by the one-party perpetuating law on multipartism (*Loi N° 90/056 du 19 décembre 1990 relative aux parties politiques*). No one will doubt that the existence of effective multiparty politics in the parliamentary system is graphical in the existence of rights such as freedom of expression, a right that permits its holders to freely criticize and make known their feelings to the government without being thrown into jail or killed, for example, by that government or anyone else. As an insightful analysis has suggested, Cameroon's 1996 Constitution truly cannot solve this country's human rights problems because it does not reflect the Cameroon people's wishes, having (as usual) been secretly drawn up and does still cloth the administration in place with excessive powers.[204] The authoritarian system is strengthened by the too many confusing laws that, in the POR's thinking, are a clear definition of democracy and its members' relationships.

One wonders if those relations are really clearly defined in Cameroon. It is not clear but it seems the too many laws are solely meant to properly define confusioncracy by concealing the absence of separation of powers; and, amusingly, the POR expects *all* Cameroonians to be very pleased with these many confusing, oppressive and incomplete laws that 'very clearly define relationships,' including incompatibilities in the functions of members of government. What would the experts all be thinking especially when the country's constitutions conspicuously talk of bicephalism, bicameralism, *congress*, incompatibilities of certain posts, etc.? It might be useful to trash out some of the confusion by first exposing the rules of incompatibilities; and then looking at membership incompatibilities in the constitutional council to see whether the case of the constitutional council makes the case for bicephalism.

The Prime Minister as Exposing the Rules of Incompatibilities

It is, of course, established practice (as embedded in article 14(5) of the 1996 Constitution) that no individual should be member of both houses of

---

204 "*Tout porterait à le penser, tant l'instabilité constitutionnelle des trente-six dernières années est remarquable.... L'avenir est en effet incertain. Elaboré dans un contexte de lassitude de l'indifférence des citoyens et formations politiques, la loi de 1996 attend d'être mise à l'épreuve des faits. Nul ne peut aujourd'hui en prévoir la fortune. Rien ne garantit son effectivité future, qui paraît subordonnée, non seulement à l'évolution du contexte politique, mais encore à la grande liberté qu'elle laisse aux dirigeants en place.*" Ondoa (1996: 11 & 14).

parliament (and that prohibits even the British Holy Trinity Lord Chancellor). Granted that the British Lord Chancellor is member of all three branches of government, he is clearly not a member of the Lower House (see Lord Hailsham, as discussed in Fossungu, 2010: 284). But what is the case with members of the executive such as the prime minister (one of the subjects of bicephalism)? This query is significant because the Cameroon Constitution in article 13 ordains that

> The office of member of Government and any office ranking as such shall be incompatible with that of [M]ember of Parliament, Chairman of the Executive or Assembly of a local or regional authority, leader of a national professional association, or with any other employment or professional activity.

This will make some Americans begin to feel that Cameroon is like their great country and, consequently, migrate to the 'advanced democracy', especially again as they would also find its enormous natural endowments very promoting of their capitalism.[205] But rushing to the alluring attractiveness and already in, these Americans will discover (too late!) that all that glitters is not gold; with one of such glittering things being bicephalism or dualism of executive heads; with Cameroon's 'glittering' even more than what an expert on comparative government (cited in Fossungu, 2010: 276) praises as the exceptional French *"unique dual executive"* which is clearly and effectively bicephal or "a divided executive", a sort of "built-in time bomb that seemed about to detonate." The confused and frustrated American then begins posing a lot of questions.

Squarely answering this bemused American's question on membership incompatibilities regarding the prime minister (if the translation is good enough), the unilingual 1991 Constitution states in its new article 26 that the POR promulgates the following law which has been adopted after deliberation by the National Assembly: … By the new article 26, the Prime Minister and other ministers, including secretaries of state, have access to the National Assembly and can participate in its debates…. Article 33 of the 1996 Constitution is the equivalent of this 1991 provision. Remember that

205 As Biya (1986: 27-28) would obviously have told them in bold print, "I can affirm that a great destiny awaits [you in] Cameroon" because of "the human and material potential of our country."

this is 1991 and forward (after legalization of paper multipartism in 1990); remember too that the POR's appointments (e.g., of the PM and other ministers, including the secretaries of state) are never vetted by anyone or organ. Are all these appointees not there in the National Assembly as the POR?

There would be no issue at all against this provision if Cameroon were parliamentary; in which case there would even be no use for any law specifically giving the prime minister and his cabinet access to the parliament (their natural home). It being otherwise in Cameroon, there are many questions the provision raises but the pressing one right now is: What about these ministers' own incompatibility as per the constitution's prohibition in article 13? The Cameroon executive branch is surely beyond its own laws; and especially its head, the POR who Fossungu (2010: 284) would say is like "[t]he ICAO President [who] would seem to be the negative form of Lord Hailsham's Holy Trinity Lord Chancellor… [because he] seems to have no House (or Organ) where he is not a member." The truth of Fossungu's analogy thesis can here be seen in the Constitutional Council (1996 Constitution, Part VII: articles 46-52) that also shows the uncomplicated way to twisted bicephalism.

Constitutional Council Case Making Case for Bicephalism?

Still in the realm of membership incompatibilities, the constitution indicates in article 51(5) that

> The duties of members of the Constitutional Council shall be incompatible with those of member of Government, of Member of Parliament or of the Supreme Court. Other incompatibilities and matters relating to the status of [its] members, namely obligations, immunities and privileges shall be laid down by law.

It looks like it was in trying to appreciate this stipulation specifically and the constitution generally that Fombad (2005: 303) questioned if it is really "a feature of the constitutional system, or it is merely an abstract philosophical inheritance that lacks both content and relevance to the realities of the country?" Fombad's query is apt because another provision of the same constitution (article 51(2)) makes present and former presidents (the current president, Biya, being the only one existing) "life members" of the

Constitutional Council. Why would a current president want to be 'a for life member' of a body that conducts presidential elections except for the fact that (as Fossungu, 2013: 131, says) he "is very desirous of preserving himself as life Emperor of the U.K. (Unconstitutional Kingdom-republic) of Cameroon"? It is the Constitutional Council that has exclusive and final jurisdiction on constitutional matters (article 46). What in a democracy (excepting the 'advanced') is not constitutional? And why is there still a 'supreme' court in Cameroon? It is also this council, as per article 48(1) that shall ensure the regularity of presidential elections, parliamentary elections and referendum operations, etc. proclaiming the results thereof. That being the case, why is there then another elections management body[206]? This arrangement would indeed seem to justify the 'ropeless Lilliputians' and 'retrogression' theories;[207] as well as elucidate numerous declarations on elections rigging.

The elections that are now being pinned to the chest in Cameroon appear to be only hoodwinking tools or "rackets" since they still clearly leave the 'governors' completely unburdened by public accountability. As some confused citizens like Keba have put it to this country's 'democrats without a democratic culture',

> They have disenfranchised us by not registering us. They have manipulated the electoral register, refused to issue cards to the few they registered, and finally refused proclaiming the results as they were. Mr. Chairman you said during the last rally in Bamenda that you will set the pace for new democracy in Africa and Mr. Biya too is setting the pace for his own sterile democracy. What was the need for this election when they

---

[206] For more on this body, ELECAM (formerly called ONEL), see Charles Manga Fombad, "Election Management Bodies in Africa: Cameroon's 'National Elections Observatory' in Perspectives" 3 *African Human Rights Law Journal* (2003), 25-51. As Ngwana (2009) has opined, "For the first time when the most important organ of our democracy, (ELECAM), is to be set up, President Paul Biya, knowing full[] well that this ELECAM was bound to fail, because he would not respect the laws setting up ELECAM, he appointed an Anglophone to head it [because] The failure of ELECAM would then be blamed on the Anglophones."

[207] See Peter Ateh-Afac Fossungu, "The Constitutional Council and the Ropeless Lilliputians" *The Herald* N° 682 (4-5 November 1998), 4; and Charles Manga Fombad, "The New Cameroonian Constitutional Council in a Comparative Perspective: Progress or Retrogression?" 42 *Journal of African Law* (1998), 172-86.

can't accept the verdict of the ballot box? [Cited in Fossungu, 2013: 70 n.69]

Deputy Kemajou (as seen in Chapter 1) could not then have been more visionary in 1959 with his prediction of what *pleins pouvoirs* would entail. Apart from refusing to 'accept the verdict of the ballot box', Kemajou's prediction of the redressing of electoral districts was done by President Ahidjo countless times (see Gardinier, 1963: 107; and Johnson, 1970: 242-243). The arbitrary redoing of electoral districts is still being done by President Biya: one of the best examples being the electoral code of the early 90s which was drawn up by the government in total disregard of the "paper opposition", an opposition which is clearly *en panne ab initio*. This arbitrary code required a circumscription in the predominantly Moslem northern provinces of the country (former President Ahidjo's region of origin) to have at least 73,000 inhabitants as against 47,000 in Sanagazone, Nyongzone, and Guinean-Savannazone, where Biya's CPDM seems to be well entrenched ("*dans le Centre, le Sud et l'Est, régions où le parti de Paul Biya est bien implanté*"[208]).

This general and quick survey of 'advanced democratic' electoral practices in Cameroon is also very essential to a good grasping of the particular case of the election of the 70 senators by IUS (indirect universal suffrage), discussed in the next Part of this Chapter. Until then, let's finish doing justice to the constitutional council's clean-and-clear road to twisted bicephalism, both of which organs raise many questions as usual. It is not logical – if there is any logic at all in Cameroon that does embrace, sleep all the time with, and define, illogicality – that the POR (who is a sure candidate in these elections) be member of the Constitutional Council. Second, since the POR himself is obviously a member of government (its head and brain for that matter); the question is also raised about the incompatibility of his functions in this Constitutional Council. This unsanctioned breach (like that of infringing the territorial integrity of Cameroon in Chapter 3) points

---

208 F. Soudan, "Cameroon: l'Opposition en panne" *Jeune Afrique* N° 1624 (20-26 février 1992), 9. See also The Herald Editorial, "Parliamentary Constituencies: Dangerous Gerrymandering" *The Herald* N° 337 (31 July-1 August 1996), 4; "Débat: Démocratie et transparence électoral en Afrique: le cas du Cameroun" *Le Messager* N° 587 (20 février 1997) 6-12; Asong Ndifor, "Legislative '97: SDF Cries Foul as Four Lists are Rejected" *The Herald* N° 446 (16-17 April 1997), 1 & 2; P. Poinsier Manyinga, "Vous avez dit transparence?" *Le Quotidien* N° 33 (29 juin 1996), 5; and E. Tasse, "Transparence ou hold-up électoral?" *Le Quotidien* N° 33 (29 juin 1996), 3.

unambiguously to the fact that the POR somewhat still stands above his own law as usual; making it hard to see how the "law is prevailing" here and how relations are clearly defined, as claimed under the rule of law and democratic society.

It can be argued for the regime that the POR is not a member of government. This theory is implicitly advanced by their always affixing '*Chef du Gouvernement*' after the president's P.M. – as if people do not know that a prime minister, if a real one, was head of government. So, goes the thesis, the POR is not the head of government. That too does not exclude the avalanche of questions. It is then inexplicable why the POR (and not the P.M.) appoints the 30% senators in article 20, as well as all the members of the Constitutional Council itself. It is also not then comprehensible what the POR is, and what the logical or explicable basis is for the POR being in the Constitutional Council. Is the POR there as a non-government presidential appointee of the POR? Cameroonians are well known to have topped the list of those who made a big mockery of Emperor Bokassa of neighbouring Central African Republic who crowned himself. Burkina Faso's President Blaise Compaoré also recently appointed himself as his own minister of armed forces, topped by the fact, again, that, as the Burkinabe POR, he is 'the supreme commander of the armed forces'. It is not clear if the Cameroonian POR's position in the constitutional council is any different from those two cases.

Affixing '*Chef du Gouvernement*' after the POR's prime minister does not fool anyone who understands that it is the POR who, while still "presid[ing] over the Council of Ministers" in article 10(1) (and not the prime minister), is also leader of the ruling CPDM party. The sure question now from the Written-Word loving Americans is, are political parties not also 'national professional associations' to also conflict with the prohibition in article 13? The best answer here could perhaps be that proffered by Fossungu; namely, that the Cameroonian authorities are quite aware of the plain fact that most, if not all, of the myriad of political parties that they have *silently* created (through the Parties Law) do not have any 'national' base, and are not at all headed by 'professional' politicians.[209]

---

[209] See Peter Ateh-Afac Fossungu, "Empty Certificates and Non-Professionals in Professionals' Job" *The Herald* N° 638 (27-28 July 1998), 4.

But that response, plausible as it is, does not eliminate the prime minster palaver because the making of the POR's Prime Minister (and not the government itself, which, in effect, is the POR) by the constitutional provisions the subject of "*une motion de censure*" and "*un vote de confiance*"[210] is of no effect since these instruments of control are not aimed at the government. Details on and the working of the motion of censure are furnished by Blondel (1985: 173-174) and Hogg (1996: 239-240) which portray that, as the Cameroonian president's prime minister does not appoint the government like other prime ministers, s/he cannot therefore, by tendering her or his resignation consequent on the *motion* or *vote*, be resigning as the government which exists *malgré lui*. A lengthy discussion of the collective ministerial responsibility that this constitution is attempting to pass for, is offered by Magstadt (1991: 91-92), Hogg (1996: 230-232), Tremblay (1993: 73-74 & 20-21), and Laski (1950: 157-166).

The inevitable conclusion then is that, absent confusion of powers, there is absolutely no way of justifying the utility (if usefulness must not be abused) of the prime ministry in Cameroon. The more especially as rather than innovate as expected of them (by emulating Prime Minister Walpole of Britain), successive prime ministers in Cameroon, in Moorhouse's (1977: 240) words, have simply behaved as "a monk [who] can[not] separate himself from what is ordained by the Rule of his order and perpetuated in the customary of his religious house." Moorhouse is not alone because the prime minister in Cameroon has also been aptly described by Boh (1991: 8) as "an overgrown 'Mass Boy' who besides the Priest, Biya, will never mature, [acting] like the messenger he is: unable to choose the message he carries and unwilling to demonstrate the intelligence we credit him with."

Because of these 'unlike-the-French-PM' characteristics, there is no likelihood in Cameroon of the "difficulties" that both Blondel (1985: 167) and Magstadt (1991: 102) have noted about the French system: namely, that of its presupposition of the president and parliament being of the same party whereas the election of both does not coincide. A Université de Yaoundé II lecturer (Ondoa, 1996: 13-14) has similarly pondered and raised the issue in the Cameroonian scene. Using the example of then President Mitterrand and Prime Minister Chirac, Ondoa (1996: 14) has noted the "*grand risque de tension que n'autorisent ni le radicalisme actuel des partis politiques ni la profonde déchirure de la*

---

[210] See 1991 Constitution, article 26 (*nouveau*); and 1996 Constitution, article 34.

société politique, ni la fragilité de la démocratie camerounaise." There can be no doubt that the said political radicalism in Cameroon (at the time) might represent a potential cause for concern in such an eventuality. But there appears to be no way the Cameroonian president can be obliged to appoint anyone but whomsoever he likes. Nothing in the constitutions and other laws, nor any known convention, obliges the president (like other presidents or kings/queens or governors-general) to appoint from the party or coalition thereof enjoying majority in the National Assembly. There are no criteria whatever. As all the texts on the issue can plainly show,[211] "The President of the Republic shall appoint the Prime Minister and, on the proposal of the latter, the other members of Government. He [president] shall define their duties... terminate their appointment… [and] preside over the Council of Ministers" (1996 Constitution, article 10 (1); and 1991 Constitution, article 9 (*nouveau*)). Two points to note here.

First, when the prime minister and the other ministers in Cameroon are appointed (as they often, if not always, are) at the same time, it is simply not known how and when the said proposal of the appointed P.M. could be or was made. Second, the likelihood of conflict clearly does not therefore exist. To emphasize again, there isn't anything that obliges the POR to appoint anyone but whosoever the POR desires, whether or not the appointed person is a member of parliament or even a human being. None of the appointees so far has ever been parliamentarian at the time of their appointment. (Is that not even the reason for a law giving him and other non-assembly ministers access to the National Assembly?) And the appointed P.M., to stay in the post, can never clash with his/her boss on whatever matter (see Delancey, 1989: 57). This point is sufficiently reflected in the fact that, very unlike the various other heads of government, the Cameroonian prime minister "shall be the [mere figure] Head of Government and shall direct its action" (1996 article 12(1)). This African Prime Minister does not formulate but simply "implement the policy of the Nation as defined by the President of the Republic" (articles 11 and 5). And it is the government – and not the POR who is the effective head of it – that

[211] See, in addition to the various constitutions already cited, *Décret N° 91/282 du 14 juin 1991 portant les attributions du Premier Ministre* [P.M. Decree]; *Décret N° 91/069 du 09 avril 1992 portant organisation du gouvernement* [Government Organization Decree]; and *Décret N° 92/070 du avril 1992 portant réorganisation de la Présidence de la République* [Presidency Reorganization Decree].

is "responsible to the National Assembly under the conditions and procedures provided for in Article 34 [which deals with motion of censure] below" (article 11).

The deformation here is clear enough because only the policy-defining organ or office must have to be responsible to Parliament regarding those policies, if the system has to be parliamentary or even semi-parliamentary at all. Failing this, the P.M. post must simply be scrapped. Otherwise, the entire system becomes merely a hoodwinking enterprise.[212] Being answerable to Parliament brings in the vote and censure instruments, as well as parliamentary procedure fortified by other offices, e.g., those of speaker and of senators. As these instruments and offices are purely absent or ineffective in the Cameroonian context, there is no other reason other than confusion of powers for using them in the constitutions and laws. This country's parliament exists merely for rubber-stamping the POR's acts.

This book consequently disagrees completely with the thesis from Cameroon's "Federal Counsel (**Procureur de la République**), representing the Federal Government in public prosecutions and later, as Director of Cabinet in the Ministry of Justice" (Enonchong (1967: xii, bold is original) that would seem to have misled the others theorizing similarly that Cameroon's constitutional system is to all intents and purposes a hybrid between the French and American systems, insofar as the concept of the separation of powers is concerned (Enonchong, 1967: 94-95). Leaving the US aside, Cameroon cannot even be a hybrid of the French system and any other on the globe since it is simply what I have termed 'a very nasty clone of the French system' in the sense that this off-spring of General de Gaulle's blatant "*détournement de procédure*" (Pactet, 1991: 327) has further been very negatively deformed in Cameroon. This takes Cameroon not only very far away from France but also even further away from the parliamentary and congressional systems – both of which are marked by separation of powers, being apart only in the manner of doing so. This separation is absent in Cameroon largely because of the selfish attitude of politicians generally but

212 "*Car, logiquement, seule l'autorité chargée de définir la politique de la nation doit être comptable devant le Parlement. Cette solution assises dans la plupart des démocraties procède simplement d'une sagesse. Dès lors, deux démarches apparaissent: supprimer le poste du Premier Ministre ou lui donner les droits qui découlent de ses obligations à l'égard de l'Assemblée Nationale. Faute de l'avoir fait, l'on a dénaturé le régime semi-parlementaire proclamé, institué et hypothétiqué les chances de stabilité du texte de 1996.*" Ondoa (1996: 14).

particularly the 'Anglophone' ones who busy themselves too much fighting over the PM garbage, just as they would surely do and might already have begun doing over being the POR's appointed (rather than the Regions' elected) senators.

Bicameralism and the Advanced Government Algebra

The Cameroon senate's 'politics without politics' and its unique recruitment mechanisms (elections plus appointments) are bound to raise many questions. But the main one here concerns the exact meaning of the 'indirect universal suffrage' that will be used in electing some of the members of the 'to-be-created' senate. This book generally demonstrates that Cameroon's advanced government is 'advanced' solely because the very essence of it necessitates a parliament which is not representative of the people; with its one-chamber parliament now to be bicameral (as it is claimed), with a senate as the upper chamber. A survey of senate politics around the globe shows that members of this chamber are *all* either elected or appointed. Cameroon's democracy is so advanced that it combines both election and appointment – the POR appointing 30% while the regions elect 70% through indirect universal suffrage (IUS).

It is argued here however that at the end of the day it is effectively a 100% presidentially appointed senate, the idea of the regions electing 70% of the senators being a mere political attention-grabber. Reinforcing the main thesis of parliament not being representative of the people (but of the POR), this view is predicated on (1) the fact that elections generally in Cameroon are only farcical exercises, with appointments being paramount and (2) the idea that indirect universal suffrage is meaningless without an *initial* direct universal suffrage in regard of the organ or person through which to thereafter elect indirectly. Therefore, the mathematical conclusion is that indirect universal suffrage (IUS) can only properly be what Fossungu calls one of the system's shorthand phrases[213] for direct universal suffrage (DUS) which, in Cameroon's advanced government algebra, takes the form of IUS = DUS = 100% POR's Senate (with IUS really meaning "*I* am *US*" and DUS being "*D*o it for *US*"). Essentially then, since *I* am *US,* I'll *D*o it for *US*.

---

[213] See Peter Ateh-Afac Fossungu, "Why Certain French Shorthand Expressions Must Disappear from Our Discourse" *The Herald* N° 641 (3-4 August 1998), 4.

Most readers must already be asking so many questions concerning the allusion to there being an advanced government in Cameroon, having an algebra of its own that must detain attention. I am not surprised by the reader's mood and would duly sympathize with this frame of mind because Cameroon's latest constitution, as well as its numerous predecessors, must leave only the ignorant without an avalanche of questions. Like the others, this part of the book attempts to provide some distinctive insights into the country's not-too-familiar 'advanced democracy', with the set purpose of assisting perplexed experts with their countless perplexities. That is, by sort of graduating them from the elementary school of constitutional government as practised in most parts of the world into the advanced (or secondary or hidden meaning) one that has Cameroon as its place of practice. The politics of the senate as well as senate elections that provide us with the meaning of indirect universal suffrage will entail (1) a brief history of the senate in Cameroon, including finding out whether the envisioned Cameroon senate resolves what has been Canada's long standing constitutional issue – the Triple-E Senate – a topic which will smoothly carry us into one-half of one of the three 'E's, namely, (2) elections/appointments of senators.

The Senate in Cameroon History

The Cameroonian upper chamber is yet to be actually created and operating;[214] but experts such as Mback (2007: 71-74) have already extensively discussed 'The Formation of the Senate and the Question of Its Legitimacy', as well as its doubtful powers. The 'gambling' that is involved in the creation of a senate in Cameroon would be better grasped through (1) the speaker's role and (2) the Canadian issue of Triple-E.

1. The Role of the Speaker

One can be sure that the absence of this revising chamber (senate) in the pre-independence ALCAM (*Assemblée Législative du Cameroun*) was very instrumental in an easy acquisition of *pleins pouvoirs* (open-ended emergency powers) that have since made sure that bicameralism or any form of separation of powers remains an unknown thing to Cameroon. The then prime minister of French Cameroun, Ahmadou Ahidjo, acquired these open-

214 See "Biya Sets Overdue Senate Vote for April [2013]", available at http//www.cameroonjournal.com. The question that remains is: why only now, 17 years after the 1996 Constitution?

ended emergency powers with the firm backing of France that was relentlessly bent on destroying all the nationalists or patriots. One of such targeted patriots was the indefatigable, influential and outspoken Deputy Daniel Kemajou who was tactically replaced by Mabaya as President (the equivalent of Speaker) of the pre-independence unicameral ALCAM. This replacement (like the recent one of the Constitutional Council replacing the world's most 'unsupreme' Supreme Court in article 67(4)) had been effected in preparation for the *coup* on parliamentary democracy that was to be staged by way of the acquisition of *pleins pouvoirs* in October 1959.

The role of the speaker in a parliamentary democracy cannot be overstated. King has indicated that in the American legislature, for instance, any member may speak for as long as s/he likes, on whatever subject s/he chooses, during any debate. In this way, a legislator may prevent a proposal by making long speeches, reading whole chapters of books, journals, and the like. But in the parliamentary systems of Britain, Australia and Canada (for example), it is the Speaker, and not the individual member, who decides on what is "in order" so that every member keeps to the subject under discussion.[215] Some other critics of the American system like Mallory (1984: 273) have frowned on the absence of this 'speaker-discipline' feature; with Moorhouse (1977: 257) even narrating the story of one of the American legislators that was doing the obstruction using "A book she had been reading, which she proceeded to describe chapter by chapter before reviewing at length her conclusions; which caused the… [bored guest Canadian Speaker] to look up from his plate at last and say, 'Do you know, I think you've totally misunderstood that book'." The office of the Speaker is thus one of the most important safeguards of the effective working of parliamentary procedure. It is plain then why ALCAM's 'speaker' Kemajou had to be taken out of the way; the more especially as there was no second or revising chamber.

Even being stripped of his position as president of that Assembly, Daniel Kemajou did not simply turn his back on the country and progeny, like the others.[216] As previously said, the goal of what he aptly described as 'this

---

[215] H. King, *Parliament and Freedom* (London: John Murray, 1953) at 122-23. For an elaborate discussion of the Canadian Speaker's role and other attributes, see Mallory (1984: 274-77 and the numerous texts cited therein).

[216] A typical example of those turning their backs is the businessman-turned-politician, André-Marie Mbida (first Cameroonian prime minister). See Benjamin (1972:

criminal law, this despicable law' (*pleins pouvoirs*) has been to make sure that bicameralism (or any other form of separation of powers) remains a thing unknown to Cameroon. Nelson *et al* (1974: viii) have then indicated how, thereafter, "All seats in the unicameral national assembly, which has little powers, [have been] held by members of the unified party led by [the] president...." Thus as Konings (1999: 299) has also noted, in the framing of the federal constitution, the Southern Cameroons proposal for a bicameral legislature was rejected, and a unicameral System was adopted. The choice was justified on the grounds of economy and efficiency, but it is most likely that Ahidjo saw the proposal as a threat to the centralised character of the constitution, as well as a means to impede the federal government from ruling without regard for human and other institutional rights. This fact alone must now place a big question mark on the recent (prospective) creation of a senate in Cameroon. So why now talk about or introduce a senate in this country? The critics think it is a mere ploy with which to effectively concentrate even more powers and keep the "paper multiparty" parliament in absolute check; blaming the poor leadership for not even trying to learn from Canadians who would just be as willing and ready to offer help in several domains, including recruitment for the senate.

2. *Triple-E Senate in Cameroon?*

Anyone who keenly follows events in Canada must be aware of the challenges to its continued existence as a single internationally recognized state. These challenges include the "Triple-E Senate" calls from Western Canada, "Distinct society status" from Quebec, capped by the hotly debated question of Quebec's threatened UDI (Unilateral Declaration of Independence) in the event of a successful sovereignty vote; and "Meech's third issue: aboriginal self-government."[217] All these challenges are not only sources of conflict; they are also reinforcements to the fact that Canada is a

213); and Richard A. Joseph, *Radical Nationalism in Cameroun: Social Origins of the U.P.C. Rebellion* (Oxford: The Clarendon Press, 1977) at 343-345 & 347.

[217] Claude Denis, "Shaping What Future for Canada? A Prospective Analysis of the Federal Government's Constitutional Proposals" 3:3 *Constitutional Forum Constitutionnel* (Winter 1992), 45-48 at 46. See also John Borrows, "Constitutional Law From a First Nation Perspective: Self-Government and the Royal Proclamation" 28:1 *University of British Columbia Law Review* (1994), 1; and Bob Freeman, "The Space for Aboriginal Self-Government in British Columbia: The Effect of the Decision of the British Columbia Court of Appeal in *Delgamuukw v. British Columbia*" 28:1 *University of British Columbia Law Review* (1994), 49.

veritable federation, with a parliament that is representative of the people and includes an existing and operational senate.

In Cameroon, on the other hand, there seems to have been sufficient preparation to make sure that, if and whenever the authorities decide to actually create it, the senate (like the Constitutional Council) must be packed with 30 presidential appointees out of the 100 (or all of them – as shown below). "The Senate," declares the 1996 Constitution rather joyfully in article 20(1), "shall represent the regional and local authorities"; with article 20(2) making each region to be "represented in the Senate by 10 (ten) Senators of whom 7 (seven) shall be elected by indirect universal suffrage on a regional basis and 3 (three) appointed by the President of the Republic." There are ten regions. Therefore, there shall be 100 senators, 30 of whom are the POR's direct appointees. I will leave aside many of the grave issues that the article 20(2) provision could raise and mention and discuss only a few here; namely, the issues surrounding Canada's Triple-E senate (the province of this section) and the meaning of indirect universal suffrage employed for electing the 70/100 senators (discussed in the next).

Quite apart from the fact that its actual eventual existence is greatly in doubt, the Cameroon Senate does not even attempt to meet the Triple-E demands in Canada. Triple-E stands for the senate being 'elected, equal, and efficient'. The demands for these three E's have been found by Meekison (1986: 18) to be the "piece of unfinished business which is now number one on the 'hit parade'...[and] is Canada's most long-standing constitutional question, going back well over 100 years." A political science professor at the University of Alberta has indicated that the Province of "Alberta [is] the birthplace of Triple E", regretting the "unfortunate" and "disturbing tendency to view the constitution as *the* vehicle for political change [which] may be blinding Canadians to the plausibility of non-constitutional alternatives."[218] One might just have to wish that this political science

---

[218] Urquhart (1992: 67 & 68, respectively). See also Peter H. Russell, "The Politics of Frustration: The Pursuit of Formal Constitutional Change in Australia and Canada" in Bruce W. Hodgins, John J Eddy, Shelagh D. Grant and James Struthers, eds., *Federalism in Canada and Australia: Historical Perspectives, 1920-1988* (Peterborough, Ontario: Frost Centre for Canadian Heritage and Development Studies, 1989), 59; and Beverley Baines, "'Consider, Sir,...On What Does Your Constitution Rest?' – Representation and Institutional Reform" in David Schneiderman, ed., *Conversations Among Friends << >> Entre Amies: Proceedings of an Interdisciplinary Conference on Women and Constitutional Reform* (Edmonton: Centre for Constitutional Studies, 1992), 54.

professor were in Cameroon. His admonition could be different because, then and there, he would be overwhelmed not only by those non-constitutional alternatives but, in fact, unorthodox and *unconstitutional* or frustratingly advanced ones.

For example, the Cameroon regime will first give the Alberta professor what is known as the Liberty Law (*Loi N° 90/053 du 19 décembre 1990 portant sur la liberté d'association*) to let him feel that he is free to do this and that. But the professor would be wrong if he should start rejoicing and trying to exercise the freedoms he is accustomed to in Canada because, talking about the confusioncracy embedded in this Liberty Law, a human rights activist (Taku, 1995: 3) has indicated how, "With the enactment of the most repressive legislation in 1990 ironically called *Liberty Laws*, this government craftily turned the courts [and media] into tools of oppression with which citizens can be incarcerated without adequate safeguard for their defence." That is exactly what people get for hastily abandoning their 'un-advanced' democracy and crossing the wide Atlantic to get to the fatally-attractive "Advancing Ocean of confusing use of terminologies" (Fossungu, 2013: x).

Another apt example of the overwhelming alternatives, to save the Alberta professor the trouble of actually making the 'fatal' Atlantic crossing, would be the very senate provisions under examination here. An interesting thing, to begin with, is that the Cameroonian article-20(2) algebra is strangely *advanced* because members of all such organs are either completely appointed or entirely elected. The United States Senate is elected according to senatorial districts. Canadian senators are appointed by the prime minister. This appointed senate (against which Triple-E advocates stand[219]) is regarded in Canada as "an invaluable means of pensioning off ministers, M.P.s and others whose health and fortune have been ruined by long service in the political wars" (Mallory, 1984: 256). The appointed House of Lords of Canada's 'distant uncaring Mother' (Britain), said to be "the best club in the world", is also regarded by Crossman (1972: 54) as simply providing the British prime minister with "a useful device for retiring aging or incompetent Ministers without disgrace – purging his Government by promotion." The

[219] For some interesting comparison of the Canadian Senate to the German *Bundesrat*, see Shapiro (1995: 19-20 n. 68). See also John Uhr, "The Canadian and Australian Senates: Comparing Federal Political Institutions" in Hodgins *et al*, eds., *Federalism in Canada and Australia: Historical Perspectives, 1920-1988* (Peterborough, Ontario: Frost Centre for Canadian Heritage and Development Studies, 1989), 130-146.

German model (the *Bundesrat*) is appointed not by the chancellor but by the *Laender* or states. (I will be coming back to this German upper chamber shortly). Even in France from where Cameroon always guiltily copies without acknowledging, Blondel (1985: 168-169) tells us that senators of *le Sénat* are *all* "elected on the basis of the *département* (county) and the number of senators per *département* varies according to the population. There are two ballots. Rural overrepresentation gives the Senate an entirely different complexion from the National Assembly." Why does Cameroon not now do the wholesale transplanting from France?

Biya seems to have gotten this crazy appointment-elections idea put into his head by the 65-member Anglophone Standing Committee whose silly *advanced combination* of elections and appointments would be found discussed in Konings (1999: 311-313). On the face of it, the Cameroon senate formula somewhat meets just one-half of one of the E's in the Triple-E demands that Western Canada is well known for making. 'Triple E', as earlier said, stands for 'equal, elected, and efficient'. In other words, Albertans will quickly explain that the senate, in order to be efficient, should have its members elected, with each province having an equal number of senators in it. An elected senate is good and fine but I am inclined to think that Equal rather becomes Unequal when, say, populous New York state has the same number of senators as small (in population) Delaware. Translated into Cameroon, Sanagazone will replace New York while Nyongzone takes the place of Delaware. Once more, is there any sense in letting these states all have an equal number of senators (like was also proposed by the 65-member Anglophone Standing Committee), especially as article 20(1) makes it clear that the senator represents the Region? This is not real and sensible politics; being so only in the sense that these people are not to represent anyone other than the POR's interests of maintaining himself indefinitely in power.

It is in this regard that the German formula (like the French and American in terms of proportionality) would seem to stand out. I am here referring to the German *Bundesrat* which is the main institutional mechanism for adjusting and regulating relations between the *Bund* (federal government) and the *Laender*. Being the most distinctive feature of the German system, it is (unlike the British House of Lords) a powerful body with exclusive constitutional functions (Magstadt, 1991: 113). Directly responsible to the state governments under the Basic Law (article 50), the *Bundesrat* has wide-ranging influence on federal policies and procedures.

Members of this *Bundesrat* are not popularly elected. Rather the *Land* governments appoint representatives, apportioned on the basis of population. By article 51(2) of the Basic Law, each Länd has at least 3 votes; those with more than two million inhabitants have 4 votes, those with more than six million inhabitants 5, and Länder with more than seven million inhabitants 6 votes. That is real and sensible politics, with the constitution laying things out clearly, and not being left in the care of a subsequent unknown law as is always the case with the dictatorship in Cameroon. It is an entrenched provision (article 51(3)) that the representatives of each *Land* government must vote as a block, a provision that experts say does heavily reinforce the federal character of the German parliament. It is probably this requirement, coupled with the combination of the parliamentary system of government with the federal structure, that may properly explain why, like others,[220] Magstadt (1991: 109) has found the German system to be probably more federal than is that of the United States; with its *Laender* running more of their own affairs and receiving a larger proportion of taxes than do American states.

In the absence of a similar provision (like the German here) in Cameroon, coupled with the stark absence of an independent judiciary, concentration of powers will continue to be camouflaged as separation of powers; unbridgeable gulfs will continue to be disguised as bridged ones, as well as indefinite executive terms of office being passed on as definite and well mapped out, with the impossible never being possible in Cameroon (*impossibilité n'est pas Camerounaise*) continuing to reign high without control. And, above all, there will continue to be claims of equality and enforcement of it only in situations where it actually means inequality and oppression. Some experts like Urquhart (1992: 67) have even postulated that an equal number of senators from every province (as is to be the case with the elected *seventy* in Cameroon) "will not raise grain or petroleum prices, nor will it guarantee more successful economic adjustment policies."

Just having these equal numbers of senators (if ever) within the prevailing context in Cameroon will similarly solve nothing, except if worsening an already precarious situation does amount to an amelioration of something. For example, concerning the three per region (or thirty in total) to be

[220] See Schneider (2008: 136-38); Nevil Johnson, *Federalism and Decentralization in the Federal Republic of Germany* (London: H.M. Stationary Office, 1973); and Max Rheinsteln, "The Approach to German Law" 34 *Indiana Law Journal* (1959), 546.

appointed by the POR, there is nothing to indicate that they must be from the regions they are appointed to represent. It is for sure to be exactly like the presidentially appointed provincial governors (now called delegates of the regions) who do not need to be of the specific provinces/regions they are appointed to. It is then not very hard to see that these thirty senators do not in fact represent any region but the POR. Some critics of Cameroon politics have instead preferred to describe the entire process as *l'évolution régressive de la démocratie* which is punctuated by *la fin des élections.*[221] These specialists are not far from the point as can be shown by an informed scrutiny of senate elections.

IUS Equals DUS, Since Appointment Plus Election Equal Appointment: You Think That Is Impossible Mathematics?

As I have shown earlier, elections in this country are mere ludicrous exercises. In short, the so-called indirect universal suffrage (IUS) in article 20(2) for their election boils down in reality to a 100% presidentially appointed senate. IUS is just a shorthand for something else; and it is not like Cameroonians have not been duly warned by the experts about 'advanced democratic' shorthand expressions and their real (or secondary) meanings. But it seems the experts have been dismayed by the fact that Cameroonians would hardly ever grow up; or at least do so as quickly as is necessary to catch up with (if not be in advance of) the Ahidjo-Biya advanced democracy. The 'indirect universal suffrage' or IUS is simply one of the nicely couched shorthand methods of advanced (or *secondary* meaning) democracy for saying that since "*I* am *US*, I'll *D*o it for *US*". Hence, IUS = DUS. This is the Advanced Government Algebra that many people in this country (and the rest of the world?) find very hard to comprehend, perhaps, because Biya (1986: back cover) thinks "Since independence, most African countries have been characterized not by seething intellectualism but by political...tyranny." I will therefore try to move toward the supposedly absent 'seething

---

[221] See Abel Eyinga, *Cameroun, 1960-1989, la fin des élections: un cas d'évolution régressive de la démocratie* (Paris: L'Harmattan, 1990); Boniface Forbin, "Senatorial Election: From Frying Pan to Fire!" *The Herald* N° 592 (3-5 April 1998), 4. On elections procedures generally, see Shiv Lal (1976); Roy Pierce, *Choosing the Chief: Presidential Elections in France and the United States* (Ann Arbour: The University of Michigan Press, 1995); Michael Dummett, *Voting Procedures* (Oxford: Clarendon Press, 1984); and Mark Ratner, "Democracy under Question: Would Proportional Representation Better Reflect the Will of Canadians?" 86 *McGill Daily* N° 65 (24 March 1997), 2.

intellectualism' (in the midst of 'an impressive Third World literacy level' that Biya (1986: 11) brags about) by more elaborately explaining how the shorthand is what I say it means, with an incensing employment of two interconnected factors: first, the existing political culture of unfettered presidential appointments and, second, the decreed absence of political development on the part of the regional people.

1. Political Culture of Unfettered Appointments

Like that of an individual, the character of a government, according to Dawson (1970: 3), is shaped by the two primary forces of heredity and environment; and the study of a government, again like that of an individual, must perforce devote some attention to parentage and the special associations which have had direct contact with each particular institution. Although this important statement from Dawson does not directly define political culture, it is nevertheless a significant indicator to it; as well as a warning to those who fail to pay the required amount of attention to non-constitutional factors that have been found to be overriding, if not exclusive, in Cameroon. The political culture of a society, according to the experts in the field, embodies the distinctive attitudes and approaches of its people toward politics, these attributes having been shaped by historical traditions, demography and geographical circumstances. Political culture thus refers to the attitudes that influence people's political behaviour or colour the overall nature of a political system.[222]

In Cameroon (as it would generally be common with what some critics would call in French "*pays décretés*" or "*pays ordonnancés*") there is a political culture of unfettered presidential appointments. Like Konings (1999: 298-99), Delancey (1989: 57) tells the story of these appointments better when he states that the current

[222] Michael Tucker, *Canadian Foreign Policy: Contemporary Issues and Themes* (Toronto: McGraw-Hill Ryerson Ltd., 1980) at 2. For a more extensive discussion of political culture, see James D. Seymour, "The Government of China" in Michael Curtis, Gen. ed., *Introduction to Comparative Government* (New York: Harper and Row, Publishers, 1985), 385, at 406-412; and John S. Reshetar, Jr., "The Government of the Soviet Union" in Michael Curtis, Gen. ed., *Introduction to Comparative Government* (New York: Harper and Row, Publishers, 1985), 283 at 296-301.

obedient position of the legislature [of Cameroon] was in part a result of the constitution and in part a result of the nomination and legislative electoral process. Because there was no real separation of powers in the constitution, the president could play an important role in the legislative process through his ability to propose legislation and to delay or prevent the passage of legislation he did not like. Moreover, in many instances he had the power to legislate by decree without reference to the National Assembly and even could declare a state of emergency on his own and rule entirely by decree. The president, moreover, did not need to seek legislative approval of his appointments: He appointed his ministers, his governors, his judges alone, and they in turn were entirely dependent upon him and his favor if they were to remain in office. The National Assembly had no role to play in the process and could exert no pressure on it. Of course, this made the appointed judiciary subservient to the presidential will.

In a country with such an entrenched culture, it is but normal that presidentially decreed/appointed officials always claim superiority to "elected" ones. Very apt illustrations to this effect can be seen even in Cameroon's 'federal' era wherein the appointed 'federal' inspector claimed superiority to the Southern Cameroons Prime Minister (initially elected through the Legislature – though lately appointed like the inspector himself). This story of the appointed 'federal' inspector in West Cameroon claiming to be boss to the region's initially elected prime minister is not new.[223] As an expert on Cameroon's judicial system (Anyangwe, 1987: 130) also puts it, "the Federal Inspector in West Cameroon was always a Francophone and because he tended to behave like an overlord there was legitimate indignation among West Cameroonians that they were being regarded and treated as a vanquished or colonised people."

This superiority complex of appointed officials is still the case today with "elected" city councillors and their presidentially-appointed bosses ('ambassadors') – the mayors or government delegates. "Take for instance

---

223 Konings (1999: 302) has indicated how Ahidjo had succeeded in creating an administrative system that basically ignored the 'federal' nature of the country [largely because] The federal inspector in West Cameroon, a Francophone, considered himself the equal of the state's prime minister, and there was a running battle for jurisdiction between the two officials until the late 1960s.

the installation of a Government Delegate like Caven Nnoko Mbele [a high school teacher] over elected councillors in Kumba or the appointment of Dr. Maikano [as a Government Delegate] in Garoua. Is this [not] stealing? This is pure terrorism. And it thrives on our collective torpor, calculation, fear and resignation. We only bark... and even bark stupidly and calculatingly."[224] This passage seems to say it all. The blame is therefore not solely Biya's. Any sensible person must really be wondering what honest and intellectually active individual will allow him/herself to be unilaterally appointed in this way to lord over the people's elected officials, especially in this era of the pinning of the high level of literacy and democracy to the chest. Some critics must then be correct indeed to have posited that spending many years in school does not *per se* make a person educated. For instance, which of these two people – the person appointing and the appointee – should be blamed for perpetuating power concentration by not knowing what decentralization, elections, etc. do properly entail? Aren't both guilty for the regression? Eyinga (1996) who has written several books on Cameroon's regressive politics sees no difference between the appointed government delegates and the real mayors since the different appellations are merely to confuse (*"On les appelle les délégues du gouvernement, mais ce sont les vrais maires dans les communes*").

As presidential appointments have come to take precedence over elections in this country, no one should then doubt that only the POR's 30 senators are to matter in Cameroon's senate, with the device also furnishing an effective allurement for the 'elected' 70/100 senators to curry for. The story of the yet-to-be appointed 30 senators in Cameroon has prospectively been more elegantly and tersely narrated by some protocol critics (Moorhouse, 1977: 242) who would parallel their attitude to that of Her Majesty's Ambassador. "He is the Queen's Man, as no one else is, and some Ambassadors never let anyone forget it. He is entitled to a nineteen-gun salute on ceremonial occasions, which is only two blank cartridges fewer than his sovereign gets from the Royal Horse Artillery in Hyde Park, but nineteen more than the [elected] Prime Minister gets anywhere." The snobbish

---

[224] Barry B. Fohtung, "Waiting... No! Inventing 1997 (I)" *Cameroon Post* N° 0021 (20-26 August 1996), 8. See also Asong Ndifor, "Fru Ndi Tells France to Advise Biya" *The Herald* N° 310 (13-15 May 1996), 1 (reporting how Fru Ndi called on France "to advise President Paul Biya to revoke the appointment of government delegates to Councils won by the opposition"); and Bonny Kfua, "France, Democratise Cameroon" *The Herald* N° 366 (7-8 October 1996), 4.

attitude of these 'ambassadors' of the POR makes it very alluring becoming one of them. Are elected national assemblers not even already regarding themselves as the POR's representatives in their constituencies, as seen above?

An English writer on diplomacy has come to the conclusion that hc can adequately explain why these people always feel that they should rather be appointees (than elected representatives) and, hence, ambassadors of the POR. As the POR's ambassadors, the diplomacy expert (Moorhouse, 1977: 257) writes, they get the feeling that "there never was a more elite body of men in the[ir] world [called Cameroon]. As a word suggesting rare distinction, there is nothing to compete with 'Ambassador', judging by the frequency with which it is attached to first-class hotels, night-clubs, expensive drinks, cigarettes and other luxuries throughout the [entire] world." This snobbish or ostentatious feeling of appointed politicians has been discovered to be heightened nowhere around the globe than in Cameroon, the entrenched home for democracy without democrats; a country wherein democracy that can simply not go must still go. In short, a state marked by politics without politics.

2. Politics without Politics

Whether one adopts James Madison's definition of politics in essay number ten of *The Federalist Papers* (1787) or the view espoused by Indian independence leader Mahatma Gandhi (1869-1948), Cameroon's 'politicians' are not captured. None of those two schools of thoughts has any application in this country because there is absolutely no constant struggle waged by individuals or groups for economic power and advantage. Neither is there any conviction in this country that the cause of justice is best served by political institutions that unite society in a common effort to achieve an equitable distribution of resources. Clear demonstrations of the unavailability of both of these theses can be found in Cameroon's Bible of Political Theology – Biya (1986: 43-47, and 10-11 & 78, respectively). But that is not all that defines politics without politics in this country.

It appears that Cameroon's advanced democrats always think that all people on earth are like them who pass through a class in school and the next minute cannot remember a thing; people who say a thing now and the very next minute forget what they have just said. I guess that is always what happens when you are trying to endlessly confuse others. Congressmen (or 'national assemblers') and senators are essentially to be local politicians. But the senators in question even appear to be more tied to their localities. This is because (1) that is even the rationale for their being from *provinces* (or the regional and local authorities) being made the *basis* of their membership of the senate. And (2) unlike their lower counterparts (the national assemblers each of whom, paradoxically, "represents the entire Nation" in article 15(2)), senators represent their provinces or regions as per article 20(2). So those senators to be oblivious of this fact must have to simply cease to be politicians (assuming that there are even any politicians in Cameroon at all). That is precisely why one always finds an American senator or representative being identified with his or her party (D – for Democrat or R – for Republican) and home state (e.g. TX, CT, MD, MI, NC, MA, NM, WA, VA).

Local politics, no doubt, is never played for the highest stakes (such as on questions of war or peace with other nations). For instance, it is not Debundschazone (South West Region), but Cameroon, that takes the decision regarding the senseless Cameroon-Nigeria conflict over the oil-rich Bakassi peninsular. Or as when, for instance, the United States of America attacks part of Quebec: not Quebec but Canada decides on the question of war or peace with the attacking country. But the similarities of the two levels of doing politics, according to Banfield and Wilson (1963:2), are still great enough to enable someone learn something about the greater national game from studying and practising the lesser. One can even see this from the fact that most American presidents have been state governors prior to becoming Number one American. It is, of course, only so obvious that one cannot understand the national political scene without a sound knowledge about its workings at the local level. Does this thesis not also largely explain the mess we have in Cameroon where *chefs d'état* have always been 'appointed' from nowhere? How can they properly "manage" Cameroon when they have never even been able to correctly "manage" a small quarter in their village or place of residence? That has to simply stop, if this country hopes to be well governed.

Kneier (1939: preface) of the University of Illinois has then pointed out that, to correctly study and/or practice municipal government and administration, it is advantageous that the student and/or practitioner be acquainted with some of the materials with which public officials must deal, such as constitutional provisions, state laws, charters, municipal ordinances, and court decisions. Why the officials concerned must be acquainted with the instruments here listed is self-evident. But one is told by Kneier (*ibid*, emphasis added) particularly that the recommended acquaintance will not only help to kindle interest and make the student/practitioner of this "second best science" appreciate the practical side of municipal government. It also – and this is a very important point to note – *encourages independent and critical thinking about the problems with which such officials are confronted.* It is here that stiff problems of comprehending the algebra of advanced democracy do arise.

The first question that must now be posed concerns how Cameroon's so-called elected senators are then going to understand the national political system without knowing something about how it works locally (which also significantly means their being able to understand their regions' prerogatives, rights, obligations, and preoccupation). This inevitable query finds its appropriateness in another conspicuous portion of the same 1996 constitution (that claims in article 1(2) to be decentralizing Cameroon) by which there is to be no political development of the people of the regions. This 1996 Constitution (in addition to its article 56 already discussed in Chapter 3 regarding sharing/transferring of jurisdiction) also stipulates in article 55(2):

> Regional and local authorities shall be public law corporate bodies. They shall have administrative and financial autonomy in the management of regional and local interests. They shall be freely administered by councils elected under conditions laid down by law. The duty of the councils of regional and local authorities shall be *to promote [only] the economic, social, health, educational, cultural and sports development of the said authorities* [emphasis added].

No political development of the regions is therefore to be tolerated in Cameroon. There is first the failure here to recognize Magstadt's (1991: 47-49) "Politics and Economics [as] Two Sides of One Coin" which Couloumbis and Wolfe (1986: 347) have vigorously condemned as the unrealistic "appeal to divorce economics from politics in...[governmental] affairs." There are many other critiques of the entire provision (see, for example, Fossungu, 2013: 231-234); but I will simply follow it up with these equally important questions. First, how are these senators to do politics without politics? And, second, how are the local or regional people to exercise political rights (such as voting the 70/100 senators) that they do not possess? The first of these issues having already been largely treated above in the discussion of the political culture of unfettered presidential appointments, I will now look into the second that can be well couched in this fascinating *e-quaestion*: Indirect Universal Suffrage = Direct Universal Suffrage?

As previously said, this 'advanced' mathematical *e-quaestion*, IUS = DUS?, turns upon how the local or regional people are to exercise their voting (being political) rights – which they clearly are not to have through political non-development. Can the apparent difficulty or paradox involved here be furnishing the justification for the *indirect universal suffrage* (to be employed in the election of the 70/100 senators) in Cameroon's unique senate formula of article 20(2)? Should the answer to this question be YES, then the Great Question (to relegate other numerous queries to the background) becomes: What precisely is the meaning of "indirect universal suffrage" as used in Cameroon, and can that precise meaning (if clear-cut at all) really solve the governmental puzzle at hand?

My answer to the puzzle of the Great Question is 'Certainly NOT but Surely YES'. Of course, on the face of it, this answer will be condemned by DeCoste (1991) for not taking a firm stand as well as by Douzinas and Warrington (1987: 33) for being "epistemologically unsound and practically immobilising." But the condemnation will only be because these critics are not aware of the existence of Cameroon's Advanced School of Democracy (ASD), let alone have a sufficient grasp of its principal and only subject called *NODDometrics* which Fossungu (1998c) defines as mathematics or economics or politics, etc. as practised in the New-Old Deal Democracy (NODD). That could be precisely why "Many of you [who] must be hearing about this subject for the very first time" (Fossungu, 1998c) have been properly warned not to go seeking to study in Cameroon's ASD with any preconceived notions. As Fossungu's (1998c) counsel runs,

> As you prepare for NODDometrics, keep in mind that you can never be an expert at democracy to qualify for admission. You will always find yourself becoming a novice at everything. Because…the School's authorities would not even hesitate in announcing to all such experts on non-NODD democracy that they still have a lot of learning to do (preferably in Cameroon's own Advanced Democracy School) to deserve

the 'expert' title. And if, for curiosity, you were 'humble' enough to denounce your well-considered views and are admitted, this is what would follow.

Having been granted admission into the ASD (Advanced School of Democracy), the first or preliminary lesson the newly admitted to the School could learn will be that my Certainly-Not Surely-Yes answer is not unsound. With that necessary advanced information, the advanced government algebra will then continue, beginning with the elementary arithmetic that is well-known for its 'It-Cannot-Go' responses (answers which earn a sure failure grade in the ASD), followed closely by the secondary or advanced meaning algebra with its 'It-Must-Go' or 'Unchallenged Equations'.

(a) The Primary School Response: It-Cannot-Go!

The newly arrived students will discover that admission into the ASD is not so much the problem; it is the successful graduation from the School that is tough and problematic. They must then need to understand that no one can successfully graduate from this School until they can understand confusion without confusion; confusion having been defined in the Introduction of this book as the act of causing surprise or confusion in (someone), especially by not according with their expectations. The novice's expected question is of course expected: How does one even begin to grasp the meaning of confusion when confusion is used to define confusion? That is precisely (the teacher responds) why it is confusion. That is the exact reason why the authorities of this School have made understanding confusion without confusion the condition precedent for successfully graduating from the School of Confusion. It can then be seen that the newly arrived students, though disturbed, are somewhat intrigued by the teacher's explication and have decided to stay on because, to them, there is a competent, albeit 'gate-crashing', teacher on the ASD Campus attempting to aid the people who have actually abandoned or are intending to trade off their elementary democracy for the *advanced* (or *secondary* meaning) one of Cameroon. The 'secondary meaning' nature of the democracy is amoeba-like but for now I will limit it to illustrating the indirect universal suffrage that cannot-go.

Most people can be able to recall their first days in school. The following illustration would perhaps aptly say much to people on the African side of the wide and deep Atlantic (separating democracies) than to North Americans (on the other side of it) who are so used to their plain surface primary meanings of the Written Word – written words that, according to them, do guarantee their pursuit of happiness because it is left to their independent judiciary to discover the framers' intention where there are conflicting claims. Most of the admitted students can still remember how in *primary* or *elementary* school the only answer they were made to understand as being for "One-Take-Away-Two" was "It-cannot-go". (Americans will actually be saying: "That the POR be the Sole Legislator, It-Just-Cannot-Go!") Of course, it is a good thing that most people (unlike Cameroon's advanced democrats who say one thing now and the next minute forget it) can still recall those long gone school days – even as uncensored history is being prohibited in Cameroon. But as they *advanced* to *secondary* school, didn't the answer to the same quiz become "minus-one"? Could it then still 'not-go' as it used to do in primary school? As indicated earlier, I am here to help graduate a lot of people from the *elementary* school of constitutional government (where a lot of things can simply not go) into the advanced or *secondary* meaning one (where everything must simply go unchallenged). Those who do not want to be left behind must better hasten up and jump into the ASS (Advanced Secondary School) Bus that is ready and almost going even when it can truly not go.

What actually then is this Indirect Universal Suffrage device all about? It is nothing but what I have already stated above as the signification of the *e-quaestion, IUS = DUS?* If I properly understand the concept of indirect universal suffrage at all, then I would take it to signify an election by a body (usually but not always called an electoral college) which is itself, *in the first instance*, elected by Direct Universal Suffrage. Take President Barack Obama's recent re-election in November 2012 as the US President. He could not have obtained the number of electoral-college votes for New York, for instance (indirect universal suffrage), without having won the state of New York through the direct universal suffrage expressed at the polls by New Yorkers. That is one way of looking at indirect universal suffrage. Another way, which I am sure the Americans must have found not to be involving enough, would be for each state to directly elect and send the number of persons equal to their electoral-college votes; and whenever it is time to elect the US president, it is done just by those in the Electoral College. In either of these two cases, there is an initial direct universal suffrage leading to the indirect one.

Now, how can indirect universal suffrage (IUS) be possible in Africa when direct universal suffrage (DUS) is, in the first place, not possible? "It-cannot-go"! The thesis I am sustaining here takes a similar path with Fossungu's (2010: 286-87) argument against the ICAO Council President's omnipotence within the ICAO:

> The absence of separation of powers in the ICAO has been accentuated here to sustain at least two theses – the one being connected to, and defining, the other. First, that the ICAO is essentially a one-organ organization, since its both heads (but in particular the President of the Council) would appear to be all pervading. And, second, that even the acclaimed most important function of the Assembly is actually not being performed (or influenced) by it but, paradoxically, by the same organ (Council) whose members are supposed to be elected by that Assembly. One can say that the second point here is immaterial – arguing (as some other organizations within the UN system could successfully do) that the Assembly is in the first place responsible for the election of the Council's officers: the President and Secretary-General in particular. An argument like this one will be saying, in effect, that such a later selection has been put upon some officers (the Council's) *initially* elected by the people (or States in the Assembly). That can be a very persuasive argument indeed. But it is seriously flawed in the ICAO context in at least two respects. .... because that (those) "officer(s)" have never been elected or appointed by the ICAO Assembly [paragraphing altered & notes omitted; but emphasis as in original].

The experts are thus inclined to say 'it cannot go' in Cameroon because the local/regional people are not to be politically developed as mandated by Part X of the 1996 Constitution that creates these regional and local authorities. The local or regional people cannot then be said to be validly exercising political rights or powers or authority (voting) that they do not wield. The right to vote, as the experts all tell us, is clearly political and intimately related to popular rule. To say what I have just said in those simple terms, the 'Masters of the Word' or lawyers (the mercantile ones especially) will bombard someone with: *Nemo quod dat non habet.* Their constitutional colleagues – not wanting to look like being left out in the advanced mathematical cold by the mercantilists – will instead want to bamboozle the person with the somewhat more elegant one: *Delegatus non portior est delegare.* (You cannot delegate powers that you don't have in the first place.) So far so good with the Certainly-Not Response, the advanced democrats are now hastily reminding me to quickly proceed to the Surely-Yes part of the response that they do think (earns a pass mark or grade in the Advanced School of Democracy as it also) favours them; that is, the unchallenged equation of the secondary school.

(b) The Secondary School Answer: The Unchallenged Equation

The only equation that can then stand out unchallenged in this complicated or lengthy answer to an uncomplicated or short question is **IUS = DUS = 100% POR's Senate** (with IUS meaning, as it is in Cameroon, "*I* am *US*" and DUS being "*D*o it for *US*"). Hence, since *I* am *US*, I'll *D*o it for *US*. The motto in Cameroon has, since the 1959 *pleins pouvoirs* law, changed from "Let's do it" to "Let the POR (President of the Republic) do it." This exposed 'hidden' motto is thus the actual motto of Cameroon; not the 'Peace-Work-Fatherland' that is nicely covering it in article 1(4) of the 1996 Constitution.[225] Were it otherwise, why is IUS also involved in every other "election" of the regions' officials[226] but not in that of their bosses, the delegates of regions? By article 58,

> (1) A delegate, appointed by the President of the Republic shall represent the State in the Region. In this capacity, he shall be responsible for national interests, administrative control, ensuring compliance with laws and regulations, as well as maintaining law and order. He shall, under the authority of the Government, supervise and co-ordinate civil services in the Region.
>
> (2) He shall exercise the supervisory authority of the State over the Region.

---

225 This covering motto being itself, according to Fossungu (2013 : chapter 5), another shorthand for something else, namely, that Cameroonians must remain forever on the farms and Cameroon forever an agricultural nation – also being one of the handy tools for preventing constitutional democracy.

226 One must note that the regions' divisional delegates are also to be elected by indirect universal suffrage under a 'to-be-provided-for' law: 1996 Constitution, article 57(2).

Yes, indeed, even in Germany's 'integrated and shared federalism' there is "Federal Supervision of Länder Administration" (Schneider, 2008: 146-48). But how are these "new" Delegates of Regions in Cameroon any different from their "old" predecessor – the equally presidentially appointed Provincial Governors? An expert on governance (Delancey, 1989: 70) warned Cameroonians in 1989 that (because of their bellytics) nothing would have changed since "in many respects Biya did not alter the system he inherited, he merely tried to make it operate more effectively. The old laws and decrees remained in place and the ability of the president to concentrate all power and authority in himself remained. Just as he had ordered the police to relax, so too he could order them to tighten up." It must be noted that operating a dictatorship more effectively can only mean more dictatorship like never before but under the coat of democracy.

The change in names and other appellations is therefore only an advanced means of forestalling effective multiparty politics that is also another means of separating powers. Thus, with such a 'name change' (and/or creation of the senate, PM post, provinces-to-regions), Tanyi (1990: 61) posits that the 'regional delegate' (and/or senator, and/or PM) "is his [POR's] investment [in power concentration], his very livelihood [in the midst of 'multiparty politics']. The company [called Cameroon] is usually identified with his person, a situation which is exacerbated by the fact that the company, together with all official documents, carries his name."

As is usual with anyone who is well-groomed in the communal arrangements for genuinely advancing a country, Tanyi (1990: 62) could not therefore have ended his legitimate suspicion and bewilderment regarding these new power-concentrating creations in Cameroon called prime minister, senate, and regions without an extremely important puzzling question-and-answer session.

> If, for instance, after a successful year, the director [general] decides to buy a new car for himself, who is there to stop him? Obviously, his beloved wife [the cronies], the minority [power] shareholder would not dare to raise a finger! [Political] Business matters have always been above the comprehension of the average Cameroonian housewife [the cronies]. She is yet to know the annual turnover of the company in which she holds shares! Her most pressing concerns relate, usually, to her monthly food allowance and school fees for the children.

This passage explains perfectly the belly-politicking that is so rife in Cameroon, being exacerbated, entrenched and encouraged by unfettered presidential appointments; a system wholly or partly maintained as a veritable instrument of denying history. Anglophone politicians should normally be scrutinizing and dismantling such devices but, since they are not politicians but *bellyticians*, they very much prop up the system with their so-called Northwest-Southwest Divide.

Closing Remarks

Once more, if the Cameroon POR decides to cut and nail a new constitution for himself, who is there to stop him? Is it the intended revising chamber of parliament? In view of Cameroon's political culture of unfettered presidential appointments, it is suggested that the yet-to-be-created Cameroon upper chamber cannot live up to the functions that it is normally supposed to perform. This is especially so as it would in effect be a hundred per cent appointed body since only the thirty per cent members that are openly appointed by the POR would really matter. Their privileged position as 'the POR's ambassadors' would inevitably furnish reason for the seventy per cent to spend all their days in that senate currying for the POR's attention so as to eventually join that club of 'the POR's ambassadors' rather than occupy themselves with what the senate's functions are. Mallory (1984: 247) cites Sir John A. Macdonald in *Confederation Debates* 1865 as defining the role of the Senate in the Anglo-American world as a crucial balancing mechanism, a revising chamber meant to check and restrain the impulse of its fickle partner, the House of Commons/Representatives or the *Bundestag*. Cameroon's invented version can simply not do this job when it is hardly distinct from that fickle partner proper.

In fact, the other ALCAM deputies had tragically failed in 1959 to understand Daniel Kemajou who would rather die in dignity than live in slavery and dishonour. Cameroon consequently continues to live the tragedy that Kemajou alone could see then: the death of the parliamentary form of democracy and the birth of the other type known as advanced democracy. Since then, as this study has shown, the Cameroonian president could do and has been doing just anything with 'this criminal law, this despicable law' (*pleins pouvoirs*). Since the acquisition of these *pleins pouvoirs*, Cameroon, instead of becoming "a more open, more tolerant and more democratic political society" (Biya, 1986: 140), became what Archer and Reay (1966: 106) reprimand as a state with a

> government that attempts to bring, where it has not already brought, all the institutions of a nation to the service of itself. Courts are useful, only if they are corrupt; universities are tolerable, only if they are controlled… illustrat[ing] the helplessness of an individual in a system which has no interest in individuals, or in justice between them, and has the power to pervert the only institutions to which the individual can appeal… [a government] where power is delegated to agents who have no responsibility; and where that power, with the blessing of government, is left to brutalise and corrupt, as all power does, when there are no institutional restraints upon its exercise.

This is exactly how Cameroon's division of governmental competence at Foumban in 1961 has 'advanced' to what the Cameroon POR (Biya, 1986: 28) now proudly describes as the "very sophisticated division of labour among the authorities." I am simply not sure Adolf Hitler, if he came to Cameroon today, would accept that he had as much 'enabling' powers as the Ahidjo-Biya 'full and complete powers'. But I have shown how the Germans (from whom there is much to be learnt by Africans) have come back to democracy and constitutionalism after 'their own less-full version of Paul Biya'.

Conclusion

> However critical and vigilant a student of social institutions may be [Antonio Cassese has appropriately warned], sooner or later he falls into the trap of believing that his own reconstruction of reality actually reflects it as a coherent and flawless whole and that indeed the object itself is as smooth as the mirror. Reality intrudes continuously, but he glosses over the cracks or simply hides them by theoretical contrivances. The present book is of course not immune from this propensity, nor from other flaws. This I say without any undue trepidation: I remember all too well Hegel's warning that the words of the Apostle Peter to Ananias's wife ('Behold, the feet of them which have buried thy husband are at the door, and shall carry thee out') also apply to all scientific works – which are ineluctably destined to be eroded by subsequent scholarship [Cassese, 1986: 396].

I must again stress that doing things right (especially in combining federalism and the parliamentarianism) in Cameroon may require careful visits to Germany to discover how the Germans did it after the Nazi catastrophe that is not much different from the Biya regime. The Alliance for Democracy and Development (ADD) has made the point that there is no way we can succeed in Cameroon if we don't go federal. It is important to stress that successfully going federal in this country and continent cannot just entail affixing 'federal' to the country's name; it must have to involve the democratic spirit because I must not shun repeating that democratic governance is a *sine qua non* for the federal form of state organization. Anything else will be as chimerical as the 1961 Foumban 'Federal' *République du Cameroun*; it will be as confusing as claiming advancement in democracy (like the ruling CPDM) at the same time that they are attacking and/or faking self-determination and federalism in preference of what the critics have called ultra centralization. It has been essential to draw heavily from abroad to sustain not only this salient point but also the principal question of how to go federal from the unitary centralized form.

Whether or not the ADD's enlargement of federalism involves regaining lost Kamerun territories, it is hard to believe that while some French-speaking Cameroonians would be talking of the enlargement of federalism some English-speaking Cameroonians (notably the SDF leadership) would be seeing just the opposite of federalism. The SDF four-state federation project would not only 'diminish' federalism; it actually prevents it from existing altogether, at least, from the standpoint of the English-speaking minority (Debundschazonians and Savannazonians). The federalism issue has largely become known in Cameroon as the 'Anglophone problem' since they are mostly at the forefront of the quest for federation, a form of state that they rightly regard as essential for the protection of their cultural rights as a minority. It is not exactly clear then how the SDF four-state project furthers this desire, by submerging them into the two French-speaking Wourizone and Bamboutouszone. As this book has shown, the reverse is instead the goal and one gets the impression that the SDF is purely out to please the majority of Francophones and, as it would foolishly think, get 'elected' to power. This same silly attitude or trend (of seeking to obtain Francophones' favours even at the expense of the cultural community) has also been traced to the English-speaking Cameroonian leaders who have be shown to have (1) failed to provide the exquisite 'third force' in the FRC and (2) killed the 1961 'federation' or FRC in 1965 through their frenzied rush to the creation of a 'unified single national party' with Ahidjo.[227] It has been essential to link and discuss these issues a little further in the book as they are also clearly indicative of what it takes to successfully go federal in Cameroon.

Cameroon has been shown to be completely on its own unique planet of both state form and governmental system. But it has been doing all in its *pleins pouvoirs* to present itself as the median to the two main democratic systems of governance (parliamentary and congressional). Cameroon wants, at one and the same time, to pass for all of the above systems and yet is none of them. All the apparent heads of power separation and democracy in Cameroon are not real, being simply what critics have categorized as the "paper system". Cameroon is not any of the governmental systems (parliamentary, congressional, and neo-presidential) that it is attempting to pass for not only because of the stunning absence of any iota of separation of powers of whatever sort. Anchoring this analysis also on the Federal Constitution has been important in indicating that the 'separation of powers

[227] The false impression is also given to the wider public by Ngwana (2009) that the one-party state was forced on "Anglophones who were used to the multiparty system of government suddenly found themselves in a one-party system of government (the CNU monster) with its dictatorship and suppression of human rights."

mind game' strategy is not an innovation brought about by the recent 1996 Constitution. It finds its roots or equivalents in all the other constitutions before it, including the 'federal' one from which all of them are descended.

Federalism proper will propel development in Cameroon as in Africa. But the federation has to be created now, from scratch, with emulation being sought especially from Belgium, Canada, Germany, and Switzerland. If properly instituted as I have indicated and followed to the letter (through an independent and knowledgeable judiciary), federalism is also an appropriate medium for properly instituting equality, justice and freedom in governance in this country and continent. All this cannot be done through the ceaseless calls for a return to the 1961 Federal arrangement. As this book has amply demonstrated, there was no federation created in 1961 in Foumban and therefore there is none for now returning to. A federation, as I have abundantly shown, does not exist simply because 'federal' is affixed to the name of a unitary centralized country. If it were to be so, then, by the same Foumban logic, the USA would not be federal because of the word 'united' in its name. Indeed, as Wheare (1963: 1) has concluded, nowhere in the US Constitution does there appear the term 'federal' or 'federation'; and yet it is generally regarded as 'unreal' if any discussion of the concept of federalism fails to include the United States of America. Canada and Australia are also federations although no 'Federal Republic of' is affixed to their names. Conversely, France is one of Europe's renowned 'highly centralized unitary' states even as no "united" or *unie* appears in its *République Française.* I would therefore rather have democracy without a federation (United Kingdom) than have a 'federation' or whatever else without democracy as was the case in Foumban where leadership non-charisma and the uniting of one history were installed and confirmed.

I believe and hope that this book would, while helping Africans and other Third World peoples to be aware of certain basics of federalism, also provoke further and more refined analyses on the issues it has raised. Truly, the bulk of the intellectuals in Africa in general have failed to even deserve that appellation (intellectuals) because their great many responsibilities towards the population have not been properly discharged. Instead, these elites have engaged in both justifying and participating in most of the political activities responsible for the current malaise in Africa. Most of these intellectuals have sat and watched, for example, while the bulk of African leaders claim over and over that federalism is not African and must be shunned because it simply does not promote national unity in Africa. Nothing could be further from the truth and some of their twisted facts have been laid bare in this contribution.

I have kicked against the nationalist form of government for its tendency to be discriminatory and totalitarian. But nationalism, as Couloumbis and Wolfe (1986: 81) explain, is not always a negative force and can be greatly helpful if it aids people to unite with others in the pursuit of the common good. That is nationalism in its genuine and modern sense. In this sense nationalism becomes a behaviour pattern that reduces individualism and alienation and thus provides the individual with a sense of identity and belonging. Such a sense of belonging cannot be realized by merely forcefully effacing the heritage of a portion of the country's population. Therefore, Africans, it has been firmly suggested, must simply separate once and for all the concepts of state and of perfect nations and make their states truly pluralistic societies. Doing so necessarily requires the federal devolution or, failing that, a properly decentralized form of governance. Both of these concepts are nonsensical in the absence of separation of powers, especially judicial independence.

The African human rights and nation-building situations have been demonstrated to have degenerated to the current frightful stage principally because those claiming intellectualism (and up to whom the "common folks" do look for guidance and deliverance) would, instead of doing just that, have themselves joined in actually hoodwinking those same people. As a result, most constitutional scholarship in Francophone Africa particularly (if any at all) on the issues would appear to be very apologetic in regard of the rights-toying authorities in place or those that preceded them; and (in) directly linked to the foregoing, very sheepish and only reminiscent of what has been castigated as rank nostalgia – including the uncontrollable urge, especially within the academia and media, to only always paint angels out of colleagues or mentors. Clearly, if those who committed the blunders of the fifties and sixties could be excused because of their situation at the time, those of us who would continue today to perpetuate them could hardly be. This attitude simply does not augur well for any positive change in Africa and the Third World generally as far as governing with due respect for human rights would go. Democracy is another name for such human rights-respecting mode of governance; a system which, in poly-ethnic societies like most African states are, is practised through federalism. Federalism is itself impracticable, if not impossible, without an independent arbiter or judiciary.

It is now time for the creation of 'solid federal edifices' in Africa; constructed from scratch, drawing from the places and principles I have indicated above. It is my belief that Africa should be uniting itself, not further degenerating into so-called independent mini-states. I also believe that, to be able to free themselves of the all-embracing confusion and consequent human rights abuses that have become characteristic of their society, Africans, in the words of Reno (1994: 8), must now all rededicate themselves and take the spirit that can touch lives, that is supportive and say: "Yes, we can do it. We can make a difference. We can move forward [toward an authentic multicultural federation in this continent]. We can make the law real, and frame the law so that it serves people." As Biya (1986: 32) also weighs in, "no [truly] patriotic citizen [let alone those knowledgeable in legal-constitutional matters] can [afford to] remain indifferent [in the making of this difference]." In June 1971, a year before the 'fusion of Cameroon' rather than the 'enlargement of the federal system in Cameroon', Draper had predicted that Africans can now hardly avoid making a decision about whether or not to become involved: whether or not they will make something happen, whether they will help something happen, or whether they will let something happen. Citizen participation is concerned with the development of communities and self-growth of individuals within them. Such endeavours may culminate in greater political and economic independence, in increased social security, or in improved living conditions, but its significance especially lies in enhancing human dignity. These goals are inseparable from the challenges of maximizing human rights to all.[228] This is indeed what I believe Africans of all shades have to do, if the reign of confusion and terror has to end in their various countries; states that would then be competently qualified and placed to consider pulling together in federation(s) for the benefit of the African People.

Having shown also here why and how most communities have adopted federal unions in order to 'escape from our impeding misfortune', the important issue now becomes that of whether or not the Third World generally and Africa particularly would be ready to consider altering their anti-federalism posture in the face of the evident and real "threats".

---

[228] James A. Draper, "Introduction." in James A. Draper (ed.), *Citizen Participation: Canada* (Toronto: New Press, 1971), 5, at 8–9.

Fossungu even wondered as far back as 1999 if Africa's "impending misfortune" resulting from irreversible trends in international air transport would not be enough for Africa to rethink its attitudes towards meaningful federalism and the effective pooling of resources.[229] In refuting the charge that his audacious suggestions (of the proper way for the ICAO that is lodged at 999 University Street in Montreal, Canada, to help the Third World generally and Africa in particular help themselves) would amount to keeping them out of the ICAO Council, Fossungu passionately argued:

> Even keeping this prestigious Council membership aside, international air transport is currently going through a period of dynamic change as a result of increasing competition, trans-nationalization of business, globalization of the world economy, and the emergence of regional economic and political groupings, privatization of service industries, and the introduction of new global trading arrangements for service sectors. Necessitated by the ever-changing technology in the field, the international air transport industry is now faced with the almost irreversible trend of oligopolization and extremely high investment. Against this scenario alone, would one not naturally think that the time may be ripe for developing countries in general, and Africa in particular, to take a more balanced and serious look at the possibility of pooling resources together in order to jointly operate more efficient, competitive, and viable air transport agencies? Only by doing this could we hope to hear of "African Tigers" that could even smell (let alone eat) the lunch and/or supper of U.S. and EU flag carriers.
>
> Could joint air transport organizations or agencies (which the Chicago Convention even implores the Council to encourage) not provide a better nucleus and locomotion (than the Organization of African Unity (OAU) Charter presently does) for the eventual emergence of a United States of Africa (USAF)? Would the world's complex metamorphoses outrun Africa's ability to devise new mechanisms of legal, political, and social cushions? Would Africa not be flexible enough to adjust its perceptions to changing global realities? Would Africa not be able to exchange conventional mental habits for ones more suitable for

---

[229] See Peter Ateh-Afac Fossungu, "999 University, Please Help the Third World (Africa) Help Itself: A Critique of Council Elections" 64 *Journal of Air Law and Commerce* (1999), 339-75 at 361.

understanding unconventional circumstances or phenomena? What, if at all, could Africa learn in this regard from the European Union's experiences? Would "Mama Africa" never wake up from her long sleep?[230]

Once more, I believe and hope that this modest book would, while helping Africans generally to be aware of certain basics of federalism formation and operation, also provoke further and more refined analyses on the multitude of issues it has raised and/or addressed.

---

230 *Id.*: 359-60 (note omitted). See also John K. Akokpari, "Globalisation and the Challenges for the African State" 10:2 *Nordic Journal of African Studies* (2001), 188-209.

References

Ackerman, L.W.H. "Constitutional Protection of Human Rights: Judicial Review" 21:1 *Columbia Human Rights Law Review* (1989), 59.

Anyangwe, Carlson. *The Magistracy and the Bar in Cameroon* (Yaoundé: PANAG-CEPER, 1989).

Anyangwe, Carlson. *The Cameroonian Judicial System* (Yaoundé: CEPER, 1987).

Anyefru, Emmanuel. "Paradoxes of Internationalization of the Anglophone Problem in Cameroon" 28:1 *Journal of Contemporary African Studies* (2010), 85-101.

Appiagyei-Atua, Kwadwo. *An Akan Perspective on Human Rights in the Context of African Development* (Unpublished Doctor of Civil Law Dissertation, McGill University, 1999).

Archer, Peter and Lord Reay. *Freedom at Stake* (London: The Bodley Head, 1966).

Arthurs Report, *Law and Learning: Report to the Social Sciences and Humanities Research Council of Canada* (1983).

Awasom, Nicodemus Fru. "The Reunification Question in Cameroon History: Was the Bride an Enthusiastic or Reluctant One?" 47:2 *Africa Today* (2000), 91-119.

Awasom, Nicodemus Fru. "Politics and Constitution-Making in Francophone Cameroon, 1959-1960" 49:4 *Africa Today* (2002), 3-30.

Azebaze, Alex Gustave. "Paris au secour de la 'démocratie avancée'?" *Le Messager* N° 590 (3 mars 1997), 9.

Azeng, Randy Joe Sa'ah. "Federalism is Best Option for Cameroon – Garga Haman Adji" *The Herald* N° 468 (6-8 June 1997), 6.

Banfield, Edward C. and James Q. Wilson. *City Politics* (Cambridge, Mass.: Harvard University Press and The M.I.T. Press, 1963).

Barcroft, Peter A.A. "The Presidential Pardon – A Flawed Solution" 14: 11-12 *Human Rights Law Journal* (1993), 381.

Berkeley, Humphry. *The Power of the Prime Minister* (London: George Allen and Unwin Ltd., 1968).

Benjamin, Jacques. *Les camerounais occidentaux: la minorité dans un état bicommunautaire* (Montréal: Université de Montréal, 1972).

Bissonnette, Bernard. *Essai sur la constitution du Canada* (Montréal: Les Éditions du Jour, 1963).

Biya, Paul. *Communal Liberalism* (London: Macmillan, 1986).

Bjornson, Richard. *The African Quest for Freedom and Identity: Cameroonian Writing and the National Experience* (Bloomington & Indianapolis: Indiana University Press, 1991).

Blondel, Jean. "The Government of France" in Michael Curtis, Gen. ed., *Introduction to Comparative Government* (New York: Harper and Row, Publishers, 1985), 115-190.

Boh, Herbert. "Open Letter to All Who Fight for Freedom and Democracy: No Price Is Too Much for Freedom" *Le Messager* N° 029 (July 18, 1991), 8-9.

Brain, Robert. *Bangwa Kingship and Marriage* (Cambridge: Cambridge University Press, 1972).

Bringer, Peter. "The Abiding Influence of English and French Criminal Law in One African Country: Some Remarks Regarding the Machinery of Criminal Justice in Cameroon" 25:1 *Journal of African Law* (1981), 1-13.

Cassese, Antonio. *International Law in a Divided World* (Oxford: Clarendon Press, 1986).

Charette, Fédérick. *Les driots collectifs – de quel droit?* (Thèse de Doctorat, Université de Montréal, 1996).

Chitepo, Herbert W. "Developments in Central Africa" in David P. Currie, ed., *Federalism and the New Nations of Africa* (Chicago: University of Chicago Press, 1964), 3-28.

Couloumbis, Theodore A. and James H. Wolfe. *Introduction to International Relations: Power and Justice* 3rd ed. (Englewood Cliffs, N.J.: Prentice-Hall, Inc., 1986).

Crossman, R.H.S. *The Myths of Cabinet Government* (Cambridge, Mass.: Harvard University Press, 1972).

Davidson, Basil. *Africa in History: Themes and Outlines* rev. & exp. ed. (New York: Macmillan, 1991).

Dawson, R. MacGregor. *The Government of Canada* [5th ed. revised by Norman Ward] (Toronto: University of Toronto Press, 1970).

DeCoste, F.C. "Taking A Stand: Theory in the Canadian Legal Academy – A Review of *Canadian Perspectives on Legal Theory* edited by Richard F. Devlin (Edmond Montgomery Publications, 1991)" 29 *Alberta Law Review* (1991), 941-69.

Delancey, Mark W. *Cameroon: Dependence and Independence* (Boulder: Westview Press, 1989).

Denning, A.T. *The Road to Justice* (London: Stevens & Sons Ltd., 1955).

de Smith, Stanley A. "Federalism, Human Rights, and the Protection of Minorities" in David P. Currie (ed.), *Federalism and the New Nations of Africa*, (Chicago: University of Chicago Press, 1964), 279-341.

Dickson, Brian. *The Rule of Law: Judicial Independence and the Separation of Powers* (Address to the Canadian Bar Association, August 21, 1985).

Douzinas, Costas and Ronnie Warrington. "On the Deconstruction of Jurisprudence: Fin(n)is Philosophiae" 14:1 *Journal of Law & Society* (Spring 1987), 33.

Dumont, Hugues, Nicolas Lagasse, Marc van der Hulst, and Sébastien van Drooghenbroeck. "Kingdom of Belgium" in Ahktar Majeed, Ronald L. Watts and Douglas M. Brown, eds., *Distribution of Powers and Responsibilities in Federal Countries* (Montreal & Kingston: McGill-Queen's University Press, 2008), 35-65.

Dunlop, C.R.B. "Literature Studies in Law Schools" 3 *Cardozo Studies in Law and Literature* (1991), 63.

Eko, Lyombe. "The English-Language Press and the 'Anglophone Problem' in Cameroon: Group Identity, Culture, and the Politics of Nostalgia" 20:1 *Journal of Third World Studies* (2003), 79-102.

Eleazu, Uma O. *Federalism and Nation-Building: The Nigerian Experience, 1954-1964* (Elms Court: Stockwell, 1977).

El Obaid, Ahmed El Obaid. *Human Rights and Cultural Diversity in Islamic Africa* (Unpublished Doctor of Civil Law Thesis, Institute of Comparative Law, McGill University, 1996).

Endali, Solomon. "Is Ekindi Suffering from Political Confusion?" *The Herald* N° 327 (8-9 July 1996), 4.

Enonchong, H.N.A. *Cameroon Constitutional Law – Federalism in a Mixed Common-Law and Civil-Law System* (Yaoundé: Centre d'Édition et de Production de Manuel et d'Auxiliares de l'Enseignement, 1967).

Etinge, C.N. "Proposition for the Agenda of a National Conference" *Le Messager*, **Special Political Issue** (6 June 1991), 6-7.

Eyinga, Abel. "Le régime néo-colonial actuel a atteint un autre niveau dans la lutte contre la conscience nationale" *La Nouvelle Expression* N° 338 (30 août 1996), 6-7.

Flanz, Gisbert H. "West Indian Federation" in T.M. Franck, ed., *Why Federations Fail: An Inquiry into the Requisites for Successful Federalism* (New York: New York University Press, 1968), 91-123.

Fohtung, Barry B. "The Gambler" *Cameroon Post* (11-18 December 1995) 11.

Fombad, Charles Manga. "The Separation of Powers and Constitutionalism in Africa: The Case of Botswana" 25:2 *Boston College Third World Law Journal* (2005), 301-42.

Fombad, Charles Manga. "Cameroon's Emergency Powers: A Recipe for (Un)constitutional Dictatorship?" 48 *Journal of African Law* (2004), 62-81.

Fombad, Charles Manga. "Protecting Constitutional Values in Africa: A Comparison of Botswana and Cameroon" 36:1 *Comparative and International Law of Southern Africa* (2003), 83-105.

Fossungu, Peter Ateh-Afac. *Understanding Confusion in Africa: The Politics of Multiculturalism and Nation-Building in Cameroon* (Bamenda, Cameroon: Langaa Research Publishing Common Initiative Group, 2013).

Fossungu, Peter Ateh-Afac. "Separation of Powers in Public International Law: Is the International Civil Aviation Organization (ICAO) Out of or Within the United Nations System? A Critique of ICAO Assembly Elections" 35 *Annals of Air & Space Law* (2010), 267-96.

Fossungu, Peter Ateh-Afac. "The ICAO Assembly: The Most Unsupreme of Supreme Organs in the United Nations System? A Critical Analysis of Assembly Sessions" 26 *Transportation Law Journal* (1998), 1-49.

Fossungu, Peter Ateh-Afac. "Lesson in Advanced Government" *The Herald* N° 650 (21-23 August 1998a), 4.

Fossungu, Peter Ateh-Afac. "The Foumban Machination" *The Herald* N° 593 (6-7 April 1998b), 10.

Fossungu, Peter Ateh-Afac. "Doing *Noddometrics* in the Advanced School of Democracy" *The Herald* N° 608 (15-17 May 1998c), 10.

Franck, Thomas M. "East African Federation" in T.M. Franck, ed., *Why Federations Fail: An Inquiry into the Requisites for Successful Federalism* (New York: New York University Press, 1968a), 3-36.

Franck, Thomas M. "Why Federations Fail" in T.M. Franck, ed., *Why Federations Fail: An Inquiry into the Requisites for Successful Federalism* (New York: New York University Press, 1968b), 167-199.

Gardinier, David E. *Cameroon: United Nations Challenge to French Policy* (London: Oxford University Press, 1963).

Geary, Christraud M. *Things of the Palace: A Catalogue of the Bamum Palace Museum in Foumban (Cameroon)* (Wiesbaden, Germany: Franz Steiner Verlag GMBH, 1983).

Gobata. "Western Democrats and African Dictatorships" *Cameroon Post* N° 0021 (20-26 August 1996), 7.

Gorji-Dinka, F. "The Gorji-Dinka Concept of a New Social Order" *Le Messager* **Special Political Issue** (Thursday 6 June 1991), 5.

Gorji-Dinka, F. [interview] "Echoes from Exile: SDF is the Party that Keeps Biya in Power, Says Fon Fongum Gorji Dinka on Political Asylum in London" *The Herald*, (6-9 June 1996), 6.

Gros, Jean-Germain. "The Role of the Military and France in Cameroon Politics" *The Herald* N° 288 (26-28 February 1996), 6.

Hogg, Peter W. *Constitutional Law of Canada* 4th Student ed. (Toronto: Thomson Canada Limited, 1996).

Johnson, Willard R. *The Cameroon Federation: Political Integration in a Fragmentary Society* (Princeton, N.J.: Princeton University Press, 1970).

Kneier, Charles M. *Illustrative Materials in Municipal Government and Administration* (New York: Harper & Brothers, 1939).

Kommers, Donald P. "The Government of West Germany" in Michael Curtis, Gen. ed., *Introduction to Comparative Government* (New York: Harper and Row, Publishers, 1985), 191-281.

Konings, Piet J.J. "The Anglophone Struggle for Federalism in Cameroon" in L.R. Basita and J. Ibrahim, eds., *Federalism and Decentralization in Africa: The Multiethnic Challenge* (Fribourg: Institut du Fédéralisme, 1999), 289-325.

Konings, Piet and Francis B. Nyamnjoh. "The Anglophone Problem in Cameroon" 35:2 *The Journal of Modern African Studies* (1997), 207-29.

Lantum, Dan N. "Dr. Bernard Nsokika Fonlon: An Intellectual in Politics" *Le Messager* **Special Political Issue** (Thursday 6 June 1991), 20-22, continued in *Le Messager* N° 028 (20 June 1991), 11-13.

Laski, Harold-J. *Le gouvernement parlementaire en Angleterre* [Translated by Jacque Cadart and Jacqueline Prélot] (P.U.F., Paris, 1950).

Lenaerts, K. "Constitutionalism and the Many Faces of Federalism" 38 *American Journal of Comparative Law* (1990), 205.

Le Vine, Victor T. *The Cameroon Federal Republic* (Ithaca and London: Cornell University Press, 1971).

Le Vine, Victor T. *The Cameroons – from Mandate to Independence* (Berkeley: University of California Press, 1964).

Le Vine, Victor T. and R.P. Nye. *Historical Dictionary of Cameroun* (Metuchen, N.J: The Scarecrow Press, 1964).

Loewenstein, Karl. *British Cabinet Government* (London: Oxford University Press, 1967).

Magstadt, Thomas M. *Nations and Governments: Comparative Politics in Regional Perspective* (New York: St Martin's Press, Inc., 1991).

Majeed, Ahktar. "Introduction: Distribution of Powers and Responsibilities" in Ahktar Majeed, Ronald L. Watts and Douglas M. Brown, eds., *Distribution of Powers and Responsibilities in Federal Countries* (Montreal & Kingston: McGill-Queen's University Press, 2008), 3-7.

Mallory, J.R. *The Structure of Canadian Government* (Toronto: Gage Publishing Company, 1984).

Mback, Charles Nach. "One Century of Municipalization in Cameroon: The Miseries of Urban Democracy" in Dickson Eyoh and Richard Stren, eds. *Decentralization and the Politics of Urban Development in West Africa* (Washington D.C.: Woodrow Wilson International Centre for Scholars, 2007).

Mbinglo, A.O. "Of Mbile, Bakassi and Southern Cameroons" *Cameroon Post* (8-14 October 1996), 8.

Meekison, J. Peter. "Federalism and the Constitution – Some Personal Reflections" in Michael Owen, ed., *Salute to Scholarship: Essays Presented at the Official Opening of Athabasca University* (Athabasca, Alberta: Athabasca University, 1986), 5-19.

Mirkine-Guetzévitch Boris and Marcel Prélot. "Préface" in Harold-J. Laski, *Le gouvernement parlementaire en Angleterre* [Translated by Jacque Cadart and Jacqueline Prélot] (Paris: P.U.F., 1950), vi-xiv.

Moorhouse, Geoffrey. *The Diplomats: The Foreign Office Today* (London: Jonathan Cape Ltd., 1977).

Ndi Chia, Charly. "We May Not Be the World But We Are the People" *Cameroon Post* N° 0274 (11-18 December 1995a), 4.

Ndi Chia, Charly. "Why Gov't Is Bent on Destroying North West Traditional Authority – Dr. Nantang Jua" *Cameroon Post* N° 0274 (December 11-18, 1995b), 6.

Nelson, Harold D., Margarita Dobert, Gordon C. McDonald, James McLaughlin, Barbara Marvin and Philip W. Moeller. *Area Handbook for the United Republic of Cameroon* (Washington, D.C., 1974).

Newman, Peter C. *The Distemper of our Times – Canadian Politics in Transition: 1963-1968* (Toronto: McClelland and Stewart Limited, 1968).

Ngwana, A.S. "Cameroon: Genesis and Reality of the Anglophone Problem", available at http//topics192.com/2009/02/cameroongenesis-and-reality-of-html.

Ntenga, George Chebe. "Cameroon Calling: Who is Destroying National Unity?" *The Herald* (10-11 March 1997), 4.

Nyo'Wakai. "Former Judge Nyo'Wakai Talks to the Messager on the Cameroonian Judicial System" *Le Messager* **Special Political Issue** (Thursday 6 June 1991), 18-19.

Ofege, Ntemfac. "Constitutional Revision: Vistas of Anglophone Exclusion and Presidential Hypocrisy" *Cameroon Post* N° 0274 (11-18 December 1995), 8.

Ondoa, Magloire. "Commentaire" 25 *Juridis Périodique* (*Revue de Droit et de Science Politique*) (1996), 11-14.

Pactet, Pierre. *Institutions politiques Droit constitutionnel* 10e édition (Paris: Masson, 1991).

Pearsall, Judy ed. *The New Oxford Dictionary of English* ((Oxford: Clarendon Press, 1998).

Pearson, F.S. and J.M. Rochester. *International Relations: The Global Condition in the Late Twentieth Century* 2nd edition (New York: Random House, 1984).

Peaslee, Amos J. *Constitutions of Nations* Vol. I – Africa (The Hague, Netherlands: Martinus Nijhoff, 1974).

Pomerance, M. *Self-Determination in Law and Practice* (The Hague: Martinus Nijhoff, 1982).

Pougoué, Paul-Gérard and Maurice Kamto. "Commentaire de la Loi N° 89/018 du 28 juillet 1989 portant modification de la Loi N° 75/16 du 08 décembre 1975 fixant procédure et fonctionnement de la Cour Suprême" 1 *Juridis Info (Revue de la Législation et Jurisprudence Camerounaises)* (1990), 5.

Reno, Janet. "Remarks: Address Delivered at the Celebration of the Seventy-fifth Anniversary of Women at Fordham Law School" 63 *Fordham Law Review* (1994), 5.

Riemer, Neal. *Political Science: An Introduction to Politics* (New York: Harcourt Brace Jovanovich, Inc., 1983).

Rovere, Richard H. "Foreword" in Charles Peters and Nicholas Lemann (eds.), *Inside the System* 4th ed. (New York: Holt, Rinehart and Winston, 1979).

Rubin, Neville. *Cameroon: An African Federation* (Praeger Publishers, New York 1971).

Russell, Peter H. *The Judiciary in Canada: Third Branch of Government* (Toronto: McGraw-Hill, 1987).

SCFAQ: "Southern Cameroons Frequently Asked Questions", available @ http://www.southerncameroons.org/index3.htm (last visited in March 2011).

Schneider, Hans-Peter. "The Federal Republic of Germany" in Ahktar Majeed, Ronald L. Watts and Douglas M. Brown, eds., *Distribution of Powers and Responsibilities in Federal Countries* (Montreal & Kingston: McGill-Queen's University Press, 2008), 124-154.

Scott, Stephen A. in David Schneiderman, ed., *After Allaire and Bélanger-Campeau* (being a Symposium) as reported in 3:1 *Constitutional Forum Constitutionnel* (Winter 1991), 14-16.

Shapiro, Evan Joel. *The Supranational Challenge: Federal and Decentralized Unitary States Within the European Union* (Unpublished LL.M. Thesis, McGill University, 1995).

Shiv Lal. *A Scheme For Ideal Elections and Separation of Powers for Developing Democracies* (New Delhi: Institute for Electoral Studies, 1976).

Simon, Richard and Martin Papillion. "Canada" in Ahktar Majeed, Ronald L. Watts and Douglas M. Brown, eds., *Distribution of Powers and Responsibilities in Federal Countries* (Montreal & Kingston: McGill-Queen's University Press, 2008), 92-122.

Southall, Roger. *Federalism and Higher Education in East Africa* (Nairobi: East African Publishing House, 1974).

Stark, Frank M. "Federalism in Cameroon: The Shadow and the Reality" 10:3 *Canadian Journal of African Studies* (1976), 423-442.

Stevenson, Garth. *Unfulfiled Union: Canadian Federalism and National Unity* 3rd ed. (St. Catherines, Ontario: Gage Educational Publishing Company, 1989).

St. John-Stevas, Norman. "Foreword" in Humphry Berkeley, *The Power of the Prime Minister* (London: George Allen and Unwin, 1968) 7-11.

Taku, Charles Achaleke. "Lawyer Alerts British Gov't: C'wealth Systems Are Being Destroyed in Cameroon" *Cameroon Post* N° 0274 (11-18 December 1995), 1.

Tamanaha, Brian Z. "The Folly of the 'Social Scientific' Concept of Legal Pluralism" 20:2 *Journal of Law & Society* (1993) 192-217.

Tanyi, Gerald Bisong. "Directors' Duties to Act in the Best Interest of the Company: Changing Attitudes" 2 *Juridis Info* (*Revue de Legislation et de Jurisprudence Camerounaises*) (1990), 59-62.

Tiruchelvam, N. "Introduction" in N. Tiruchelvam and R. Coomaraswamy, eds., *The Judiciary in Plural Societies* (New York: St. Martin's Press, 1987), vii.

Tixier, Gilbert. *A Comparative Study of the Economic Policies of the Cameroons and Ivory Coast* (Paris: International Institute for Economic Research & LGDJ, 1974).

Trager, Frank N. "Introduction: On Federalism" in Thomas M. Franck (ed.), *Why Federations Fail: An Inquiry into the Requisites for Successful Federalism* (New York: New York University Press, 1968), ix.

Tremblay, André. *Droit Constitutionnel: Principes* (Montréal : Les Éditions Thémis, 1993).

Urquhart, Ian. "On Senate Reform" 3:3 *Constitutional Forum Constitutionnel* (Winter 1992), 67.

Verhelst, Thierry. "Guaranties constitutionnelles relatives à l'individu face à la justice dans les États d'Afrique francophone" 15 *Journal of African Law* (1971), 113-131.

Wade, H.W.R. *Constitutional Fundamental* (London: Stevenson and Sons, 1980).

Waindim, Jude. "Gwangwa'a's Cry of the Destitute," *Cameroon Post* (11-18 December 1995), 4.

Wambali, M.B.K. and C.M. Peter. "The Judiciary in Context: The Case of Tanzania" in N. Tiruchelvam and R. Coomaraswamy, eds., *The Role of the Judiciary in Plural Societies* (New York: St. Martin's Press, 1987), 131.

Wheare, K.C. *Federal Government* (London: Oxford University Press, 1963).

Williams, John M. and Clement Macintyre. "Commonwealth of Australia" in Ahktar Majeed, Ronald L. Watts and Douglas M. Brown, eds., *Distribution of Powers and Responsibilities in Federal Countries* (Montreal & Kingston: McGill-Queen's University Press, 2008), 9-33.

Williams, Patricia J. "Alchemical Notes: Reconstructing Ideals from Deconstructed Rights" 22 *Harvard Civil Rights-Civil Liberty Review* (1987), 401.

Zang-Atangana2, Joseph-Marie. *Les forces politiques au Cameroun réunifié: Tome 2 - L'expérience de l'UC et du KNDP* (Paris: L'Harmattan, 1989).

Legislation

Federal Constitution: *Loi N° 61-24 du 1er septembre 1961 portant révision constitutionnelle et tendant à adapter la constitution actuelle aux nécessités du Cameroun réunifié.*

1972 Constitution: *2 June 1972 Constitution of the United Republic of Cameroon.*

1991 Constitution: *Loi N° 91/001 du 23 avril portant modification des articles 5, 7, 8, 9, 26, 27, et 34 de la Constitution.*

1996 Constitution: *Loi N° 96-06 du 18 janvier 1996 portant révision de la Constitution du 02 juin 1972.*

www.ingramcontent.com/pod-product-compliance
Lightning Source LLC
Chambersburg PA
CBHW032127020426
42334CB00016B/1073
* 9 7 8 9 9 5 6 7 9 0 1 5 9 *